Before God

Before God

Exercises in Subjectivity

Steven DeLay

ROWMAN & LITTLEFIELD
Lanham • Boulder • New York • London

Published by Rowman & Littlefield
An imprint of The Rowman & Littlefield Publishing Group, Inc.
4501 Forbes Boulevard, Suite 200, Lanham, Maryland 20706
www.rowman.com

86-90 Paul Street, London EC2A 4NE

Copyright © 2020 by Steven DeLay

All rights reserved. No part of this book may be reproduced in any form or by any electronic or mechanical means, including information storage and retrieval systems, without written permission from the publisher, except by a reviewer who may quote passages in a review.

British Library Cataloguing in Publication Information Available

Library of Congress Control Number: 2019950644

ISBN 9781786613165 (cloth) | ISBN 9781538148143 (paperback) | ISBN 9781786613172 (epub)

And we know that all things work together for good to those who love God, to those who are the called according to his purpose.

Romans 8:28

Contents

Address		ix
Prayer		xi
1	Divine Things and the Fluidity of Thought	1
2	The Interlacement of Self and God	13
3	What Is the Problem of Intersubjectivity?	41
4	Forgiveness	73
5	Making Peace	97
6	A Sketch of Silence and Evil	117
7	Suffering and Salvation: A Note on Art	151
8	The Light That Lights Every Man	163
Index		185

Address

As phenomenology concerns itself with every appearing, why not God too, who also appears? To declare, with embarrassing presumptuousness or shallow methodological fastidiousness, that God may not enter phenomenology is idle talk more than anything revealed in the light of *Evidenz*. The stance that God be excluded from philosophy, we know well, exerts its influence because of the entrenched but unclarified modern distinction between theology and philosophy. Is this division of labor so evident as those who, invoking it, do so without thinking twice assume? It is in reflecting on ourselves that this work's eight essays (or exercises in subjectivity) deconstruct that distinction between philosophy and theology. For here, when thinking about who we are, could it be otherwise? Phenomenology puts our humanity to work completely. And work of life that it is, it is thus done in the presence of God. And so, one further word in anticipation of the pages to follow: remember that we are laid bare, not just when we ourselves are writing, but when reading too. May you, reader, feel it to be so!

Prayer

O Lord God in Heaven, You establish the thoughts of those who commit their works unto You. Please, Lord, I ask that You establish my thoughts in the pages to follow. May this work bring You glory, and may it touch those who read it, bringing them hope and joy. Amen.

Chapter One

Divine Things and the Fluidity of Thought

Philosophy thinks existence. In the course of thinking about that existence, whether it be a matter of humanity's or our own, God comes to mind. What, then, could cordon off philosophy from God, securing it from God's unwanted or unwarranted intrusion? Is there a reasonable principle, a sound methodological choice maybe, or even just a good rule of thumb, which, ever at work, is responsible for keeping them apart? Is there something more maintaining their distance than the mere personal resolve of those who, for whatever their reason, have instituted it? That philosophy and theology make two sometimes is pronounced with the confidence suggesting it were a truism.[1] And yet just a brief recounting of the history of existentialism shows that nothing could be less obvious.

Usually, we know, it is suggested that the boundaries between philosophy and theology shed clarity on things. Understanding philosophy's own relation to God is said to be among them. If it is stated that God should not enter philosophy, one widespread view takes such a position to be straightforwardly innocent enough. Methodologically, so it claims, it falls to theology (and not philosophy) to bother with God. Philosophy and theology, so the thought continues, make two. For on the one hand, there is a thing we call theology that concerns itself with God. On the other, there is what we call philosophy, which does not. But what explains this distinction exactly? On closer inspection, it appears to be more terminological than substantive. Are philosophy and theology really so distinct? One compelling reason for thinking they are not is to appreciate how the preceding way of trying to distinguish the two is mostly theoretical. What results is a distinction failing to capture life, or having any significant bearing on it. The division is artificial, and, foreign to how we know existence to be, it seems not so much to crystallize from existence naturally, but to be an imposition upon it. When we wrestle with the meaning of human existence, from a birth none of us has chosen, to the death to which we are all delivered, and thus in turn the question of what such a death might bring in the hereafter, could anything be more ideological and stilted than the conviction that, ignoring God, claims philosophy thereby finds its purpose? How could it be that by deciding not to bother with God, philosophy brings understanding to things? And yet, ever since Kant's critical philosophy at least, that commonly has been taken to be the case.

And so, philosophy neutralizes the question of God. Bracketing the existence of God (and not in the unique sense Husserl meant by it in §58 of *Ideas I*), this neutralization occurs so thoroughly that, as a matter of principle, our relation to God is not allowed to be posed seriously even *as a question*. Most often, God is treated as a nonentity. Without even mentioning the decision, things proceed smoothly as if God does not exist, as if God's existence remains irrelevant to whatever philosophical matter is before us. For this a-theology, such an exclusion of God is seen as a consummation of philosophy's autonomy. It is said to be thinking's apotheosis. There will be more to say about the nature of such autonomy later, for reckoning with Heidegger's view of the relation between philosophy and theology demands it. But let us begin where we find ourselves presently, which is faced with the commonplace that God should be relegated to theology. Cutting against the grain, we ask: is the elimination of God's part in philosophy laudable, or is it not thinking's decay?

It is well-known that increasingly much (maybe most) of philosophical thought is methodologically atheistic. Any accounting of how that has become so would need to reckon with the progressive stages of the historical transformation responsible for it, including its perhaps most pronounced moment: the crisis of culture following the killing fields of the world wars. Such was the landscape that gave rise to existentialism. It is interesting to note that existentialism's assessment of the place of God in philosophy is ambivalent, however. Sartre and Camus of course were atheists. The inexistence of God almost is axiomatic to their thought. The same is in a way true of Heidegger, who we know, however, resisted the existentialist label. It would, to be sure, be incorrect to deny that existentialism is associated with atheism. Many of its most prominent figures held to an atheistic view of man. Still, the history is mixed. For the existentialists were not by any stretch unanimous in repudiating God from philosophy. It often is the existentialists themselves who come immediately to mind when considering exceptions to the atheistic trend of modern philosophy: in the nineteenth century, there were Kierkegaard and Dostoevsky. In the twentieth, Shestov and Marcel. Even the figures whose thought is defined by the rejection of God (Nietzsche, Camus, and Sartre) are unrecognizable apart from the question of God. Existentialism was not solely atheistic, and its strand of atheism was far from jocular. The existentialists who denied God's existence took that rejection seriously. Now, it is true that definitions are not always helpful. Sometimes they do not clarify matters. But it seems appropriate here to hazard one. Existentialism, then, as we have thus far understood it, is thought that thinks the human condition is in reference to the only frame of reference that matters absolutely: to God. But if that is right, is not the thesis that philosophy thinks atheistically suspect?

Furthermore, while it might almost seem to be too obvious, it should be mentioned: probably without any significant exception, every existential thinker of any influence over the last two centuries has not evaded the question of God but has begun by facing it squarely. Existentialism's atheism was never born of indifference to the question of God. Who we are as individuals is defined above all, no less for Nietzsche than for Kierkegaard, not by whether, but in how, we respond to it. The existentialists all saw that. Whether with the atheistic existentialists for whom God was said to be a corpse whose death we must move beyond, or with the Christian existentialists for whom God remains the living One to whom we owe all, existential philosophy emphasizes that any thinking equal to existence ought to face the question of God. Even just a quick survey of existentialism, thus, suggests that philosophy grapples with divine things. And for good reason. If it is impossible for any individual life to evade the question of God entirely forever (to ignore it is not to escape it), how could a philosophy that aims to understand human existence do so itself? The question of God starts looking like it may be philosophical, after all. For to think a philosophy worthy of the name could excuse itself from facing the question of God by appealing to the ideal of methodological atheism, or the authority of scientific naturalism, or whatever else, is for existential philosophy an excuse. Or better, it is an illusion. Just as each of us eventually deals with God, so must any philosophy of existence. An existence lived apart from God is possible. Of that there can be no denial. But a philosophy that made no mention of God at all would not *be* an existential philosophy.

These opening reflections have in the name of existentialism challenged the general contention that God cannot justifiably enter philosophy. Before drawing any firmer conclusions on the matter, however, we must say something about Heidegger, who, more than anyone, insisted on an inviolable demarcation between philosophy and theology. On March 9, 1927, he delivered the famous essay "Phenomenology and Theology," which, in keeping with that year's *Being and Time*, conceives philosophy as a science. But, as that text notes, philosophy is not a science like others. There are ontic sciences, notes Heidegger, sciences of beings responsible for investigating a given region of entities. In his terminology of the time, these are "positive sciences." Philosophy for its own part is a science too, but it remains nevertheless quite different. Rather than investigating beings, it is the science of being: "It is evident from the idea of science as such—insofar as it is understood as a possibility of Dasein—that there are two basic possibilities of science: sciences of beings, of whatever is, or ontic sciences; and *the* science of being, the ontological science, philosophy."[2]

Theology and philosophy are thus each a science, says Heidegger. Yet they are different in kind, for whereas theology is a positive science, philosophy is the science of no particular entity, but rather being itself. And there is more. What kind of science is theology, we ask: what is its *positivum*? Heidegger's answer is as surprising as it is provocative: theology systematically thematizes the historical form of Christian faith as a style of lived existence. Theology, then, is not the science of God as we might expect. For Heidegger, theology is indeed a science, the science of faith! To treat theology as a science of faith has consequences peculiar to how philosophy sees human existence and relates to the question of God. When it is understood properly, as he hastens to emphasize, philosophy now is methodologically atheistic, because, as an inquiry into the meaning of being, it does not occupy itself with any region of beings or any particular being, including even God himself. Philosophy does not deny God's existence. It is just that God is orthogonal to the business of philosophy.

It does not take much, however, to notice a tension in Heidegger's position, one his own remarks later in that same essay evince clearly. It might be conceded that ontic sciences exhibit all the distinguishing characteristics he attributes to them.[3] It might even be further conceded that, so defined, theology is one among these sciences of beings. And finally, we might go further still, granting that, so defined, philosophy is not a science of beings, but the science of being. Does this entail that God is prohibited from entering philosophy?

There are reasons for denying that the conclusion follows. Keeping God at arm's length from philosophy is not so easy. First, to locate philosophy within the horizon of scientificity is to downplay that, going back to Socrates, philosophy was never primarily a quest for scientific knowledge. Rather, it was a task concerning how to live the good life—what Kierkegaard would call "subjective" knowledge, not "objective" knowledge.[4] As the ancients well understood, philosophy is a *way of life*. And that means it involves, arguably, what Heidegger in the name of scientificity wanted to eliminate from it. It is not just that Heidegger swerves away from a venerable view of philosophy, but that, in doing so, the resulting notion of philosophy contradicts its own stated aspirations. In the interest of removing any metaphysical vestige of worldview from philosophy as phenomenological ontology, Heidegger succumbs to a distinctly modern one, namely, the worldview according to which we are able to extricate ourselves from such metaphysical presuppositions. Contrary to its explicit intent, philosophy as a science of being is deeply metaphysical in the very way the same worldview philosophies it criticizes are.

A second reason for doubting philosophy and theology can be kept apart follows directly from the first. It would be one thing had Heidegger claimed that theology is numbered among the ontic sciences, and so just in that regard differs from philosophy, which itself is unconcerned with beings. But he does not leave things there. As the 1927 essay under consideration makes plain, the initial claim that theology and philosophy are irrelevant to one another is betrayed by his later comments characterizing that relation in starkly antagonistic terms. If theology is the science of faith, and if faith itself is the "mortal enemy of philosophy," then, as Heidegger himself seems to suggest, it is difficult to see how theology and philosophy could play nice: "as a specific possibility of existence, [faith] is in its innermost core the mortal enemy of the form of existence that is an essential part of philosophy and that is factically ever-changing. Faith is so absolutely the mortal enemy that philosophy does not even begin to want in any way to do battle with it."[5] It would seem philosophy and theology will not be friendly neighbors after all.

In addition to this second reason, we may cite a third. It pertains to the status of thinking in philosophy. Or more specifically, the objection concerns this way of bracketing God from philosophy, since there is an instability in the very concept of philosophy itself as Heidegger understands it. In one breath, he insists that philosophy is atheistic only insofar as it neither decides for nor against God's existence. The atheism is purely methodological, says Heidegger. But here it must be admitted that he is talking out of both sides of his mouth. For, as he goes on to say, faith is the mortal enemy of philosophy! It would be a mistake to think there is not something of substance beneath Heidegger's dramatic language. This way of seeing faith and philosophy as opposed to one another underscores a genuine incommensurability between the methodological atheism of philosophy *qua* science of being, on the one hand, and seeing human beings as Dasein, whose whole of existence is initially independent from God, on the other. The image of man Heidegger takes for granted is hardly neutral.

That there is a more virulent atheism at work in his conception of philosophy becomes apparent when pondering what exactly is supposed to distinguish uniquely its mode of thinking. If for Heidegger philosophy is "the free questioning of purely self-reliant Dasein,"[6] this characterization of human existence is itself dubious from the perspective of faith. To be sure, Heidegger claims that faith cannot seriously enter into philosophical questioning, because the one who lives by faith takes oneself already to have an answer to the question "Why something rather than nothing?"—hence, whoever has interpreted life through the lens of faith cannot face up to the anxiety of existence. But that very anxiety, as stated repeatedly in *Being and Time*, is said to be the consequence of Dasein's fundamentally unsettled mode of being-in-the-world. This conceals within itself more than it admits. To say that Dasein is anxious fundamentally is another way of saying that there is no ultimate answer to the question of who we are. But to say *that* is not at all to bracket the question of God, but to reject directly the idea that we are made in the image of God. There is nothing neutral about the decision, which is why it is of no small significance to stress that it *is* a decision. In a word, the supposed methodological atheism of phenomenological ontology is not so metaphysically innocent as Heidegger makes it out to be. As it inadvertently emerges in the context of the analysis of anxiety, the existential analytic takes a stance decidedly against God. In seeing anxiety as the fundamental mood of human existence, it may do so only because, having interpreted that existence as perpetually enigmatic, it rejects the Christian view of ourselves as beings-before-God.[7] It is not unfair to suspect that, contrary to whatever he may say, for Heidegger, the existential analytic's explicit rejection of man as made in the *imago Dei* drives his methodological aspirations for a philosophy as the science of being, not the other way around.

This observation leads to a further remark concerning the reputed autonomy of philosophical inquiry presently at issue. What is praised as philosophy's self-reliance, as its capacity to question for questioning's sake, takes that questioning to be sensible because it assumes there are no answers of the kind that would make such questioning otiose. But once again, *that* is to take a metaphysical stand, since it is to commit oneself, however tacitly, to a view of man's relation to reality. Man is thought to be without essence, without end, and without any measure except the one he gives to himself as the result of wrestling with the enigma of his existence by questioning. Such a view is not so innocent. It rests on a commitment, which, if mistaken, leads whomever follows it badly astray. We can agree with Heidegger that it would be a mistake to short-circuit questioning where questioning is still necessary. This happens when, presuming ourselves to possess answers to questions we do not, we call inquiry to a premature close. But to claim questioning *must* be kept ever open is effectively to commit oneself to the idea that there are no answers. It is easy to see the danger. If there *are* answers, it would be a terrible mistake to go on questioning as if there are not!

For Heidegger, that there is no ultimate answer to the meaning of existence takes on the status of something like a dogma. Faith is the enemy of philosophy, he claims, after all, precisely because it is said to misdirect us from interrogating the insoluble enigma of being Dasein, lulling us instead into a false security by which we come to believe naively that we have answers to matters we do not. It is a story we have heard many times. However, it is just as possible to see things differently. According to this other way of appraising the situation, the existential analytic is foolish or even stubborn, for it persists in asking some questions only because it refuses to recognize that there *are* answers! Would not a Revelation truly worthy of its intent slake our thirst for answers? As the 1927 essay on phenomenology and theology attests, Heidegger never seems to recognize that it is possible to ask amiss in *two* ways: either because we cease questioning authentically when we should have continued on (it is this that worries him), but also just as potentially because we may continue questioning when there is no longer any need to.[8]

Given what we have seen of phenomenological ontology's rejection of our fundamental condition as being one before God, it makes sense why Heidegger distanced himself from existentialism as vehemently as he did. In a crucial way, the atheisms of Sartre and his own are miles apart. Superficially, Heidegger's methodological atheism might seem hospitable to a theological view of human existence compared to Sartre's view of the *pour-soi*, but on closer look, it actually is the Sartrean formulation that takes more seriously the idea that the final horizon of human existence is theological. Whereas Heidegger basically decides against God while pretending he has not (it cannot go without noticing that in the 1927 essay he mentions the occurrence of revelation), never offering an argument to justify his fundamentally atheistic characterization of human existence, Sartre attempts to do so. At the very beginning of *Being and Nothingness*, he criticizes the ontological argument, arguing that God, who from Anselm to Descartes was thought to be a necessary being, in fact is an *impossible* being. Although Sartre's portrayal of human existence refuses to accord any positive reference to God, it does so only after having tried to establish that methodological choice by showing that there is no God. As for Heidegger, his existential analytic simply deploys an atheistic characterization of man by invoking a background distinction between philosophy and theology that itself presupposes the kind of substantive atheism he claims the existential analytic does not enact. Without ever squarely admitting to it, the stated methodological atheism of Heidegger's philosophy hinges on a thoroughgoing denial of faith, which is simply to say that it *does* take a stance against God. This spells trouble for the idea that the existential analytic was safe to set aside God. And it casts further doubt on the prospects of formulating a methodologically atheist philosophy. As Jean-Yves Lacoste has commented, "Being-before-God can be claimed as the ultimate mystery of existence; philosophy can be criticized as incomplete if it makes no mention of God's name."[9] *If* God exists, and *if* faith is true, then to bracket God when characterizing our fundamental being-in-the-world is not to describe, but to distort, what makes us who we are.[10]

Of course, there is a wholly different way of seeing the relation between philosophy and theology worth mentioning, albeit briefly. It is one that itself disagrees with Heidegger's own particular way of separating them. But with him it agrees that the two must be separated. We have in mind the various Aristotelian theologies. For that tradition, it is true that theology deals with God in a way philosophy does not sufficiently, but it is not the case that philosophy sets aside God entirely. At the very least, for philosophy there are the rational deductions of God's existence. Beginning in the Middle Ages, we know, distinctions between faith and reason, the supernatural and the natural, were taken to determine the methodological difference between theology's and philosophy's content. There is natural reason, which reveals to us its truths, that God exists, or other basic divine facts, for example. But this is all. To know more, we will need something extra besides natural reason to reveal it to us. It is here that theology comes in, relying as it does on a divine donation beyond what we otherwise would see or understand independently of the faith that believes it. And usually, it is here also that the further distinction between grace and nature comes into play. But all of these distinctions only get us so far. At bottom, the existential question inevitably arises: how do I, as an individual, relate myself to God, and to these divine matters that present themselves as revealed truths? Do I accept them, or not? And if I do, on what basis do I decide? As for deciding such questions, the division between faith and reason is of no significant experiential help. Even if it is a theoretical distinction drawn to keep our intellectual domains from crossing into one another's respective spheres of influence, these divisions of labor do not honestly represent the position of the individual who must confront the question of God. Here, the distinction between faith and reason could not be any less instructive.

To begin with, as Lacoste has noted, there are many things that everyone agrees are rational to believe yet depend on our accepting them. And that act of acceptance invokes our capacity for freedom. Even rational conclusions that we seem to reach by reason alone appeal to our freedom ultimately. When faced with a good argument for something, we *concede* to it— which is why, when we do not but should, there is something wrong with our not doing so. We cannot say so straightforwardly, then, that some things are believed without being rationally known (faith), while other things simply are known rationally without any serious concern about whether it took an act of faith to do so (reason). It is true that many states of affairs, like the cat sleeping on the bed at my feet, compel my belief—in everyday life, most of the time the question whether to believe what is before us never seriously arises. But with knowledge of God, it is different. As Lacoste has said, because rationality appeals to freedom, even arguments that ordinarily are thought to belong to the province of natural reason appeal to a logic of consent, not constraint: "To be able to agree that God exists, we must decide freely, and must make up our minds."[11] Even thinking is choosing, and as for choosing, that is a matter of our willing, which itself in turn is always emblematic of what we love. Love and reason are not so unconnected. As Lacoste thus notes, the *logos* of love is already at work in judgment and thinking, even in something as initially apparently cut-and-dried as rational deductions of God's existence. It might be overstating things to say that faith is being exercised to its fullest, but it is operative at least minimally in an inchoate form.

If, then, this implicit role of love in reasoning about God's existence were not already decisive proof that simplistic distinctions between faith and reason do not hold, there is more. Contrary to what a popular truism asserts, neither can we say so confidently that there is reality as everyone experiences it (nature), but some further one only discerned subsequently by some (supernatural). Natural theology asserts that the Creator is revealed through creation. Is such a revelation natural? Fine, but then it is natural knowledge of something beyond nature itself! The supernatural has already intruded. Nor may we say that we know God as First Cause (natural reason) only to know him later and better as the God of Jesus Christ (faith). There are plenty of people who are acquainted with Christ without ever having to read a word of theology and who have never bothered to reason their way to God's existence in accord with the principles of what some philosophers mean by natural reason. We cannot always say, then, with the tradition of Aristotelianism, that philosophy lives by natural reason, theology by faith. As the ordinary believer knows (*connaître*), Revelation changes everything: in the wake of the life, death, and Resurrection of Jesus Christ, philosophy too is done under the gaze of God, whether it acknowledges so or not.

If both theological Aristotelianism's and Heidegger's failures to demarcate philosophy from theology show that it is not so easy to police thought on God, does that mean everything is thrown into a state of conceptual disarray? Are we unable then to say with any confidence whether some questions are philosophical, while others are not? These anxieties are understandable. But they are overstated. Even if we do not have the kind of solid distinction Heidegger or others wanted, things are not nearly as confusing without it as someone might think. For instance, concern over the ontic status of numbers obviously is a philosophical one. And the question of how many angels can dance on the head of a pin is a theological concern if there ever were one. But when our concern turns to the majority of matters, any such clear division recedes. And that is okay. It just means we are willing to meet things on their own terms, rather than on those our methodological provisos wish to foist on them.

It is to existentialism's credit that it has taught us why, when concerned with questions of our human existence, divine things cannot safely be set aside. When thinking about questions of ultimate human significance, attempting to draw any such distinction between theology and philosophy would be beside the point, even counterproductive. What matters is not locating some rigid boundary between philosophy and theology, but describing things as they are. The goal is seeing the truth, that of the human condition as it is. In putting ourselves into question in the way such inquiry demands, it would be a mistake to think God can be neglected. Here in this context, methodological atheism rests on a mistake.

We may mention a final word with that result now in mind. There is something of an irony in that, very often, it is those speaking in the name of such methodological atheism, who, desiring to purge God from philosophy, end up thereby resorting to dogmatism to do so. They are too assured that the wall between theology and philosophy is as firm as they wish that it were. It always is worth remembering that definitions treating philosophy and theology as distinct did not come down off the mountain with Moses. Drawn in the minds of men, neither are they written in stone.

NOTES

1. The *locus classicus* of this idea is found in Dominique Janicaud's now dated, but still influential, essay in *Phenomenology and the "Theological Turn": The French Debate*, trans. Bernard G. Prusak (New York: Fordham University Press, 2000).

2. Martin Heidegger, "Phenomenology and Theology," in *Pathmarks*, ed. William McNeill (Cambridge: Cambridge University Press, 1998), 41.

3. Specifically, he states three: first, that a certain being has already been disclosed as a possible theme of theoretical objectivization; next, that this disclosure is prior to any theoretical apprehending; and, finally, such "prescientific comportment" involves an understanding of being (Heidegger, "Phenomenology and Theology," 42).

4. The distinction appears in one shape or another across Kierkegaard's corpus. For its most famous and direct formulation, see *Concluding Unscientific Postscript to Philosophical Fragments*, vols. 1 and 2, trans. Edna Hong and Howard V. Hong (Princeton: Princeton University Press,1992). It is throughout his journals, too.

5. Heidegger, "Phenomenology and Theology," 53.

6. Ibid.

7. Even supposing that Heidegger is right that anxiety implies a finitude initially closed off to God, it does not follow that it cannot be interrupted by a Revelation that transforms it, dispelling the enigma of man's meaning. See, for example, Emmanuel Falque, *The Guide to Gethsemane: Anxiety, Suffering, Death*, trans. George Hughs (New York: Fordham University Press, 2019).

8. Walter Hopp has reminded me why Camus, too, is susceptible to similar criticisms. As with Heidegger, for Camus the un-answerability of ultimate questions is a dogmatic commitment. Anyone who is honest with himself, Camus says, will act on what he knows only, but we know nothing. An inconsistency is lurking in what Camus contends. For instead of living as if he does not know whether God exists (or whether life has a meaning), Camus says instead that he shall live as if there is no God and that life has no meaning. But that is to confuse *not knowing that P* with *knowing that not-P*. Moreover, Camus still insists that he wants answers to the questions that he insists are unanswerable. Thus, there is something transparently self-serving about the entire thing: he enjoys (from his perspective) the best of both worlds. He garners the respect due to a seeker of wisdom, while remaining entitled to live a life of voluptuousness. This approach is a clear instance of Iris Murdoch's insight that behind the existentialist's despair really is "elation"—or "intoxication" as Kierkegaard described it in *Judge for Yourself!*

9. Jean-Yves Lacoste, *The Appearing of God*, trans. Oliver O'Donovan (Oxford: Oxford University Press. 2018), 101.

10. For another way to this same conclusion, see the refutation of Heidegger's methodological atheism in Tarek R. Dika, "Finitude, Phenomenology, and Theology in Heidegger's *Sein und Zeit*," *Harvard Theological Review* 110, no. 4 (2017): 475–93. As Dika says, attempts such as Heidegger's to purify phenomenology of theological content inevitably fail, since, "For

atheism to be possible here, it would have to be possible, not only not to 'believe' in God, but not to relate to one's finitude in light of the idea of God. This is not a requirement even the most methodologically rigorous phenomenology of finitude has thus far been able to satisfy. To take the finitude of the human being as one's methodological starting-point, and to characterize such a method as 'atheism,' presupposes that finitude is phenomenologically accessible immanently, i.e., prior to and independently of any relation to a transcendence that exceeds it in power," 492. In order for Heidegger's existential analytic to eliminate any theological residue from ontological finitude, it must not reintroduce the ontic content of what it has tried to modify ontologically. In short, "The ontological concept of finitude cannot have as part of its content the experience of oneself *coram Deo*," 493. However, finitude presupposes a power beyond itself (Dika says "transcendence"), a perspective that accordingly is *not* radically immanent. With Descartes, he thus concludes, it must be conceded that infinity is prior, not just formally but experientially, to finitude. Methodological atheism has been shown to be a dream. For another work that assesses the Heideggerian attempt to purify phenomenological concepts of their theological content, see Ryan Coyne, *Heidegger's Confessions: The Remains of St. Augustine* (Chicago: University of Chicago Press, 2015).

11. Lacoste, *The Appearing of God*, 88.

Chapter Two

The Interlacement of Self and God

Faith, which works by love, is the reclamation of our humanity, the acceptance of our being-before-God. To be oneself is to be laid bare, at heart, by God. He seeks always to bring us back to ourselves. And for that reason, his call resounds within our depths. It is difficult to believe there has been someone who has not at some time in his life experienced it, for here any such exemption borders on the unthinkable, since to be alive, as the one who lives in faith comes to recognize, is to have felt the weight of that claim immemorially, even during the long span, maybe even many years, in which it was ignored or suppressed. This call, which happens as a self-revelation by making us acutely aware of ourselves, never allows for the possibility that we may succeed entirely in not hearing it. Struggle as we may to silence it, each of us cannot escape that we must answer it, either in the form of an embrace or a rebuff. It is with this divine call in mind, and with language consciously reminiscent of Fénelon, Malebranche, and Kierkegaard who had considered it too, that the French philosopher Jean-Louis Chrétien, while in the midst of a rich meditation in *The Ark of Speech* exploring the interplay between silence and listening, observes with the admirable clarity characteristic of his style that it is "only because God has encountered us, has come to meet us, that we can turn away from him, or try to turn away from him, and forget him."[1] Supposing that we do not hear God, is it because he has not spoken, or is it not rather because we do not want to hear what we know he says? The truth is so simple, which explains its incredible power to humble us when we finally have let it reach us. God, we see, was always there waiting for us even when we were not yet prepared to be there for him.

How, then, could it ever be possible to speak truthfully about ourselves while simultaneously ignoring the question of God's existence? Despite the implausibility of being able to do so, attempts have been made. One common line of such reasoning, frequently rehearsed and even apparently somewhat innocuous at first, is said to favor the conclusion that an adequate reckoning with our human existence only demands reference to what (or who) we are said to be when where we are is understood solely as being-in-the-world. We begin by noting the heart of the argument's professed insight. Statements as the one above (that everyone knows the call of God), it says, should be dismissed as ungrounded theological assertions, or at the least seen to be less than bona fide philosophical claims. *Homo religiosus* is not outright irrational, maybe, it will concede, but from its perspective the faithful witness is bound to seem somehow artificial. And for good reason, so this thought continues. For according to this perspective that sees human existence as fundamentally atheistic, as not characterized ultimately by the felt need for God, the most compelling reason for finding any suggested mention of our being-before-God safely set aside philosophically is that the world of experience makes no real room for that encounter. To begin with, as someone persuaded by such a thought no doubt will note, no one sane denies that we all find ourselves in the world. And if those without belief in God are to be taken at their words, it must also be noted that the world is not, at least immediately anyway, somewhere God as a matter of course appears. As J. L. Schellenberg's atheistic argument from divine hiddenness insists, for instance, and as generally is held to be the case (Pascal aside), there are nonculpable unbelievers.[2] The idea to many seems credible. And not without its apparent reasons: are not there those who will go an entire lifetime claiming never once to have encountered him?

Hence, the appearing of God in the world is not a revelation occurring in the dazzling, intuitive light of what Husserl meant by his notion of *Evidenz*. To the contrary, for, were God disclosed obtrusively in the world, were "divine things" (as Justin Martyr would say) clearly and distinctly manifest alongside the other things that are, we would then be forced to conclude that whoever went on living without (or apart from) God is like the patient in the mental ward, who, wandering the halls aimlessly at night, despite every evidence presented him to the contrary, denies the world's existence, maintaining it is an illusion. If there are those who can be believed when they report knowing nothing of God, we find the profession coherent, to whatever extent we do, because the world, as they observe correctly, is a place where God's existence is ambiguous because it is not so obtrusive. God is not encountered as a chair, a parrot in a cage (as Kierkegaard sardonically remarked), a law of logic, or a value. Of course, to the believer God is not hidden (or no longer is). But we can see why someone might think that God is hidden. As Jean-Yves Lacoste has noted in this context, God does not impose himself on us, which accounts for why it remains possible to choose not to have anything to do with him.[3] If God is to appear, his presence is (at least some of the time) one we must seek.

Being-in-the-world makes God's presence sufficiently faint to grant plausibility to the statement of those who deny any acquaintance with God. And yet, at the same time, while it must be noted that no one denies that we are children of the world, and while indeed almost everyone would not concede that God's existence is far from self-evident in it, we cannot shake off the lingering sense that there is something amiss. Must we confine our efforts to make sense of the human condition to what appears obvious to the one living in the world without God? Nothing could be less obvious. Certainly, we are in the world, and the world appears initially to be a place where God does not appear. The validity of these statements deserves to be acknowledged. But that validity notwithstanding, there is something unsatisfying about an attempted accounting of our existence that purports to assign, finally and decisively, the last word on existence to our thrownness into a forsaken world. It is worth noting that in his letter to the Romans, Paul highlights that the visible world discloses the glory of God. Those who claim not to see, he says, are blinded by the darkness of their own minds. Contrary to what is sometimes assumed, Paul's claim is not some banality of natural theology. It is, rather, a phenomenological claim that deserves careful consideration, and which repays the efforts we make to explicate it. The place to begin is with the unbeliever's own claim, according to which God is hidden. God is hidden, yes, in that denying seeing divine things is not as embarrassing as denying not seeing the chair in the room, but while God is not visible, he nevertheless appears despite that invisibility *through* visible things. It will be our task to see what Paul's statement means.

To start, a total concession to the idea that the absolute horizon of existence is being-toward-death would be premature. And to resist it does not demand that we challenge any of its key assertions about God's unobtrusiveness in the world. Granting for the time being that God's presence in the world is ambiguous, we are still free to doubt whether such a view has succeeded in meeting its stated aim of excavating the most intimate mode of that existence. We are in the world, yes. About that it is correct. And for many of those whose existence is taken today to be entirely quotidian, such an existence, an existence of being-in-the-world, is one lacking the knowledge of God or any rapport with God. That, too, fits with such an account. But because being-in-the-world is the typical mode of existence, it does not follow that we may bracket (much less eliminate) the significance that the possibility of living being-before-God contributes to our understanding of what it means to exist in the world. Is being-in-the-world the entirety of what we are, and fundamentally so? Does the world enjoy the last word on existence? Nothing we have read in the celebrated accounts of human existence in *Being and Time* or *Being and Nothingness* provides reason to think that the decision to undertake an analysis of humanity apart from God is irreproachable. In saying that we are inscribed in a world where God does not appear, are we thereby committed to also saying that another way of existing, one subverting the logic of such being-in-the-world, is not a real option? Existence for Heidegger and Sartre is one essentially without God. But need it be?

To make progress on deciding, it will be necessary to revisit an old issue, that of the world's meaning as a *phenomenon*. In short: what is the world? When viewing the world as a phenomenon, as we mean to do here, the question becomes quintessentially phenomenological, which is why beginning with Husserl's own investigations into the matter, those who have thought in the wake of his legacy have never ceased being preoccupied with it. For phenomenology, the problem of the world must be awakened philosophically *as a problem*. In the present philosophical context, here as ever, to raise that problem is to do so by approaching it with the readiness to acknowledge that, whatever common sense suggests, the world as a phenomenon is one whose meaning deserves full treatment and a nuanced answer. What is the world, and what about it veils God?

An elementary thing worth noting here is that the world, if nothing else, is a perceptual world. Our most basic mode of contact with it is sensorial. It does not take reading Merleau-Ponty to recognize that the perceived is that which originally surrounds us. That God does not appear, then, is not so much evidence counting against his existence necessarily, as it is an indication that, given who he is, his appearing will not be a matter of mundane visibility. Even the child understands God is invisible. Shrewd adults who have come to believe there is no God are always tempted at this point to make a joke, observing wryly that God, who is invisible, is really the believer's imaginary friend. But if we later were to decide that God truly is a figment of our imaginations, it would be bad reasoning to think so just because he is invisible. Does a thing's invisibility, without further ado, cast doubt on its existence? Experience counsels otherwise. We encounter invisible things incessantly (the backside of the chair), and that they are invisible never gives us pause. Their invisibility is no reason to doubt them. Numbers are invisible, for example. So, too, the laws of logic. Anyone who jeered at the mathematician for taking the existence of numbers seriously because they were invisible would be guilty of a very basic, even ghastly, misunderstanding of the situation—such a comment would betray an ignorance of what numbers are. The one who did not comprehend that numbers exist invisibly, and then mistook his disappointment on not encountering one in his living room as he does the sofa, as if their visual absence were an indication they were unreal, is not someone gathering evidence in favor of his suspicion that none exist, but someone confused about what he was looking for, and consequently has been failing to find. Is not a similar kind of misunderstanding perhaps at work when, being reminded that God is invisible and thus not among the things we can expect to appear alongside the visible items of our environment, atheism ignores this point, and still persists adducing the absence of God in the visible world as proof of God's inexistence? In reply, it will be insisted (and rightly so) that nobody, nor for that matter the unbeliever, ever seriously expected God to be visible next to a cat, or on the table, or inside the refrigerator. Looking out my living room window onto the street, I see cars and trees, but that I do not see God too, that is no surprise. What the one as yet unacquainted with God means by his absence (or a lack of evidence for his existence), then, has nothing to do with something so simple as that. But if that is so, then it no longer is fair to make the usual wisecrack about God being imaginary in response to the believer who reminds the skeptic that God is Spirit, and thus invisible. What God's invisibility amounts to, consequently, is a matter of some nuance. We have made no small progress if, in this context, the unbeliever sees that the sphere of invisibility is not to be conflated with the imaginary and illusory.

This lesson about God's mode of appearing is important, and though it may seem obvious, it was necessary to state it, for it is a mistake that many repeat, albeit in a more sophisticated philosophical fashion than in the somewhat comical, everyday way just alluded to. Nevertheless, the lesson stands. Tracing the most basic form that mistake takes has highlighted the imperativeness of avoiding it. The danger of confusing God's invisibility with his inexistence, then, we may take to be surmounted. But there is another. For as vital as the lesson that God appears invisibly is, we must also guard against a possible misunderstanding that arises when overcorrecting in the opposite direction. That God is invisible does not mean he is unperceivable, or that encountering him does not call upon our powers of perception. On the contrary, to appreciate why God does not appear visibly in the world is to see how knowing God requires the art of perception. As with any encounter, perception is in play.

Sometimes, perception can be more than a matter of registering what without further ado announces itself. There must also be the willingness (and ability) to perceive. When this is so, the perceived exerts a demand not only on our senses, but on our entire being. What we feel is there to be perceived solicits every faculty to confirm the premonition of its presence. In such cases, the *logos* of discernment is intellectual, aesthetic, and moral. Our capacities of judgment, taste, and will are all put to work, as when we listen to a Beethoven sonata, view a Kandinsky, or interpret a delicate remark from a friend. Understanding something technical (a mathematical theorem), refined (an artwork), or precious (a gesture of kindness in the time of need) requires a will to understand. Unless attention is exercised, what appears will not. There can be failures to perceive because what we thought was there is not. Equally, though, there can be failures to perceive because we are oblivious or unreceptive to what is there. Someone coldhearted and self-absorbed is prone to overlook the good that others show him, just as the one with a novice ear is unlikely to notice the full richness of one of Stamitz's compositions like *La chasse* due to its apparent simplicity. Perceiving can be an achievement, a success won after considerable training or struggle on our part.

Here inevitably, the question arises. How is God's own obscure presence in the world to be understood? What explains that God's presence eludes those it is said to? Does whoever claims not to know God fail to perceive because there is nothing to be perceived, or is the presence of "divine things" something forever there, waiting to be encountered when our discernment has been cultivated? Is God's not appearing in the world to be explained by his nonexistence, or because, ever ready to appear, God only appears elsewhere and otherwise than as the one locked into the mode of being-in-the-world expects?

There are reasons for concluding that God's elusiveness is similar to the subtleness of a great symphony or mathematical proof—perceiving will take both effort and discernment. Let us consider the most essential of these reasons. First, paradoxically, that God appears discreetly is constitutive of who he is. God, who is love, does not impose an encounter with himself, because to do so would be incompatible with the love defining him. If he seems distant to the one who does not yet know him, it is because God can only be near when we have already drawn near to him—even in the case of an instantaneous and unexpected conversion, we must not flee or shrink back when God has taken the initiative to surprise us.[4] The point at issue is not so provocative as it seems. It is even sensible. To note it simply reminds us that if we ever are to close whatever experiential gap we feel between God and ourselves, how else will we be able to do it except by loving him? Hence, if God will be known, he must be loved. This phenomenological axiom is sufficient to disqualify any statement that purports to adduce the inexistence of God, while never having approached him in faith genuinely. Scheler was right, strictly in virtue of phenomenological principle, when he was to identify (following the examples of Augustine and Pascal) the logic governing the *ordo amoris*: whereas other matters must be known before they may be loved, such is not the rule with divine things, for which it is necessary to love them in order first to be known.[5] It is a truism that almost seems banal when stated so plainly. Nevertheless, it deserves to be underscored once again: no one who does not love God can know him.

Our saying so invites a natural concern that may be put as an objection. Does not the contention that God must be loved to be known beg the question? This objection misfires, however, for it proceeds as if what were at issue is a matter of propositional truth. Perhaps then a circularity charge would bear on things. But when it comes to the knowledge of God, we are concerned with knowledge by acquaintance, with knowing God in a way not unlike the way we do another human person. We are not concerned with an entity whose existence must be demonstrated by deductive argument, but with someone whose presence is to be sought and enjoyed.[6] The concern is one of desire, not abstraction. If one were to attempt to sidestep this point, insisting it is irrational, unfair, or otherwise dubious to expect everyone to begin his journey toward God without having a demonstration in hand, they would never get started with the search. The one enthralled to rational demonstration has not looked only to not find. Rather, he persists looking in a way that guarantees he will come up empty-handed inevitably, so long as he wants to. Even in the case of rational arguments for God's existence, as we have noted with Lacoste, such demonstrations never coerce. Because here we are not on the terrain of certainty, our thought must always still decide whether to accept the conclusion proposed to it. The exercise of reason, as Lacoste says, depends accordingly on our freedom, which in matters regarding God accordingly appeal to love. Knowing is entwined with what we *want* to know, or *want* to be. In a very subtle yet relevant way, just affirming an argument's conclusion takes an exercise of love.

The significance of reason's presupposing the free exercise of love cannot be overstated. For one, the familiar Freudian accusation of "wish-fulfillment," it follows, is a double-edged sword, as apt to cut against the skeptic's affective integrity as it is said to cut against the believer's intellectual integrity. If it is always possible to allege that faith believes what is false because it desires it to be true, it is just as intelligible to claim that unbelief fails to believe because it wants what is true to be false. If I believe, my affirmation to know God may be discounted by others as an instance of believing what is not there simply because I want to love it. At the same time, the denial of God's existence might equivalently be interpreted as someone's not wanting to love what *is* there. Contrary to what many unbelievers in a Freudian spirit say, it is not so easy to show one's personal unbelief is rooted in a rational assessment of what everyone can agree is what the evidence impartially indicates, and not a reluctance to love—and thus *obey*—God. Schellenberg's question of culpability, here, is germane. We should ask ourselves: when we resolve not to love God without first satisfying the condition that God be demonstrated (as if his existence should be subjected to such efforts), is God's subsequent failure to appear his fault or actually ours?

Face-to-face with another person, for example, there can be no seriously doubting that he exists. Choosing to withhold our love from him on the grounds that we had not yet been given adequate demonstrative reason to think he exists would be cruel, and it would be mad. A demand for that sort of demonstrative assurance is out of order. We find ample reason for believing the other exists because he appears right before us. Seeing is believing. As someone whose mode of givenness is visible in the flesh, in looking on him we have met him on his terms, in accord with his mode of appearing (here we may ignore the possibility that even the revelation of another human involves a rapport with the invisible). Should God be the exception to the rule? He, too, must be encountered according to the fitting phenomenality. And if God has addressed us in love, then as we have been saying, his call will be heard only when we have made ourselves ready to receive that love by showing ours. If we are sealed off to what God has spoken, and hence insensitive to his way of making himself heard, no wonder we will not hear from him.

To note that the genuine *logos* of our existence is one set to work by love is no small thing. It runs counter to the idea, for example, as Heidegger contended in 1927, that the fundamental mood of existence is anxiety. To emphasize the importance of love in how we make judgments, draw rational conclusions, weigh evidence, and desire to see or not see what we want to, is to accentuate the point we have been making in these pages: neither foundationally nor absolutely is existence defined by being-in-the-world. To the contrary, it is our being-before-God that is so. God's failing to appear self-evidently to everyone straightaway does not belie this thesis. If anything, it reinforces it. Just as love discloses more than what otherwise would appear without it, so the one who does not want to know God will not. Traditionally, if philosophy's main tendency has been to characterize faith in terms of propositional belief in God's existence, it seems better to put faith in terms emphasizing the experiential stakes of the knowledge of God. It is a knowledge opened, sustained, and deepened through love, at once both by ours for him and in his for us.

We now return to the original claim that insofar as God fails to appear in the world, it is owing to this absence of appearing that those who report not possessing knowledge of him do so. For instance, when questioned as to what he would say to God if asked why he had not believed, Bertrand Russell answered, "Not enough evidence God! Not enough evidence!" There is reason, however, for doubting that Russell's unbelief was really epistemic. Given the eidetic connection between faith and love, it strains credulity to think that there has ever been someone who genuinely tried, straining with every fiber of his being, to seek God only to discover not to find him. Russell's own jocular attitude was not that of someone who had tried with everything inside himself to pursue God only to be crushed by a realization that there was nothing to find. Agnostics are sometimes haunted profoundly by what they are concerned might indeed be the real absence of God. There are comparatively few atheists who seem to be saddened by God's absconsion—that difference between agnosticism and atheism is telling, and not obviously in the atheist's favor. It is difficult not to form the impression that, for Russell personally, there was a total lack of seriousness about the matter, as if he were playing a game or toying with an intellectual puzzle. When we look at the aged Russell in his interviews, we do not see the figure of some wise man we should expect to have found God if anyone can. What we see instead, truth be told, is something still very adolescent. It is worth mentioning that many of the most renowned atheists report having decided to be done with God in their teens. Usually, this biographical nugget is interpreted retrospectively as evidence of what then was their intellectual precociousness. But is that what it really suggests? Even in his latest years, Russell the man created an impression, on television and radio anyway, that was shallow and superficial, even calculated. To be sure, there is plenty of erudition in the sort of intellectualism for which he had become so famous. But there is very little love of God in it.

Noting what we have on the relationship between love and knowledge, it is necessary to shift the focus some. It will be noted that looking into the most intimate dimension of the self's structure usually is phenomenology's jurisdiction (Ricœur's *la question du sujet*), yet it is necessary to offer some remarks whose distinctively religious pedigree will lead some readers to claim they accordingly lie beyond the bounds of phenomenological reason. It might even seem to concern a subject thoroughly unphilosophical, one residing entirely on the distant shore of what we today term patristic theology. To capture adequately not only the experience of being-in-the-world but also of existing before God, it is necessary to discard the conceptual and theoretical partitions traditionally installed between philosophy and theology. In approaching the question of our relation to God, and how the ever-present possibility of establishing such a relationship is constitutive of what it is to exist, we may appeal to things as we all know and experience them as the existing human beings we are. Hence, we ask once again: why do those who claim not to know God not hear the divine call?

One answer, and the one probably that has enjoyed the most favor since the Reformation, is to see nothing surprising or amiss in a professed ignorance of God's call. According to this mentality, it is only natural (in every sense of the term) not to hear God, either because there is no God calling to us (atheism), or because, though God exists, we are not immediately poised, in what it calls our unregenerate state, without any further ado, to hear him (Augustinianism). In short, it suggests we are born without ears to hear. Taking deafness to be our natal condition can be seductive for many reasons. And the allure of its apparent explanation of unbelief has led diverse (and mutually competing!) causes to enlist it—Augustine, Calvin, Plantinga, on the one side, Voltaire, Camus, and Sartre, on the other. That this way of interpreting the human condition as originally forsaken from God has appealed to so many philosophers and theologians is incredible, given how badly it fails to withstand serious scrutiny. A simple *reductio* shows the point. Assuming we have always already found ourselves in a world estranged from God, as if such a separation were a regrettable birthright, then this alienation from God, which is said to be our natural condition, should imply that, when languishing in the gall of bitterness and the pits of despair, those who remain morally depraved should not experience any guilt over transgressions that this form of forsakenness treats as inevitable anyway. But that is not how things are. If moral darkness characterizes our original standing, then why do those who claim not to have any acquaintance of God's call, after having committed a wrong, naturally attempt to cloak it from others (and even ourselves through rationalization)? If committing such acts were inevitable, why then are they not treated as natural, without any shame or regret? Why do we feel guilt for what we have done if we were not responsible for our having freely done what we did? If we were not at liberty to leave off from doing evil and to do good instead, why does everyone know the crushing feeling of being overwhelmed by the shame that haunts even the mere remembrance of past wrongs? Rational regret is possible only where necessity was lacking.

Kant in *Religion within the Bounds of Mere Reason* emphasizes this point when examining the nature of radical evil. He says, "The human being must make or have made himself into whatever he is or should become in a moral sense, good or evil. These two [characters] must be an effect of his free power of choice, for otherwise they could not be imputed to him and, consequently, he could be neither morally good nor evil."[7] He expands by noting, "duty commands that [one] be good, and duty commands nothing but what we can do."[8] For, as he explains, "if the moral law commands that we *ought* to be better human beings now, it inescapably follows that we must be *capable* of being better human beings."[9] But a view that sees evil as inherent to our nature (in the sense that it was imposed on us without our freedom) would be to undermine the basis of both virtue and moral accountability. Hence, while recognizing the universal human propensity to evil, Kant takes care to emphasize the existence of a comparatively more fundamental predisposition to good: radical evil arises from the free decision to improperly order our maxims in response to the felt conflict between reason and sensual incentives. To be sure, the rational origin of such evil remains inexplicable to us, says Kant. But that is fine, and it is not an objection to this account of evil's origin. For there are limits to our understanding, and, if evil inherently is irrational, there is little surprise that the decision to subordinate the moral law to sensual incentives remains mysterious: at bottom, there is no *reason* why anyone should, because doing so is fundamentally irrational.[10]

That the origin of radical evil presupposes a freedom just as radical is ancient, going way back before Kant. This idea in Kant that evil ultimately is rooted in freedom, and not our nature, is one the early Christian church universally taught before Augustine. Irenaeus of Lyons, the understudy of Polycarp the disciple of John, was among the earliest observers to note this eidetic connection between freedom and responsibility. In his Fourth Book of *Against Heresies*, it states that everyone's nature is such as to enable us to "hold fast and to do what is good." Unequivocally, an ability to choose the good pleasing in the sight of God is emphasized in an adjoining portion of that same text: "Man is endowed with the faculty of distinguishing good and evil; so that, without compulsion, he has the power, by his own will and choice, to perform God's commandments."[11] Handed down to the early believers by written epistle and through taught example, the idea at stake could not be more Johannine: "Little children, let no one deceive you: he that does what is righteous is righteous even as [Christ] is" (1 John 3:7). The remarks of Irenaeus, which reflected what was handed down from the apostles directly, imply that whatever estrangement from God we do experience occurs only after we have learned to discern good from evil and, by our own decision, have chosen knowingly to descend into the latter. In a text entitled "First Epistle," Clement of Rome (who knew Paul and hence formulates an early statement of Pauline teaching), addresses a question to us of basic concern. What, he asks, must we do to be found worthy of God's promise of eternal life? In answering that question, Clement accentuates how doing good before God is not only possible. It is expected. Just as Irenaeus would later emphasize the link between love and faith, Clement notes one between faith and the unhindered human ability to choose between right and wrong. Salvation, then, is something we must work out in fear and trembling, for as Clement stresses, because it is a question of the love of God, true faith is put to work by doing good: "But how, beloved, shall this be done? If our understanding be fixed by faith toward God; if we earnestly seek the things which are pleasing and acceptable to Him; if we do the things which are in harmony with His blameless will; and if we follow the way of truth, casting away from us all unrighteousness and iniquity, along with all covetousness, strife, evil practices, deceit, whispering, and evil-speaking, all hatred of God, pride and haughtiness, vainglory and ambition."[12] The next century another Clement, he of Alexandria, expressed the same view in his "Valentinian's Vagaries About the Abolition of Death Refuted." Those who find themselves separated from God have no one but themselves to blame, he states. Alienation from God is the consequence of a perversion of the will through the misdirection of our attention and desire. It is not, as Augustine was later to claim, the immemorial consequence of our having been born with a weakened will that twists our desire. As Clement makes clear, "estrangement is the result of free choice." [13]

The idea that the earliest patristics reject, namely, this idea of a human nature unable to obey God because of an inherent corruption, appears in many forms throughout the subsequent history of philosophy. The doctrine's reach is not limited only to the arcane and premodern, theological context. Regularly, we encounter it on the daily news. Crooked defense attorneys, for example, employ a variation of the idea when they try to convince jurors that their client was in some regard unable to avoid doing what he did, either because of bad brain chemistry, upbringing, or a cocktail of the two. Children, we all know, resort to a similar defense strategy when caught by their parents doing something they should not have done. It is not a foreign experience. Is there anyone who at some point has not tried justifying what he did by claiming he could not help it? And it is this very mindset that many, even in nominal adulthood, do not outgrow, when at work they lie and gossip, or in private cheat on their taxes and spouse, living a life of basic disregard for what is right, while accepting no responsibility for the consequences of deciding to do the wrong they have done. What the Christian philosopher Justin Martyr noted of his time is no less true today. Our surroundings, he noted, can corrupt us by obscuring the good we might otherwise have seen. As he states in "Dialogue with Trypho," "For [God] sets before every race of mankind that which is always and universally just, as well as all righteousness; and every race knows that adultery, and fornication, and homicide, and such like, are sinful; and though they all commit such practices, yet they do not escape from the knowledge that they act unrighteously whenever they so do, with the exception of those who are possessed with an unclean spirit, and who have been debased by education, by wicked customs, and by sinful institutions, and who have lost, or rather quenched and put under, their natural ideas."[14] A lack of moral consensus does not show there is no fact of the matter, just that there are many ways to have missed the mark.

Is there, then, something in our nature making us incapable of being better than what the standards associated with average everydayness suggest? There is no short supply of reasons for thinking that we can do better. In fact, there is precedent for thinking that today's normal—what, for example, Kant called an "unsociable sociability"—is not normal at all. It is deeply abnormal, in that it is pathological, a deviation from nature, no matter how common it becomes. If failing in virtue were truly due to a depraved nature from birth, that fact was unknown to the earliest patristics, who, without exception, never spoke of such a thing. Encountering them today, the modern reader trained to see everything through the Augustinian lens of most systematic theology will be shocked by how the writings of the earliest Christian philosophers approached the life of faith from a premise asserting that, even before the new birth, we are always already able to do the right thing. That is why we are guilty before God if we do not. For them, it is not *phusis* that sets us onto the path of wrongdoing, but rather our own free unwillingness to yield ourselves to good. A very early follower of the way, Ignatius of Antioch (a disciple of John), notes exactly that when writing in reference to those who become evil: they *become* evil. They are not born so. As he says there, the wicked are "made such not by nature, but by their own choice." The natural human freedom to do what is good finds expression in other texts besides Ignatius's "Epistle to the Magnesians." No less a church authority as Eusebius, for instance, when commenting on human nature, is quick to emphasize that far from constituting the inner secret of our being, evil remains contrary to it even after the Fall. We have not been cursed with moral depravity, but with mortality. And however what is meant by death here is interpreted (as physical or spiritual), it cannot be anything that hinders our power to do good. That capacity remains in us intact and unmarred. " But when a man acts wrongly," as Eusebius says, "nature is not to be blamed; for what is wrong, takes place not according to nature, but contrary to nature, it being the work of choice, and not of nature!"[15] Far from being a fact of natural necessity, the reputed inability to hear and heed God in the form of his moral imperatives, as these early patristic writings show, is a myth, for being evil simply is a function of the unwillingness to do good. Disobedience to God and the moral law is choice, not a *fait accompli*.

Additional writings from this period emphasize the power of individual freedom to overcome evil surroundings by nevertheless clinging to what is good. As Justin says, "[God] created both angels and men free to do that which is righteous, and He appointed periods of time during which He knew it would be good for them to have the exercise of free-will; and because He likewise knew it would be good, He made general and particular judgments; each one's freedom of will, however, being guarded."[16] Is not that our own situation? Today is thus so; each day is another opportunity to work what is good, freely! Disobedience is the result of a resolution on our part, not a fate extraneously constraining us. This trove of early patristic theology is perennial, for it contradicts, incessantly and unambiguously, the later theological constructions of concupiscence and total depravity. In another early apologetic voice as unimpeachable as that of Lactantius, we read the same lesson, when he observes, without the slightest reservation, "We should be free from vices and sin," since, as he immediately explains, "no one is born sinful."[17]

As he hastens to clarify, our natural affections (sensual incentives) become vices only as a result of being deployed as maxims taking precedence over moral ones. Hence, free choice alone is responsible for determining the shape our character will assume. We sculpt ourselves. The account of Lactantius explains why Origen, following the identical logic to that same conclusion, had already rejected the idea of inbred depravity. Such a notion is gnostic heresy: "We are responsible for being bad and worthy of being cast outside. For it is not the nature in us that is the cause of the evil; rather, it is the voluntary choice that works evil."[18] And in a comment from his *First Apology*, Justin agrees, noting in chapter 24 on the subject of God's care for men that "in the beginning [God] made the human race with the power of thought and of choosing the truth and doing right, so that all men are without excuse before God; for they have been born both rational and contemplative."[19] God shows us a great kindness in having made us able to taste the deep sweetness of doing good. As uplifting as these reassurances are for someone who wants to break free from the spiritual jail brought about by the discouraging thought that it is unattainable to be righteous, in reply to the pessimists and naysayers, one early Christian voice offered simple counsel. Do not be told you cannot do what you know you can: "And do not wonder that a man can become an imitator of God. He can, if he is willing."[20] No one, he notes, may dismay us by saying we cannot be so. It is possible to do the truth.[21]

And we need not resort just to the patristics for that assurance! As it happens, the truth is as available to us as it was to them. We are no less human than they, and eternal truths abide across time, even when (and indeed above all) they have fallen into disrepute. The interlocking testimony of common sense (one can only be held responsible for what it is possible to do), our hearts (guilt when we do wrong, joy when we do what is right), and the Holy Scriptures ("Depart from evil and do good, so you will abide forever" [Psalm 37:27]) all harmonize, reinforcing the patristic sentiment, as we have seen. Nothing hinders us from doing what is good, and certainly not a concupiscence inherited from Adam.[22] If we want to be good, we will. It is up to us. And therein consists the truth's real sting—evil does not befall us as a calamity; it is something that we chose.

The mist of centuries of theological systematizing has obscured this simple, sobering experiential fact. Attributing the supposed alienation from God to a fallen nature, and hence an accompanying impaired will or inherently perverse desire, these views locate the source of sin in a corruption said to be linked indissociably with the reality of embodied existence. But is being incarnate to be handed over to evil? How could such an idea running so contrary to what our own experience, the writings of the earliest Christian philosophers, and the words of Scripture, have overtaken us? The history leading us here is known. From approximately the fourth century beginning with Augustine, on through to the eleventh century's invention of substitutionary atonement in Anselm, then on to the Reformers like Calvin and Luther, human depravity has been a plank of theological anthropology's characterization of our being-before-God. Probably more than any other single idea, it determines the frame by which our place within the world has been viewed. The very label of "Pelagianism," which still today functions as an accusation and which had already become synonymous with heresy after Pelagius had challenged Augustine, Jerome, and Ambrose, is a view that, by defending man's unhindered natural ability to choose the good, stood in line with the consensus of Christian thinking theretofore. Holding to our natural ability to know and do what is right, Pelagius followed the example of Justin, Irenaeus, and Clement of Alexandria. If there was any threat of heresy at the time, it rested with Augustine, who, denying the existence of an unhindered natural ability to obey God, attacked the biblical anthropology of the heart. Where Christ always spoke of our being expected to have a good and noble heart, modern Augustinian theology speaks otherwise. Ever since Augustine, the various systematic theologies and church creeds tinged with a quasi-Manicheism Augustine never fully overcame have, from Aquinas's *Summa* to the Reformation's *Westminster Confession of Faith*, maintained that being born is to be born fallen as a sinner.

This volley of patristic references requires us to catch our breath. What role do the propositions they assert, which from a modern perspective are liable to be dismissed as obsolete theological claims, have here? The worry is only compounded by another fact: is not this meant to be a phenomenological inquiry? Yet remarks concerning our being-before-God that invoke notions such as sin, metaphysical freedom, and eternal immortality and responsibility will no doubt appear naive and, from a specifically transcendental philosophical perspective of Husserl or Heidegger, as lacking in philosophical rigor. Are they not assertions without *Evidenz* (Husserl)? Invoking them, have not we resorted to a domain of positive beings, thereby violating the methodological atheism (or metaphysical neutrality) of phenomenological ontology (Heidegger)? Or, to put the same point in the form of a question, what legitimate role, if any, do observations regarding being-before-God have in what aims to be a *phenomenological* account of subjectivity? If that truly is the goal, would it not be better for everyone involved (for the philosophers and the theologians alike) to reserve such issues to revealed theology? Or, more to the point, what philosophical basis is there for not excluding these theological phenomena from the present phenomenological consideration of *la question du sujet*?

This family of objections is familiar. It fails to persuade, however, for many reasons. First, it may be observed that this methodological objection uses the terms "phenomenological" and "theological" as labels for two supposedly different modes of inquiry without ever specifying, much less justifying, their breezy use. Here, adjectives come to substitute for description or historical and conceptual explication. Second, and more troublingly, in taking another look, we see that such an objection may be turned back against itself. Rather than proceeding as if God cannot enter the phenomenological field save for exceptional circumstances, why not reverse that adage and stipulate instead that, until convincing reasons are given, God must be included in our accounting of subjectivity, and not just in an auxiliary capacity but essentially? Thus, where Heidegger recommended methodological atheism as philosophically crucial to transcendental phenomenology, why cannot we claim the opposite and insist on a methodological theism? It could be claimed that presupposing God is to presuppose too much. But how is taking the inexistence of God for granted (or at least the irrelevance of his existence to phenomenology) not also a philosophical presupposition, and a very serious one at that? The suspicion that there is nothing at all neutral about methodological atheism only intensifies when, as seems right, we highlight that for phenomenology the issue always should remain one of appearing. If so, by what authority can God's phenomenality be discarded as illegitimate, as unimportant to phenomenological philosophy's concern? Where

Heidegger insists that we must interrogate ourselves as beings-in-the-world without God, why may we not insist instead that, if we are being honest about who we are, such an inquiry will remain incomplete, ignoring as it does our existence in the presence of God?

Why the second route is to be preferred to the first becomes evident when taking stock of the bad consequences attending the Heideggerian approach. To ignore the question of God (and "neutralizing" the question in the name of phenomenological method is just an elaborate way of doing this) would place us on shaky ground immediately, since, in the last analysis, to insist that phenomenology has no need to deal with what is treated as a matter for revealed theology is to neglect what, at least potentially, can be brought into the light of *Evidenz*. No doubt someone deeply invested in a certain understanding of transcendental phenomenology will want to uphold the modern division between reason and faith. What lies open to the evidence of reason is universal and attestable, whereas matters of faith are not—so the argument goes.[23] But that is to disparage faith as if it were blind, which it is not. Faith has its own form of evidence, the "evidence of things not seen" (Heb 11:1). The Pauline insight does not say that faith is blind or without evidence. It says, instead, that faith's evidence is unseen, which from even the Husserlian perspective is hardly scandalous, since the *eidos* is an ideal item of invisibility. As Husserl has taught us, what appears is by no means relegated to the visible. Then of course there is a further problem with the objection at issue. For even were we to overlook that faith indeed possesses its own evidence, one is still stuck having to explain why what is given to faith in evidence is irrelevant to the traditional phenomenological interest in evidence. Are faith's experiences unrelated to the objective of making sense of our being-in-the-world? Nothing could be any less obvious! It should be remarked that what is disclosed in evidence to faith changes how we see what else appears. Faith is not limited to one specific domain of beings or evidence that can be cordoned off neatly from everything outside it. A faithful life, led by its distinctive form of evidence, involves a comprehensively new way of seeing things in their totality, one with wide-reaching implications for how we grasp everything, including matters that from the perspective of methodological atheism will seem to have nothing to do with faith but with what it considers reason.

Heidegger would object not so much to the preceding appraisal of faith as evidentiary as he would to the suggestion that such evidence belongs to philosophy. To incorporate the evidence of faith into philosophy, for him, results in what thereby no longer is philosophy in the proper sense, but rather an instance of a *Weltanschauung*. But here Heidegger is wrong. It does not take much to see that no neutral perspective exists in the sense Heidegger's criticism implies, which is why the worst of all worldviews may be the one that, in characterizing philosophy as it does, takes itself to have suspended all worldview, as if it were a paragon of metaphysical neutrality. For a very long time it has been something of a commonplace in hermeneutic circles that the greatest blindness of Husserl's own philosophy was the presupposition that it is possible to liberate ourselves from every presupposition. Cannot the same be said against a philosophical mode of inquiry that, inveighing against the metaphysical commitments of others, fails to notice it is guilty of having its own? Arguably, the most pernicious of philosophical worldviews is the one that takes itself not to be one.

Consequently, to "methodologically" discount the reality that God could be present evidently in our quotidian dealings is, it seems, not to uphold pure phenomenology's philosophical rigor but to be blind to what shines forth as the noon day. To neglect the appearing of God on the unclear division between reason and faith is the desertion of phenomenology. And a feature of everyday experience makes that distinction's unfoundedness clear. Take as our example the encounter with the face of another person. In seeing the other's face, the eyes of faith claim to perceive, however dimly, the condition of his soul. The face of others is theopathic. We can discern the light of the Spirit when it is present in the visible features of the one who bears it.[24] The reverse is true as well. Its absence appears in the furrowed features of the anxious one, who, shrouded in darkness, is struggling to hide from the light. Now, is to say so a metaphysical construction? Or is it rather a phenomenological description? Is the evidence it claims to adduce for its claim relevant to the essential and universal contours of intersubjective experience, or is what it claims something to be bracketed from consideration because of a methodological stipulation having to do with separating philosophy from theology?

Of course, any suggestion that the visible face of the other reveals what we have claimed it does will be met with arguments insisting that things are to the contrary. But just because not everyone sees something (or claims not to see it) does not mean that those who say they see have not. There are many who deny there is a soul, deny there is a God, deny any acquaintance with God's call, and so dismiss the idea that the other's face discloses something invisible within others, and hence themselves when they are seen by others. Is it that such things are really just "seeing things" (in the sense we mean when referring to a hallucination or illusion) or is it the case that they are there and that those who do not see them are blinded by their own metaphysical commitments? For those who do not have eyes to see such things (or who claim not to see them), the face is a surface, not an icon. Insensible to what experience is capable of revealing, they fail to see what those of faith see when others appear in the light of God, namely, before any of us has uttered a word saying what he is thinking or feeling or believing, because we are exposed to one another, we are, to some degree at least, capable of being known to one another before ever saying anything at all. To be sure, an encounter with others takes place within a linguistic horizon. It is pregnant with the promise of speech. The face, however, expresses itself before any vocal utterance is exchanged. The face speaks. What we carry deep within ourselves is exteriorized in the flesh of our face. And so, even if someone disputes that we can see the inner man on his face, who can deny having discerned in the face of someone the burden of a rough past, or the distinctive glowing halo of joy that portends the expectation of a sunny future? The face is a relic of a past that has left its mark, but it also shines as a beacon of the future. It is at once a confession of where one has been, what one has seen, what one has done, of what one feels is coming next. The accumulated weight of experience etches the face as much as any scar.

As for those who deny seeing what has been described, denying familiarity with the Spirit's power to announce its presence (or absence) on the other's face, what more is to be said? The aim is to give words to what goes unnoticed. That everyone does not see what we see does not change that what has appeared does, nor does it undermine the task of trying to bring that appearing to expression. Returning to the one who reports not seeing what we have said is shown on the face, it is worth noting that, very often, the skeptic's own face belies his claim of inexperience. Though he pleads ignorance, we might not be so convinced. Eventually, even if only very late in life, those who neglect the claim of God's call in their lives only end up witnessing against themselves; when they say that they have not experienced such things and know nothing of the Spirit, it is clear they have worn themselves out by trying to live without it. Hence, it would be premature to give up and say that there is no way forward to adjudicate such disagreements. It is mistaken to conclude that because one claims to experience divine things while the other does not, it follows that there is no deciding who is right. Whoever claims to experience divine things can point to further considerations. Here, perhaps the strongest evidence is the presence of divine things made conspicuous by their absence in the one who does not know them. To strengthen the suspicion that a suppression of the truth lies at the root of why those who claim no familiarity with the experience of God's call say so, we have only to look into the eyes of those who disagree most vehemently that there is such a call. What are they resisting so passionately if not precisely what they deny exists? If they knew nothing of what they plead total ignorance of, why does their style of existence confirm that they do know, but resist, it?[25]

What, we ask, does this unbelieving face show? Setting to the side whatever else it shows, notably, it shows this: the glassy sheen of shark eyes, an icy stare whose vacancy reveals a cold heart that feels itself not at peace. The restlessness can be concealed from others for a time, especially in life's early stages. But time makes it increasingly evident. Having not yet laid themselves open to God, those alone in the world begin withering away. In a glance, we gather all we need to. Here is the stare of someone who has been busy silencing God. Nothing disguises it. The strain of the smile, a tension of the lips, the dullness of the pupils, a furrow of the brow, taken together with the distinct absence of any radiance to the skin coalesces to form the unmistakable impression of a soul without joy. This is a heart whose spark has gone dim. As for the eyes, they do provide a window to a tormented and embittered soul. For they tell the naked truth, that here is a void of dread intermingled with the gloom of a hopelessness fraught with the anguish of confusion—here present before us, a brooding darkness. Though many have long denied it (Hume's atheist admirers took care to emphasize their friend's demise had been tranquil and happy), it is a notorious secret that contrary to what people say, very often the lost, overcome with terror, cry on the deathbed. And for anyone who looks out on the sea of downtrodden faces in the grocery store or office, does it come as a shock? The pain is already there, festering barely beneath the surface of the superficial social norms restraining us from admitting to it.

Tasked with the job of trying to express what we see in the face of someone estranged from God, what good are the distinctions between theology and philosophy, faith and reason? When I look at the other face and see what I see, is to describe what I see doing philosophy? Or have I now embarked on theology? The lesson is that present before what appears, no such inviolable distinction matters. In the face of the things, venerable thresholds no longer hold, and the theoretical classifications and academic schematizations imposed by the habit of custom and the influence of institution go out the window—what could be a more *phenomenological* result than that? From a perspective that prioritizes above all else simply giving words to what has been seen, it is no surprise that the distinction between philosophy and theology no longer holds. Experience is richer and more subtle than what ossified intellectual divisions of labor suggest. In coming to terms with what the other's appearing brings to presence, we see that it is not just useless, but counterproductive, to fret over whether we are on philosophical or theological territory. Maybe it is both, maybe neither. In the end, if we feel so compelled to try to name it, we might do best to say that it is phenomenological and leave it at that.

That a description of the phenomena of everyday life (as the other's face) will require us to stop fussing so much about maintaining the methodological distinction between philosophy and theology as modes of theoretical discourse, we may add a second. The history of thought (to say the history of philosophy would already be to prejudge things) suggests as much. In antiquity, such a division was unknown. Philosophy for the ancients was not foremost an attempt to provide systemic propositions about reality, but instead to live a life of wisdom. As Pierre Hadot has shown admirably, no matter which ancient school we consider (Stoic, Epicurean, Cynic, Aristotelean, or Platonic), philosophy was a way of life meant to transform one's entire being. Philosophy for them was not so much about discovering which true propositions to endorse, but for learning the right rules to live by, knowledge of how to live a just and wise existence. Consequently, belief was not assent, but transformation. It was into this existential setting that the earliest followers of Christ were able to insert their own competing understanding of "divine things." They were able to do so not only as one contribution to their immediate philosophical milieu at the time, but, as Justin claims, *the* philosophy. As a way of life, Christianity was in this sense a philosophy, even its very consummation, for it provided the best comprehensive framework in which it was possible to live truly, and well. Justin's assessment is offered not out of arrogance but of good sense. Why choose to follow any mere man, when the Incarnation has now made it possible to follow the God-man? Thus, in reference to the ancient custom of identifying one's philosophical position with the name of the one having inaugurated it, Justin notes, "each [is] called after the originator of the individual opinion, just as each one of those who consider themselves philosophers, as I said before, thinks he must bear the name of the philosophy which follows, from the name of the father of the particular doctrine."[26] It was no different for him. By following Christ, "and for this reason," he says, "I am a philosopher."[27]

As Hadot observes in "Spiritual Exercises," Justin's surrounding philosophical climate took philosophy "not as a theoretical construct, but as a method for training people to live and to look at the world in a new way."[28] But not only that. Their conception of philosophy already at once anticipates and undermines what today is taken to be among the most compelling of reasons for thinking the modern methodological division between philosophical and theological discourse is not artificial. As Justin was to note in the previously mentioned "Dialogue with Trypho," for Greek, Jew, and Roman alike, philosophy was understood to be an inquiry into "divine things." As Justin reports, his interlocutor Trypho remarks at the beginning of their conversation that a philosophy failing to account for God would be a bizarre one: "Do not the philosophers turn every discourse on God? And do not questions continually arise to them about His unity and providence? Is not this truly the duty of philosophy, to investigate the Deity?"[29] Trypho's sentiment could not be more subversive to the modern expectation according to which philosophy should be insulated from God. He offers us instead a definition of philosophy that might substitute for today's Thomistic one of theology! The idea that God could be purged from philosophical inquiry would seem, not just to Justin but everyone with whom he was arguing, tantamount to saying that we should set aside philosophizing while doing philosophy.

There are other examples of this ancient pattern. When, for instance, Paul contended for the faith in Athens, only a few who listened to what he said were convinced by it. Yet no one, not even those who mocked him, ever thought to accuse him of doing theology and not philosophy. The Stoics and Epicureans he encountered there listened intently, and while they rejected what he argued for, they did so not because they thought what he said ran contrary to a set of rules determining what constituted good methodological philosophical hygiene. For his opponents no less than for Paul himself, to exclude "divine things" from the discussion would not have been to keep philosophy safe from theological intrusion, but to abandon its very vocation.

We here may return to an earlier theme. Because God appears only when we love him, and thus not until we have loved him can it be said that we truly know him, it follows that from the beginning, for the earliest Christian philosophers, a life of wisdom and one of faith were said to be inseparable, equivalent even. All the ancient schools, as Hadot has noted, articulated an ideal responsible for normatively governing what it means to live well, or, more precisely, to live philosophically. There was thought to be a norm that involved striving after a form of existence capable of elevating those who pursued it above the quotidian life. "In this transcendent norm established by reason," as Hadot describes, "each school will express its own vision of the world, its own style of life, and its idea of the perfect man."[30] Preoccupation with perfection was not idle. An everyday life that did *not* define itself as the pursuit of wisdom was, the ancients saw, one destined to be plagued by worry, ignorance, anxiety, and fear of death. Not unlike those today who admire the philosophy of Wittgenstein, they recognized that philosophy was to be in some way therapeutic. How so exactly they disagreed, but they were united in the conviction that salvation requires more than conceptual clarity, as for Wittgenstein. Now, it will not have gone without notice that many of the virtues Hadot highlights as belonging to the Stoic or Epicurean schools—say, vigilance over the heart, attention to our thoughts, a healthy mindfulness of death, an awareness of the ultimate transience of finite things, a persistent effort to develop good habits that reinforce all these right things—are at work in the Christian life, too. Even the act of reading can be a spiritual exercise. Putting before the mind what the text is attempting to show can be an act of attention requiring serious concern, an effort synergistically entwined with other efforts commensurate with cultivating a godly mind.

There is another crucial piece to the map here as concerns reading. The ancient schools maintained that one should hold before the mind a set of handy truisms that can act reliably as guides, to be enlisted for right action in the thick of everyday life. But is that not basically what we are aiming to do when reading Scripture? When I read a psalm of David, or a proverb of Solomon, or most especially the words of Christ, I do not memorize what I encounter simply for the sake of being able to recite it later for any old reason. More important, I do so hopeful that the words might sink into my heart and mind so that what they state becomes, as it were, "second nature" in times of decision calling for discernment. When the moment of trial arrives, having the words at the ready can make the difference between truth and error, good and evil. Thus, the act of reading is a component of the philosophical life, so understood, since it is a spiritual exercise oriented toward equipping ourselves to navigate the situations of life wisely.

It is here that anyone familiar with phenomenology will see this ancient residue resurfacing in interesting ways. In reading those texts, it becomes clear that many of the great phenomenologists, in their own way, also saw the philosophical act of reflecting on the world as continuous with the effort of living as we should. For Husserl, the ultimate norm at stake was one of living a life of rational self-responsibility, a life of *Evidenz*. For Heidegger, thinking about the meaning of being in no small part entails grappling with what it means to work out the very meaning of our personal existence authentically. And for Merleau-Ponty, to pay attention to what perception makes manifest takes on a sort of ascetic tone. As he never tires of noting, it takes genuine effort to notice in a painting or a countryside what we ordinarily do not.

But it is perhaps the work of Jan Patočka that is most admirable in this regard. Citing the ancient notion of care for the soul, he routinely emphasized that phenomenological philosophy should cultivate what the ancients called a "cosmic sense" for the whole. The genuine heritage of Europe, which in this sense was one Patočka took to be Greek, was none other than philosophy as a way of life. According to Patočka, as James Dodd has commented, "It is not Christianity, nor capitalism, nor the political legacy of the Roman Empire, nor imperialism and revolution, nor even the abstract ideas of freedom and democracy, but philosophy as a way of life, defined by the care for the soul, that forms the genuine heritage of Europe."[31] We have already seen why it would be hasty to disassociate Christianity from philosophy as a way of life, as Patočka does. With that caveat in mind, the point remains that Patočka, who was to the end extremely Husserlian in his faith in the power of philosophical reason, saw how life lived under the norm of phenomenological *Evidenz* entailed embracing philosophy as a way of life, as care for the soul. Here again, the prospects of somehow dividing philosophical reason from faith could not seem dimmer. Reason and faith are entwined in the common effort of living a phenomenological life of truth.

Thus, we are led back to the methodological issue of God's role in phenomenology. A methodological atheism that seeks to characterize phenomenological philosophy as a rational discipline is certainly right to do so, and there is nothing misguided about stressing the imperative of first-person evidence as essential to living a life of reason. But its view of truth becomes very one-sided and incomplete when it refuses to incorporate the philosophical effort of making rational sense of our place in the world into a broader philosophical regime of seeking practical, which is to say spiritual, wisdom. If that more robust conception of reason was known to the Greeks, neither was it entirely lost to transcendental phenomenology, as the life and work of Patočka attest. Where we have intimated that the post-Kantian distinction between philosophical and theological discourses is less evident than one might think, and if we have tried to argue so by emphasizing how any such distinction was unknown to the ancients, and if furthermore the ancient view of philosophy was consonant with what the earliest Christian philosophers were doing, are there nevertheless not differences that must be acknowledged between antiquity and phenomenology?

Another way of getting at the issue is to ask the question: can (or should) we philosophically enter the domain of what metaphysics licenses but what transcendental phenomenology, following the example of Kant's critical philosophy, has always cautioned against? To someone with Kantian or Heideggerian sensibilities, what we have already been discussing will have seemed to be an instance of metaphysics, in the bad sense. That is especially so as some of it will have also seemed to be what it deems theological. The majority of what has been said will have appeared to lie beyond the bounds of what a transcendental philosophy concerning itself with being (or meaning) permits.

Should the cautionary comment against metaphysics in the name of phenomenology be given the last word? Only if the methodological atheism it presupposes as bedrock were as firm as it thinks. But the history of thought gives us at least one obvious example for thinking such a framework is actually built on sand. In his *Philosophical Fragments*, Kierkegaard, who never described himself as either a philosopher or a theologian but simply as a Christian thinker, deliberately did all he could to exacerbate the difficulty of understanding Socratic philosophy in relation to the Christian *logos*. He does so, in part, by stating the commitment that, of all things, salvation is the central concern of human life, and hence philosophy too. Assuming the final *telos* of human existence is eternal life (Kierkegaard was aware many would dispute this) has startling repercussions for how we understand the object of philosophy. If it would be a very strange philosophy that had nothing to say about life's ultimate point, then philosophy, it would seem, must say something about the issue of salvation, a theme that should be strictly theological were there ever one. Situating the human condition in light of salvation, is Kierkegaard still doing philosophy? Or is this now theology? His point is to reveal that the situation is ambiguous. What matters, he highlights, is not whether what we are doing belongs in this disciplinary box or that one, but whether what we are saying is worth saying, and true. As he stresses, the life that has something most worth expressing is the one led in the Spirit. Life in the Spirit, which is to say a life of wisdom, is the philosophical life. The suggestion that emerges is scandalous for any modern thought that would try, under the banner of methodological atheism, to eliminate God from philosophy entirely: to follow Christ is to be the philosopher *par excellence*. Many will see Kierkegaard's suggestion as his contemporaries in Copenhagen did, as an eccentricity not to be taken seriously. It is clear that for Kierkegaard the philosophical life finds its true bearings only in the hope of eternal life. Living philosophically, thus, involves thinking about theoretical matters carefully, but more, it involves the transformation of our entire being and way of living in light of what we think. Philosophy taken as a spiritual discipline finds its ultimate expression in ushering us into a walk in the Spirit. Where then for someone as Heidegger the notion of Christian philosophy is an absurdity, for Kierkegaard it is more so a tautology. Philosophy as the love of wisdom must begin with the fear of God, in turn enduring through the continued effort of working out one's salvation in fear and trembling. To seek wisdom is to seek after eternal life.

All this leaves unaddressed the issue of writing philosophy. What's the intention behind it? Writing philosophy, at least some of the time, now becomes an act of *psychagoy*—an "art of seducing souls." A text can speak simultaneously to many people, and with various intents. It all depends on where the author knows the reader personally to be. To continue the point that we have just extracted from Kierkegaard, a Christian philosopher will see writing as a way of communicating to others who are not yet believers why they should be, by producing a text that might stir them to begin seeking after God—in this way, the text is a call to repentance, referring the reader back to his conscience and current inward condition. The text is a *memento mori*. In appealing to his humanity and thus him individually, it brings him back to himself. As for the reader who is already a believer, the text instead can function as something uplifting, as a source that reinforces good habits and inspires the hope to press on. And of course, the act of writing is instructive for the writer himself. It would be the worst of contradictions were someone with these intentions toward others to write something that was not true of oneself. Writing, then, as with the act of reading, becomes a meditation, a form of spiritual exercise, for it is necessary to make sure I measure up to the written word I pen. "[Writing takes] the place of other people's eyes. A person writing feels he is being watched; he is no longer alone, but is a part of the silently present human community."[32] Sometimes writing as a spiritual exercise for a spiritual purpose can therefore be self-conscious, as here in this current paragraph I self-consciously explain what it is to do what I am doing, not only for my sake, but also for the sake of others who might understandably wonder what the exact intent of the text is, were I not to have alerted them.

To round out the preceding meditation on the relation between philosophy and theology, or rather how there probably is no such real distinction between the two, it suffices to restate that, for the ancients, philosophy was thought to be a form of life, one which for the earliest Christian philosophers meant an induction into the Spirit of Christ. Their texts summoned others to embark on that journey, encouraging others already on the way to continue, and testing the one writing to make sure he too is making progress on the way. A word of precaution must be made here. Nothing of what we have said is meant to imply that there is no place for abstract or theoretical discourse—work in set theory is not put in jeopardy. It remains philosophical. But such work, if done exclusively, and done totally disconnected from any attempt at an existential integration within a life striving for wisdom, becomes distraction or diversion. Not thinking at all can be a vice, but also can thinking too much about the wrong thing!

At the end of this present reflection on the appearing of God, we are returned to the question of philosophical thinking's status. What are we to say about thinking? How does it fit into philosophy as a way of life, and, perhaps more pressingly, what is thought to think? We know Heidegger's answer, which proves instructive. For Heidegger, philosophy is the freedom for thinking. Thought thinks what comes to mind, and simply for its own sake. Rather than take up concern with any domain of beings (Husserl would say a "regional ontology"), thought thinks being, which in a more contemporary idiom has become identified with meaning (*Sinn*). Philosophy, which makes no time for entities but only meaning, thinks starting from itself and for its own enjoyment. Thinking is the absolute exercise of our freedom, of man's capacity to consider not merely things as they *are*, but how they *could be*—it is to dwell on possibility.

It is with this intent of preserving philosophy's autonomy to think freely that Heidegger around the time of *Being and Time*'s publication will define philosophy as a methodological atheism, not, as he hastens to clarify, because it decides for or against the existence of God. According to him, as we have seen, it is said to remain neutral—or better, indifferent—to the question because, as an ontological inquiry into the meaning of being, it is not a positive science concerning itself with any domain of entities or a specific entity, God included. In preparing to formulate fundamental ontology's question of the meaning of being, the existential analytic thus offers an account of what makes human existence distinctive insofar as that very existence is characterized uniquely by the understanding of being we possess. Yet here, Heidegger's philosophy can be challenged, and the reason for discarding it proves strictly experiential.

The matter comes to one of seeing that Heidegger distorted the human existence he claimed to have disclosed. The point is not simply to challenge the methodological decision that philosophy should interrogate being rather than any being (including God), but to notice that, in propounding this vision of philosophical inquiry, he ends up expecting us to pervert the truth of the human experience. One is free to pose the question of being if one likes, but to claim that the question of being is the ultimate horizon for understanding the one who is capable of asking such a question, that is too much. While it is fine to ask the question of being, doing so must not lead to falsely portraying our own existence. In the last analysis, Heidegger's phenomenological ontology fails, not as an attempt to reawaken a question that deserves our neglected attention, nor even because such an attempt to redirect us back to the question seeks to get us to appreciate something unworthy of that effort, but because, in characterizing human existence as being-in-the-world without God, Heidegger's analytic distorts the very existence he purports to have captured. Surely, God must enter phenomenology—that is just to say philosophy—not because it is necessary to reverse the Heideggerian stipulation to prioritize being over entities, but because, even when examining ourselves as the entities we are with the distinct aim of fundamental ontology in view, it would be a total distortion to characterize existence as a mode of being-in-the-world while neglecting, as just as essential, our being-before-God.

It has been said that whatever else it does, phenomenology makes sense of meaning and how that sense is made. But any such attempt that did not thereby attempt also to make sense of ourselves would be a failure. Heidegger recognized correctly that phenomenology, no matter where one thinks it should lead ultimately, must start, whether or however we thematize it, with ourselves. True!

But how are we to think about ourselves? Having considered what an understanding of philosophy as a way of life means for phenomenology, we find ourselves faced again with the matter of thinking. In response, we may now say this much. We are free to think without the love of God in mind. But this does not change that God, to whom all our thoughts are known, remains even that atheistic thought's final measure. Only then, in the presence of God, is phenomenology possible.

NOTES

1. Jean-Louis Chrétien, *The Ark of Speech*, trans. Andrew Brown (London: Routledge, 1997), 55.

2. The argument has had currency in Anglophone philosophy of religion for some time. For a recent formulation of it, see J. L. Schellenberg, *The Hiddenness Argument: Philosophy's New Challenge to Belief in God* (New York: Oxford University Press, 2015).

3. For a subtle analysis from Lacoste on this point that influences the present discussion to follow, see chapter 4, "The Knowledge and Love of God," in *The Appearing of God*, trans. Oliver O'Donovan (New York: Oxford University Press, 2018), 68–90.

4. This important qualification was brought to my attention by my wife. Nothing in the idea that knowing God is one with loving God means that he will not (or cannot) sometimes make himself felt when, as an atheist, we still were not even expecting it.

5. Placing the focus on Heidegger, Lacoste takes up the question of the relation between love of God and the knowledge of him in the chapter "Existence and Love of God: Remarks on a Note in *Being and Time*," in *The Appearing of God*, 91–111.

6. See Matthew Benton, "Pragmatic Encroachment and Theistic Knowledge," in *Knowledge, Belief, and God: New Insights in Religious Epistemology*, ed. Matthew Benton, John Hawthorne, and Dani Rabinowitz, 267–87 (Oxford: Oxford University Press, 2018). See also Matthew Benton, "God and Interpersonal Knowledge," *Res Philosophica* 95 (2018): 421–48.

7. Kant, *Religion within the Bounds of Mere Reason*, trans. Allen Wood and George di Giovanni (Cambridge: Cambridge University Press, 1998), 65.

8. Ibid., 68.

9. Ibid., 70.

10. For an explanation of Kant's account of the propensity to evil locating its origins in the felt tension between the rational demands of the moral law, on the one hand, and sensual incentives, on the other, see Stephen Grimm, "Kant's Argument for Radical Evil," *The European Journal of Philosophy* 10 (2012): 160–77.

11. Irenaeus, *Against Heresies*, IV. 39. 2. Along with chapter 39, he addresses these matters earlier, in chapter 37 of that same Book.

12. Clement of Rome, "The First Epistle of Clement," in *The Ante-Nicene Fathers: The Writings of the Fathers down to A.D. 325*, vol. 1, ed. Alexander Roberts and James Donaldson, 5–21 (Grand Rapids, MI: Wm. B. Eerdmans Publishing Company, 1950), 14.

13. Clement of Alexandria, "Valentinian's Vagaries About the Abolition of Death Refuted," in *The Ante-Nicene Fathers: Fathers of the Second Century: Hermes, Tatian, Athenagoras, Theophilus, and Clement of Alexandria Volume II*, ed. Alexander Roberts and James Donaldson (Grand Rapids, MI: Wm. B. Eerdmans Publishing Company, 1950).

14. Justin Martyr. "Dialogue with Trypho," in *The Ante-Nicene Fathers: The Writings of the Fathers down to A.D. 325*, vol. 1, ed. Alexander Roberts and James Donaldson, 194–270 (Grand Rapids, MI: Wm. B. Eerdmans Publishing Company, 1950), 246.

15. Miller, *The Christian Examiner, Volume 1*, pub. James Miller, 1824 ed., 66.

16. Justin, "Dialogue with Trypho," 250.

17. Lactantius, "Of True Wisdom and Religion," in *The Ante-Nicene Fathers: The Writings of the Fathers down to A.D. 325, Volume 21*, ed. Alexander Roberts and James Donaldson (Grand Rapids, MI: Wm. B. Eerdmans), 29.

18. Origen, "Commentary on the Gospel of Matthew," in *The Ante-Nicene Fathers, Volume 9*, ed. Alexander Roberts and James Donaldson (Grand Rapids, MI: Wm. B. Eerdmans, 1950), 29.

19. Justin Martyr. "The First Apology of Justin," in *The Ante-Nicene Fathers, Volume 1*, ed. Alexander Roberts and James Donaldson (Grand Rapids, MI: Wm. B. Eerdmans Publishing Company, 1950), 172.

20. Mathetes, "The Epistle to Diognetus," in *The Ante-Nicene Fathers, Volume 1*, ed. Alexander Roberts and James Donaldson (Grand Rapids, MI: Wm. B. Eerdmans Publishing Company, 1950), 29.

21. For an account of how this expansive notion of truth—one encompassing doing, and hence not limited only to a semantic phenomenon—was already current in antiquity, and accordingly deepened and modified by the Christians, see Claude Romano, "'Faire la vérité' d'Ambroise à Augustin," *Être soi—même: Une autre histoire de la philosophie* (Paris: Éditions Gallimard, 2019), 176–202.

22. For a compelling account that challenges modern Pauline theology by showing how Paul held to humanity's natural ability to do good and did not thereby endorse the idea of a sin nature, see Pelagius, *Pelagius's Commentary on St Paul's Epistle to the Romans*, trans. Theodore de Bruyn (Oxford: Oxford Clarendon Press, 1993).

23. See, for example, John Drummond, "Husserl's Middle Period and the Development of His Ethics," in *The Oxford Handbook of the History of Phenomenology*, ed. Dan Zahavi (Oxford: Oxford University Press, 2018), 135–54.

24. "A man may be known by his look, and one that hath understanding by his countenance, when thou meetest him" (Ecclus XIX:29).

25. Jean-Luc Marion sketches the unavoidable and thereby essential role of resistance to the phenomenon of revelation. See "Thinking Elsewhere," *Journal for Continental Philosophy of Religion* 1, no. 1 (2019): 5–26.

26. Justin, "The Dialogue with Trypho," 212.

27. Ibid., 198.

28. Pierre Hadot, *Philosophy as a Way of Life: Spiritual Exercises from Socrates to Foucault*, ed. Arthur Davidson (Oxford: Blackwell, 1995), 107.

29. Justin, "The Dialogue with Trypho," 195.

30. Hadot, "Forms of Life and Forms of Discourse," in *Philosophy as a Way of Life*, 57.

31. James Dodd, "Jan Patočka's Philosophical Legacy," in *The Oxford Handbook of the History of Phenomenology*, ed. Dan Zahavi (Oxford: Oxford University Press, 2018), 396–411.

32. Hadot, "Reflections on the Idea of the 'Cultivation of the Self,'" in *Philosophy as a Way of Life,* 211. This observation about writing is enacted self-consciously in the genre of writing known as *hypomnemia*, when one writes down, as a spiritual exercise, one's daily reflections on personal observations and progress, as in Marcus Aurelius's *Meditations*.

Chapter Three

What Is the Problem of Intersubjectivity?

In the world, we are alone together. As one sits in Manchester Plaza watching people pass by to disappear into classrooms and dormitories, whether they exist never arises as a question. Not only is their existence beyond questioning, but, from the perspective of those streaming past, it is evident that one is to them as nothing—one's own existence, and not theirs, is inconspicuous. Most of the others seen are completely unknown to me, and as for myself, I remain mainly unseen. Having stepped outside the whirl of activity to look in rather than to join in, for a time our place under the sun amid the throng is like that of the ghost who hovers. Things are shrouded in anonymity to the point that, though we are not, we may as well be invisible to one another. Many do not see anyone else as they walk, preoccupied in conversation with their friends or entranced by their phones. And if someone does see, one appears to the other not as one is known to oneself in singular intimateness, but as unremarkably generic: "a guy there," an evaporating "I-think-I-have-seen-him-before." To these others who pass me by, my figure is a Gestalt of their experience, more a blurred concept than a flesh. In short, it is not just others who are anonymous to me, but I to them. Nevertheless, the anonymity is not the experience of a pure disconnect. For even its atmosphere is one of presence. As unconcerned with one another as we are, there is no metaphysical issue as to whether we are alone in the sense solipsism countenances. Despite what it suggests, it is not as if we are the last one on earth. The Cartesian problem of other minds finds no foothold here.[1]

And yet is to acknowledge the existence of other minds a misguided metaphysical problem to decide there is no problem of intersubjectivity whatsoever, that the mystery of our relation to others is dispelled entirely? Such an inference would be too quick. While there may be no denying that others exist with us (and equivalently that we exist for them), does this mean there is not a remaining sense in which, despite our being together in a world that we share in common, we are fundamentally alone? Others are known to us even when they do not recognize us, just as they know we exist when we remain oblivious to them. To see somebody else is not for that reason to be seen. Much of the time we pass each other as ships in the night. And though there is a bond uniting us and explaining why there is no seriously asking whether others exist alongside us, that existential bond does not alter the reality that each of us finds ourself handed over to a degree of isolation. Being-with-others does not eliminate solitude but presupposes it. This solitude, which remains to be assessed in what follows, is the basis of our human solidarity. We are united in the common burden of having to deal with an isolation that can be shouldered by no one but ourselves.

Let us take, as a start, a mundane experience of life. I am walking, and I encounter a stranger on the street. Even here, I never could be persuaded fully that the other is a figment of my imagination, a character in my dream, or some artificial intelligence. Who am I to him, or better, what are we for one another when we encounter each other for just a brief moment, exchanging perhaps a glance or a word, only to depart just as we had met, never to meet again? The other in such cases remains basically unknown to me. However, it would be a mistake to characterize this phenomenon of unknowing as limited to the stranger. Just the same, the circumstances associated with those we think we know well highlight it. To be acquainted with someone is not to know them without remainder. For even with those we know much better than strangers, we never reach to the bottom of their depths. The identity of the stranger I am standing beside in the parking garage elevator on the way to our cars is a question that will remain a mystery. Far from that question being resolved with a friend or beloved, however, in a way it is only intensified. Friends and the beloved are no longer strangers, but neither are they translucent. Others are traces. And so too ourselves.

This ambience of mystery characterizing our being-together is reinforced when I recognize in someone's face that who I am remains as cryptic to him as does who he is to me. In turn, there is an unfamiliarity at work when our gazes cross. But it would be an overstatement to say that there is not already some degree of a bond present between us. Indisputably, no matter how personally unfamiliar we are to one another (as when encountering a total stranger), a subtext of basic human familiarity counteracts the foreignness of meeting someone unknown. In time, then, where before there had been no experiential rapport other than the mere possibility of there being one eventually, an actual rapport does take shape. But whether it be the sort present when encountering the stranger, or the more intimate kind marking friendship, familiarity never resolves all ambiguity. The daily encounter with the neighborhood postman or cafe owner involves a persistent withdrawal. The more one gets to know somebody, or the more times one encounters him, the more the secret making him uniquely himself is felt.

It is necessary to caution against a confusion. Admitting to the secret at issue does not mean resuscitating the specter of solipsism. When confronting the elusiveness of what the other is thinking as he remains silent or when trying to interpret the motive behind a comment, I do not think that the other is irreal. Far from such uncertainty calling the other's existence into question, impenetrability accentuates that very existence. That I can experience how I remain an enigma to others reinforces the lesson. In the eyes of another, I am the other. And this experience of being the other to somebody underscores the crucial point at issue. To be sure, there always will be a disconnect separating us in that I can never melt into others, annulling all difference between us. He has his perspective, as I have mine. But that very separation presupposes a bond that nothing can possibly sever.

To repeat as already remarked, there is no disputing that others exist with me and I for them. What explains the indissoluble link? Parting ways with a long philosophical tradition that had always thought it necessary to seek a proof of the other's existence, it was Heidegger who, taking a stand against this Cartesian trend, in *Being and Time* asserts that an ontological feature of existence is being-with-others. Just in being the ones we are, he says, we are never alone but always with others. To be the individual one is means, not that one is first a Robinson Crusoe, exiled to a solipsistic consciousness far from a world without others, but rather to be *Mitsein*—a being-with-others. As these famous sections on intersubjectivity in Division I contend, the question of my relation to others in the first place is not one of establishing whether others than ourselves exist. They do exist, and entertaining the idea that possibly they do not is to distort the phenomenon. Given how Heidegger sees the issue, the task instead is existentially differentiating ourselves from the anonymous mode of inauthentic existence. The problem of others is not proving they exist, but existing in such a way that we ourselves are not reduced to an undifferentiated anonymity. As Heidegger explains, in the inauthentic mode of average everydayness, we robotically enact the social behavior of those around us, rendering us indistinguishable from others, since we have melted into the crowd. The problem of other minds is not that their existence stands in need of demonstration (as if it were dubitable), but of securing our individuality by breaking free from the tendency to conform ourselves to what everyone else says and does. The world, as he hastens to note, is not mine. Nor for that matter is it yours. It is, he stresses, ours. Or even better, it is ours precisely to the extent that it stands above either of us. Hence, Heidegger's talk of a "self-world" in the years surrounding World War I is replaced later, by the time of *Being and Time*, with language conscientiously designed to avoid the least trace of Cartesianism. The world, in short, is what we share wholly in common, as it is what in principle rules out the possibility of a solipsistic mind. As those famous sections of *Being and Time* remind us, a lucid view of the world, *as a phenomenon*, disqualifies the very possibility of others' inexistence, just as it forecloses the idea of the world's nonexistence. A world where I am the only one in existence would not *be* a world, since, as existing, others already make a claim on me, making their appearance felt in a way that eliminates the intelligibility of thinking that their existence requires further demonstration. It is in this sense that for Heidegger there is no such thing as a problem of intersubjectivity.

For his own part, Husserl was never satisfied as Heidegger with a total dissolution of the problem. That is why continually he returned to the question (for him it is a question) of how the world, which is constituted as an intersubjective space, permits the appearance of others. Husserl agrees with Heidegger that there is no disputing that others do exist. We experience the world as a place inhabited by others, he says too. But instead of taking that as a brute fact, Husserl emphasizes that it requires some explanation. It may not make any sense to begin by doubting the other's existence on the way to trying to understand how an experience of the other is possible. But an encounter with the other, or how that encounter is made possible by transcendental subjectivity, stands in need of explication, says Husserl. Thus, in his famous Fifth Meditation, he contends that it is by and through the body that our being-with-others is established. Put into possession of my own body's powers of perception and action opening me onto a sensible world, it is by "analogizing" the other's body to my own, that I come to experience the other as another for whom I am the other. The other is the *alter ego*, another I.

It is within this epistemic orientation that the problem of the other is approached by Edith Stein, too. In 1917, Stein, who was at the time Husserl's private assistant in Freiburg, published as a book what the year before had been her dissertation, *On the Problem of Empathy*. As with her teacher Husserl, the text treats intersubjectivity largely as a question of knowledge, of how we encounter others as others. Empathy is a *sui generis* act of consciousness allowing for the perception of the foreignness of others, says Stein. It is, she comments, "the experience of foreign consciousness in general, irrespective of the kind of the experiencing subject or of the subject whose consciousness is experienced."[2] Using the example of joy to illustrate the point, Stein considers the experience of encountering a joyous friend. When the friend comes beaming with joy and tells us that he passed his examination, "I grasp his joy empathetically."[3] For Stein, this is strictly perceptual. If I am already joyous for some other reason before encountering the other's news, after hearing it, my joy remains different from his. The two joys have different objects. And if I am sad, seeing his joy might not change my mood at all. Rather than initiating me into his joyousness, it might exacerbate my sadness. To empathize, then, is to see how the other finds himself in the world, but it is not for that to feel it for oneself. When seeing the other's joy does initiate us into it, no longer is this a matter of empathy, but sympathy. Following the terminology of Max Scheler, Stein accordingly notes that "we can designate this primordial act as joy-with-him or, more generally, as fellow feeling [sympathy]. Sympathized and empathized joy need not necessarily be the same in content at all."[4] Stein's analysis becomes more interesting when, in the next page over, taking up a term from the philosopher Theodor Lipps—"negative empathy"—she notes how when we fail to sympathize with what we see, this is because something in us "opposes it."[5] Something about one's current experience or an aspect of one's personality stops one from fusing with the other—for example, I am already overcome with grief over the death of a friend, so I cannot identify with this other friend's joyousness over the exam.

As Stein notes, whatever the particular reason behind it, the result is that we lack a sense of oneness. It is here, however, in trying to accommodate the felt reality of oneness, that the limitations of her own analysis of intersubjectivity in terms of empathy become apparent. Referring again to Scheler's account of sympathy, Stein claims it is not through "the feeling of oneness, but through empathizing"[6] that we experience others. To be united with others as a "we," for Stein, accordingly is a higher unity based on a plurality of relatively atomistic subjects, not an ineradicable and primordial feature of our relation with others: "The feeling of oneness and the enrichment of our own experience becomes possible through empathy."[7] The problem of others, then, including the question of sympathy, for Stein, is set within a Cartesian frame. Sympathy is rendered unintelligible, for the very possibility of sharing one and the same world is eliminated. Prioritizing a subtly solipsistic conception of empathy, I and the other are consigned to separate worlds. How so becomes especially evident later in the analysis: "Empathy as the basis of intersubjective experience becomes the condition of possible knowledge of the existing outer world."[8] This view, which is Husserl's also, takes empathy essentially to be a perceptual act presupposing a radical separation between oneself and the other, thereby denying the existential bond necessary for explaining sympathy. If later Heidegger will go too far in the other direction, it seems Stein has gone too far in this one.

Michel Henry, who was never shy about his disagreement with other phenomenologists, here as so often in other respects follows Husserl rather than Heidegger. Contrary to Heidegger's assertion that the problem of intersubjectivity is a pseudoproblem, Henry in *Incarnation* challenges such a pronouncement as too facile. "If 'being-with' must mean a 'being-with-the-other,' one cannot pull this out of a hat," he says.[9] Husserl and Stein took up the other's constitution from an overly epistemic perspective, but they were not wrong to see it as a legitimate concern. Husserl, says Henry, is not to be faulted for thinking it needs explication. But if the problem of intersubjectivity is not equivalent to the traditional metaphysical or epistemic ones, which treat the other's existence as a matter in need of rational demonstration, what is it?

For Henry, the matter comes to one of seeing how we should treat others. The issue is ethical, for it reduces to one of overcoming transcendental egoism. Solipsism is not a metaphysical position we need to refute; it is a mode-of-being-with-others that distorts that condition. It is not a philosophical problem but an existential failure. In reference to what Heidegger treats as normal, Henry notes that, in the mode of average everydayness, the world shows up in accord with my projects, but that this is shot through with a pernicious subtext. Things are undertaken with a view to myself in that the intelligibility of the situation, including a sense of how others matter to it, makes ultimate reference to my own attempts to make sense of who I am. The world is ontologically inflected in terms of my care. It is here that Henry notes how this is not obviously an inevitable (or acceptable) form of self-interest. It is a transcendental myopia, a way-of-existing that filters reality through the lens of egoism.[10] It is in this sense that what we mean by the world takes on a negative valence. John's admonition to "Love not the world: the lust of the flesh, the lust of the eyes, the pride of life" (1 John 2:15) is not just a condemnation of selfishness. It concerns more than mere desire. Such a statement, to be understood in its full radicality, must be taken in its phenomenological essence, which amounts to seeing it as a criticism of a transcendental illusion. When the world shows up strictly in conformity with my projects and desires, there is a fundamental distortion at work. Others cannot appear truly. Not loving the world, then, lays a foundation on which a genuine encounter with others is achievable. Far then from the world providing the sole site whereby we may meet others, it is otherwise. The world, in the phenomenological sense Henry identifies, is a place where others do not appear. In the world taken as a horizon of exteriority projected by one's concerns, there exist only *alter egos*, others who, reduced to furniture showing up in a milieu structured by my lusts, are made in my image. Another who shows up as an *alter ego* is not a bona fide other, but one who mirrors back myself.

All this is to say that the problem of intersubjectivity is not so much whether (or even how) we do know others, but rather the stance toward them we must adopt, given that relation being what it is. If such a suggestion sounds like something Levinas said, that is because it is. Our main concern with others is not with whether they exist. That would be bizarre. Nor is it one of knowing how we know that they do. More significant, the matter is to appreciate why, in the course of daily life, too often our way of relating to others habitually slips into treating them in a fashion contrary to what they are, and therefore how they deserved to be treated. What is it about the world, as Heidegger understood it, that explains how it is at once the place where we encounter the other and also where that relation itself is effaced?

Many texts have explored that question, but none more admirably than the beautiful essay, "Solitude et secrete. Prolégomènes à une phénomènologie du lien humain" in which the philosopher Claude Romano sketches the subtle way in which others are mysteries to us. At the beginning of the essay, he observes how the history of philosophy, following Descartes's decision to conceive selfhood through the epistemic lens of the *cogito*, has often characterized the alterity of the other as a mode of absolute transcendence. Corresponding to the other's radical transcendence, in turn, is an understanding of oneself. One is taken to be an *ego* seen as enclosed within oneself. On such a view, there is a gap, not a bond, between us. An absolute solitude (I as *ego*), on the one side, a radical secret (other as *alter ego*), on the other. As Romano accordingly observes, this cleavage in effect entails that the other exists in another world, one totally transcendent to our own. He says,

> By virtue of the epistemic cleavage between evident knowledge and knowledge subject to doubt—to which corresponds, on the ontic plane, the difference between interiority and exteriority, immanence and transcendence—the other and myself are literally no longer of the same world: there is a radical closure of the ego on itself (what Husserl rightly called by the title "egological closure") and an absolute loneliness of solipsism, on the one hand; there is an absolute exteriority of the other to oneself, on the other hand, which means that, so long as the phenomenal field is still made a matter of immanence—even if it is an "expanded" one—the other, who appears as a phenomenon in the world, is less an other than merely a sign or trace of that presence. On the one hand, an absolute solitude; on the other, a radical transcendence with regard to the phenomenal world, that is to say, a *world-for-me*, which signifies latency, hiddenness and an irremediable secret.[11]

To be sure, sometimes there is a conjectural aspect to knowing others. Romano will not deny it. But whatever transcendence is here at work, it is overstated. Turning to great works of literature to make the point, he sets out an analysis of our being-with-others inspired by passages from Proust's *In Search of Lost Time* exhibiting the way others evade our comprehension. What explains this everyday incomprehension? Such incomprehension, notes Romano, supposes a basic familiarity disqualifying the sort of absolute transcendence that Cartesian and idealist traditions have ascribed to others. It is in this context that Romano comments on the relationship between the narrator and his maid, Françoise. As he observes, though Proust's narrator describes his difficulties in comprehending her, his incomprehension presupposes a foundational intelligibility, for, "If Françoise were not already known and familiar to us in large part, if, thanks to the art of the novelist, she were not already for us this defined and identifiable being, nothing about her could surprise us."[12] To the extent that Françoise is opaque, this is only so because of a prior and ineliminable translucence: "Every opacity born of incomprehension," notes Romano, "supposes the familiarity with which it breaks; any obscurity in conduct or statement can appear only against a background of tacit understanding of the whole of that person and their actions."[13] Romano's essay on Proust raises questions regarding the relation between literature and philosophy that are not to our present concerns. Of interest, instead, is his claim that, contrary to what the Cartesian and idealist traditions have claimed, others are less mysterious than is said.

How the traditional epistemic and metaphysical problems of intersubjectivity rest on a misunderstanding becomes evident, claims Romano, when we put a question to ourselves. Is it that others fundamentally are unknowable to me because of their radical transcendence to consciousness, or is this only to the extent that, by frustrating my attempts to comprehend them, what is at stake about them is there to be seen, while I simply fail to see it? Is the apparent unknowability of the other an essential feature owing to a radical transcendence, or is it an empirical result of my failing to see? Favoring an interpretation that understands the inaccessibility of the other in terms of the latter option, Romano underscores how the other who appears as a mystery often appears so precisely and only to the degree that we have failed to see what is there to be seen. Such a possibility is taken to an extreme when, not recognizing that the other is plain and that his intentions and thoughts are thereby evident in his gestures and actions, we instead mistake there to be some ulterior motives where there really are none: "His only mystery," says Romano of such types, "is his absence of mystery, that is to say, his revelation without remainder."[14] Sometimes the only secret is that there is none! What one sees is what one gets, and if not, it is only because one has not seen.

If contrary to idealist philosophy the other is not in my mind but exists in the world with me, then our existing in the same world also involves, as Merleau-Ponty always emphasized, and as Romano will too, the other's body as inherently expressive: "The body in its phenomenal manifestation is intrinsically expressive: emotions, thoughts, and intentions are received through the intermediary of this body, a first visibility."[15] Hence, when others appear mysterious, even bordering on the precipices of the unknowable, this has more to do with the failure to see what is there to be seen: "that which masks the other from us is not his inherence outside our consciousness but wholly a matter of the facts stopping us from understanding him—beginning with our own failings."[16] The inaccessibility of the other, thus, is due not to an absolute transcendence, but to us: "Others are often much more transparent and manifest to us than our inattention, our presuppositions, our foolishness, our prejudices and our clumsiness would have us believe."[17]

According to Romano, the many interpersonal vignettes sketched by Proust suggest the same lesson: "So many failings have their source in us and in no way in the manner the other is given to us."[18] And yet to acknowledge that there is not an ontological screen absolutely separating us from others is not to deny that there is an undeniable element of mystery here. How is such mystery to be conceived? As Romano himself acknowledges, others possess an element of secretiveness: "One might even hold that the more we know the other the more he remains unknown: not knowing him is proportional to knowing him."[19] What is the sense of this unknowability, this inaccessibility?

It is "radical singularity"—the unique style of every person that makes him unsubstitutably who he is. As much as everyone's emotions and intentions are evident in gestures and expressions, and no matter how well we come to know the other's habits, beliefs, inclinations, traits, and tendencies, there is something unique about him—that *je ne sais quoi*. The other is not subsumable under a rule or category. And as Romano notes, the radical singularity explaining such irreducibility is itself related to a second feature characterizing the other's secret, namely, his freedom. Others always can surprise us, and the future is never a fate, because the other is free. And just as the other is free, so he can never be anticipated fully. The true problem others present to us, then, is not so much a matter of knowledge per se, but of coexistence.[20] Trying to know others, or to make them known, is part of attempting to live with them. In doing so, we are seeking understanding, a rapport. Thus, if Romano's analysis of how others are mysterious to us indicates how the relation to them involves a familiarity that philosophical idealism overlooks, it still remains to understand how the bond with others, which is focalized on the quest for mutual understanding, actually works.

It is this dimension of coexistence that is highlighted in the remarkable writings on the matter by Jean-Jacques Rousseau. Or better, his work illustrates the contours of such understanding by highlighting the many results associated with our failure to achieve it. On offer, in short, is a view according to which society corrupts us, thereby making it more difficult to see others, and for them to see us. Under Rousseau's pen, why comes clearly into focus. Society, he will note, habituates us into abandoning our true and natural attitude toward others. Where our natural endowment is one of compassion rooted in a love of humanity, society spoils all that, inculcating instead pride, malevolence, and selfishness. This perversion of our benevolent nature is captured in the term designating what results, *amour-propre*, a form of life which, according to Rousseau, is propelled by a self-frustrating drive for a recognition from others. It is a competitive struggle producing strife and acrimony, and eventually misery for everyone involved. As he remarks, "L'amour-propre n'est qu'un sentiment relatif, factice et né dans la société, qui porte chaque individu à faire plus de case de soi que de tout autre."[21]

But it was not first or always so, he contends. In an Edenic image of man that has struck readers as incredibly nostalgic, our original condition, Rousseau says, was good. At peace with himself in the state of nature, one thereby was at peace with others, who also were at peace with themselves. This image of the state of nature is not as Hobbes described (a warfare of all against all), but paradise. It is an original condition in which peace reigned through goodwill and mutual benevolence. And it has been lost. And it will remain that way for us so long as we are obsessed with society's notions of how life ought to be lived, standards which Rousseau himself characterizes in terms of artifice and insincerity. Because society asks us to become fake, it is only through an introspective turn into ourselves that we rediscover the real self we have put off. His text, *Les Rêveries du promeneur solitaire*, recounts this odyssey back to oneself. Accordingly, as he remarks in the Fifth Walk, it takes a state of transfiguring reverie, a forgetting of everything about the competition, strife, and nonsense of civic society, to reconnect with who we truly are. Just as the state in question is tranquil, so it is of intense solitude, one so encompassing that Rousseau himself does not refrain from likening its measure of independence and self-sufficiency to something divine: "De quoi jouit-on dans une pareille situation? De rien d'extérieur à soi, de rien sinon de soi-meme et de sa propre existence, tant que état dure on se suffit à soi-meme comme Dieu."[22] For Rousseau at least, if one is to be oneself, it will be necessary to retreat inward, far away from the machinations of society's others.[23]

A hindrance to authenticity, society acculturates us to bad rules of conduct, ones whose adoption sculpts a perspective ensuring that the recognition we are seeking from others, and which they are seeking from us, never materializes. Self-love sends us on a fool's errand. People looking for validation from others (who are themselves self-seekers) will not find it. How is it a surprise that this quest ends in disappointment? And for Rousseau, part of the disappointment is finding ourselves to be misunderstood by the very ones we had wished would understand us. In seeking the approval of others, we are met with the opposite. People misconstrue our intentions, belittle or ignore our achievements, resent us for the good that we do, and envy us for what they wish was true of themselves—the final insult, of course, is when they resort to lying, telling others things about us they know to be false.

It is in facing up to how this quixotic quest for self-affirmation fails that Iris Murdoch for her own part takes up the problem of mutual self-understanding. Only for her, unlike for Rousseau, the primary focus initially is not placed on how others misunderstand us unfairly. Rather, like Romano, she trains her attention on how we do so to others when, blinded by some failing of our own, we fail to see them accurately. Seeing others for what they are, and as they are, becomes for Murdoch a moral task. As she notes in *The Sovereignty of Good*, "Where virtue is concerned, we often apprehend more than we clearly understand and *grow by looking*."[24] Part of that growth involves learning to see, so as to better embody, the good. Seeing the good requires that we begin attempting to see things for how they are, which means admitting that perhaps we have theretofore been failing to see them. It means, says Murdoch, not permitting our vision to be clouded by our prejudices. And that requires first admitting that we might be prejudiced. In trying to see things as they are, one must exercise effort and care to spare others from being filtered through the lens of bias. Vision, then, or moral vision more precisely, demands a process of what she aptly calls "unselfing." Taking a lead from Plato, Murdoch speaks "of what is perhaps the most obvious thing in our surroundings which is an occasion for 'unselfing,'" what "is popularly called beauty."[25] Not unlike Rousseau, who sees nature as a refuge from society (he turned to plants when people were too much), so Murdoch identifies beauty, natural beauty in particular, as what releases us from illusions by first relieving us of the distorted self-conception propagated through egoism. Touchingly, she writes of the bird that calls us back from elsewhere, and to reality: "I am looking out of my window in an anxious and resentful state of mind, oblivious of my surroundings, brooding perhaps on some damage done to my prestige. Then suddenly I observe a hovering kestrel. In a moment everything is altered. The brooding self with its hurt vanity has disappeared. There is nothing now but kestrel. And when I return to thinking of the other matter it seems less important."[26] Nature's beauty, as epitomized by the bird, removes us from what was an artificial condition of quarrels, transplanting us firmly back on good soil instead.

As with Rousseau, for Murdoch the needed transformation of perspective is one of self-forgetfulness. Forgetting how we are seen by others, and instead simply seeing things for what they are, we are no longer taken in by the egoistic concern of searching for the approval of others. "More naturally, as well as more properly," notes Murdoch, "we take a self-forgetful pleasure in the sheer alien pointless independent existence of animals, birds, stones and trees."[27] Approaching the lesson's conclusion, she says, "It is a task to come to see the world as it is."[28] But this task is one achievable by anyone, and it begins with demolishing the first impediment to seeing things lucidly, namely, the screen of pride, arrogance, and selfishness characteristic of the one sunk in self-love. "The humble man," she thus concludes, "because he sees himself as nothing, can see other things as they are."[29] Seeing other things as they are, consequently, involves seeing others as they are. But what does it mean to see others as they are? No longer appearing through the lens projected by our own need for their validation, others appear in their unfiltered humanity, in the light of natural compassion and love for humanity. With the drive of self-love extinguished, they can appear without any trace of comparison or competition. Purely content to be who we are without recognition from others, they finally now can be for us what they always already should have been.

Though it has become something of a commonplace to note, it is worth remarking on the various ways in which technological society, or more precisely mass society, complicates finding mutual understanding. In a very wonderful study by sociologist and philosopher Jacques Ellul that is not widely known, his *Propaganda: The Formation of Men's Attitudes* underscores what Heidegger highlights about *das Man*, or Kierkegaard before had in his notion of "the public."[30] The individual of mass society who lives in accord with what society deems normal is not, his protestations to the contrary notwithstanding, a true individual. He is what Kierkegaard called a "cyphon," a carbon copy of everybody else. In *The Sickness unto Death*, Kierkegaard describes such an individual, who, in the grips of the despair of not willing to be himself, only has a superficial social identity. As we read, such an identity is empty:

> In a deeper sense, the whole question of the self becomes a kind of false door with nothing behind it in the background of his soul. He appropriates what he in his language calls his self, that is, whatever capacities, talents, etc. he may have; all these he appropriates but in an outward-bound direction, toward life, as they say, toward the real, the active life. He behaves very discreetly with the little bit of reflection he has within himself, fearing that what he has in the background might emerge again. Little by little, he manages to forget it; in the course of time, he finds it almost ludicrous, especially when he is together with other competent and dynamic men who have a sense and aptitude for real life. Charming! He has been happily married now for several years, as it says in novels, is a dynamic and enterprising man, a father and citizen, perhaps even an important man; at home in his own house the servants call him "He Himself"; downtown he is among those addressed with "His Honor"; his conduct is based on respect of persons or on the way others regard one, and others judge according to one's social position.[31]

As Kierkegaard's putting this fake man into the spotlight shows, mass society produces a crowd, a throng of people who, seeing themselves only in regard to how others see them, are without God and hence without any self. As for Ellul, among the most damaging illusions of such a state of affairs is that, by thinking one is an individual when one in fact is not, someone plunged into the crowd fails to recognize how one has been leveled down to something bordering on the inhuman. The experience of being reduced to the crowd leads to an overcompensation, to the attempt to assure oneself that one is more than a cog in the machine. But doing so, Ellul says, is a ruse: "Actually, just because men are in a group, and therefore weakened, receptive, and in a state of psychological regression, they pretend all the more to be 'strong individuals.' The mass man is clearly subhuman, but pretends to be superhuman."[32] Thus, as Ellul continues, propaganda that addresses the individual "apart from the crowd, is impossible."[33] And if that is so, mass society must create an individual suited to be someone primed to conform to the vision of life it wants one to live. Yet it would be misguided to claim that the pseudoindividual of mass society is propaganda's unwitting dupe. It only works, notes Ellul, because the propagandee wants to be deceived, since that is the price to pay to be released from one's true condition, which is to be a single individual fully responsible for one's existence. Any accounting of the situation must not overlook the obvious, namely, "the *complicity* of the propagandee. If he is a propagandee, it is because he wants to be, for he is ready to buy a paper, go to the movies, pay for a radio or TV set."[34] "For propaganda to succeed," he states in that same text, "it must correspond to a need for propaganda on the individual's part. . . . The propagandee is by no means just an innocent victim. . . . Rather, there is a citizen who craves propaganda from the bottom of his being and a propagandist who responds to this craving."[35] What is the source of this craving?

To answer the question, let us consider more closely propaganda's design. One must first have a look at its methods. "It proceeds," Ellul observes, with "pre-propaganda," that is, "by psychological manipulations, by character modifications, by the creation of feelings or stereotypes useful when the time comes. It must be continuous, slow, imperceptible. Man must be penetrated in order to shape such tendencies. He must be made to live in a certain psychological climate."[36] The climate is one in which the individual is saturated with cues directing and shaping his thoughts, preferences, and attitudes. The social environment, hence, is an artificial environment. It is a setting of trained response. "Propaganda," as he says, "tries first of all to create conditioned reflexes in the individual by training him so that certain words, signs, or symbols, even certain persons or facts, provoke unfailing reactions."[37] Inhibiting one's ability to think by limiting the scope of thought's content, it also impairs the capacity to think freely. Rather than thinking creatively, and for any considerable length of time, thinking becomes truncated. An individual of mass society becomes someone with a "very limited capacity for attention and awareness."[38] This is the point, since by pushing the preceding event into oblivion, and so the next one too, everyone's collective memory becomes short. As Ellul explains, "the event that has been supplanted by another is forgotten; it no longer exists; nobody is interested in it anymore."[39] Henry was to note the same phenomenon, when in *Barbarism* he observes how the news of mass media is designed to present what does not matter: "Nothing can enter into the news except under the twin conditions of incoherence and superficiality. As a result, the news is insignificant."[40] "The content of technological media," as Henry continues, "is the Insignificant, the 'news.' Tomorrow it will no longer have the least interest. There is even good reason to believe that there is no interest at the time of the event."[41]

Who today remembers Howard Dean's 2004 presidential campaign? The last war-scare with China over a potential invasion of Taiwan? The 1993 World Series Champion? Here it is crucial to note, as both Ellul and Henry do, that propaganda is ephemeral, disjointed, and superficial. It must be. As it is meant to distract whoever consumes it, it must be sufficiently incoherent and tantalizing to hypnotize. Sports and other light entertainment features will do. The goal of the hypnosis is to put the mass individual so to sleep that, mesmerized by the parade of images and blurbs before him, he forgets his own self. The job has been done when, thoughtlessly parroting what they have seen on their screens, those claiming to be "woke" are anything but! To take a most recent example, if one's conception of masculinity is sufficiently superficial so as to be extolled faithfully in a Gillette Super Bowl commercial, we are not dealing with someone who is thinking, but with a propagandee.

Distracting the individual of mass society, media open what is a surrogate reality. Propaganda is the opiate of the masses, only because it delivers all those who succumb to it from what they would otherwise experience as their intolerable condition. Behind the media world are pain and loneliness. The propagandee, as Ellul notes, "realizes that he depends on decisions over which he has no control, and that realization drives him to despair. Man cannot stay in this situation too long. He needs an ideological veil to cover the harsh reality, some consolation, a *raison d'être*, a sense of values."[42] Providing him a means to cope with his felt impotence, propaganda allows everyone to deny "his own continuity; to the same extent that he lives on the surface of events and makes today's events his life by obliterating yesterday's news, he refuses to see the contradictions in his own life and condemns himself to a life of successive moments, discontinuous and fragmented."[43] From the perspective of propaganda, the more fragmented and contradictory things become, the better. For example, the same people who one year are marching in the streets of San Francisco protesting against Bush calling for peace ("No Blood for Oil!") are the same people who, just a few years later, are now defending Obama's killing civilians in drone strikes. And so vice versa. To open a paper, to tune into a news channel, to browse the Twitter feeds, is to step into the surreal, a virtual world where nothing makes sense, where everything constantly changes, and where there is no resolution to anything. Consequently, for anyone who "tries to keep informed," as Ellul says, "a world emerges that is astonishingly incoherent, absurd, and irrational, which changes rapidly and constantly for reasons he cannot understand."[44] Mass media, which are intended to placate the consumer's need to be reassured, feeds lies by projecting a fake existence, since the one who consumes it is unable to deal honestly with his real one. "Man," Ellul concludes, "is doubly reassured by propaganda: first, because it tells him the reasons behind the developments which unfold, and second, because it promises a solution for all the promises that arise, which would otherwise seem insoluble. Just as information is necessary for awareness, propaganda is necessary to prevent this awareness from being desperate."[45]

Perceptively locating the source of propaganda's power to influence as lying in the individual's impulse to escape the pain and anguish of those who enjoy it, Ellul accordingly observes that it is only persons who are in deep despair who would ever resort to it. "Above all," he says of such an individual, "he is a victim of emptiness—he is a man devoid of meaning. He is very busy, but he is emotionally empty, open to all entreaties and in search of only one thing—something to fill his inner void."[46] "*Propaganda*," he says, "*is the true remedy for loneliness.*"[47] It is such loneliness, as Henry also says, explaining the "flight into exteriority," a "fleeing oneself and thus of getting rid of what one is" intended to avoid trauma and the "malaise and suffering" of existence.[48] As Henry notes, mass society thrives on mass media, for the latter numbs those who feel the helplessness of their condition. "The media world," he explains, "thus does not offer a self-realization of life; it offers escape. For all those whose laziness represses their energy and thus always leaves them discontent with themselves, it offers the opportunity to forget about their discontent."[49] This is why everything about propaganda is calculated to stupefy the one who encounters it. In order to produce its effect, Ellul emphasizes how "propaganda restricts itself to utilizing, increasing, and reinforcing the individual's inclination to lose himself in something bigger than he is, to dissipate this individuality, to free his ego of all doubt, conflict, and suffering—through fusion with others; to devote himself to a great leader and a great cause."[50] The goal is to evacuate the individual of all substance to the point of total stupefaction, to a point where, having no depth beneath the surface of his social identity, there is no self at all.

The absence of self becomes acutely evident any time somebody attempts to question such an individual. Trying to get him to adopt a free and thoughtful posture to an event or situation is futile. Inevitably, the effort meets with failure. "When the propagandee tries to assert himself as a living reality," as Ellul explains, "he demonstrates his total alienation most clearly; for he shows that he can no longer even distinguish between himself and society. He is then perfectly integrated, *he* is the social group, there is nothing in him not of the group, there is no opinion in him that is not the group's opinion."[51] There is not a real self here, only an avatar of one. Communication is rendered impossible. What remains is typified best by the discourse of social media: a cacophony of individuals who, disassociated from themselves, argue and bicker with others over trivial things, repeating opinions handed to them by others, all in the vain attempt to win validation from others, or else humiliate anyone who will not give it. Gladiatorial combat for the emotionally and intellectually stunted! As Ellul observes, "we see before our eyes how a world of closed minds establishes itself, a world in which everybody talks to himself, everybody constantly reviews his own certainty about himself and the wrongs done him by the Others—a world in which nobody listens to anybody else, everybody talks, and nobody listens. And the more one talks, the more one isolates oneself, because the more one accuses others and justifies himself."[52] In a lonely world without compassion, people overcome with hopelessness flee to a virtual world for escape. What they find is not a better world, a panacea. They find instead an echo chamber of screams, a place even more collectively shallow and insincere than the life they are attempting to leave behind. This other reality is just like the first. It is not the overcoming of self-love but its ugly consummation.

While it would be correct to insist against the solipsist (if we ever met one) that others exist and that we exist alongside them, it must not be overlooked that this does not annul how, in another sense, we are alone. When initially we spoke of the other as the stranger, the strangeness in question was owing to the other being neutral or unknown to us. But what about the one who does not show up that way, but rather as hostile? What about those who have become a stranger to us because they are our enemy? Nowhere is the isolation of existence more profound than in the excruciating form it takes in persecution. The opening lines of *The Reveries of a Solitary Walker*, a work Rousseau completed in the very final years of his life, capture that isolation exquisitely. Here, we see immediately, is an isolation stemming from being surrounded by others who, having shown us no compassion but rather only indifference or scorn, have become strangers to us. As the First Walk begins:

> I am now alone on earth, no longer having any brother, neighbor, friend, or society other than myself. The most sociable and he most loving of humans has been proscribed from society by a unanimous agreement. In the refinements of their hatred, they have sought the torment which would be cruelest to my sensitive soul and have violently broken all ties which attached me to them. I would have loved men in spite of themselves. Only by ceasing to be human, have they been able to slip away from my affection. They are now strangers, unknowns, in short, nonentities to me—because that is what they wanted.[53]

As ever, there is a touch of hyperbole in what Rousseau says. But he has a point. It was Rousseau's own inspiration, however, the first-century moralist and essayist Plutarch, who mapped out the terrain concerning our being-with-others in unparalleled fashion. As he notes, how others treat us can spur us to ponder ourselves. In the essay "On Listening to Lectures," Plutarch observes, to begin with, that listening is an art, demanding effort and sincerity. "For just as light is a good thing for those who can see," he says, "so is discourse for those who can hear, if they be willing to receive it."[54] Self-love, though, can deter us from listening honestly. When we are consumed with the self-concern of pride, we do not want to hear that we are wrong or that we stand in need of some correction. The peril in question is evident, Plutarch notes, with the flatterer. In listening to him, the danger is that we hear what we want to hear, which is the opposite of what we need to hear. As for the flatterer himself, he succeeds in gaining our ear only because we are already in love with ourselves. He helps us maintain our false self. In "How to Tell a Flatterer from a Friend," we read, "It is because of this self-love that everybody is himself his own foremost and greatest flatterer, and hence finds no difficulty in admitting the outsider to witness him and to confirm his own conceits and desires."[55] The flatterer simply exploits the psychological weakness of the one already intoxicated by *amour-propre*.

Beyond the danger of being told what one wants to hear rather than what one needs to, there is a further threat. In the time of need, a flatterer will prove unreliable. Because he only has an eye toward what he can get from whomever he pretends to be a friend to, he is prone to abandon anyone who has fallen on hard times. The one who has surrounded himself with flatterers comes to discover, in the dark hour, that he had no friends all along. As Plutarch says, it is good to avoid flattery, since we thereby ward off phonies (as maladjusted as Holden Caufield was, he did have a point) and avoid having to experience the cruel fate of discovering "friends that are no friends at a crucial time which calls for friends, since there is then no exchanging one that is untrustworthy and spurious for the true and trustworthy."[56] As anyone infatuated with self-love eventually comes to see, when there are no friends to come to our aid, it is because the true ones were eliminated for having tried to tell us things we did not want to hear. A real friend is the one who says what is disagreeable when it is necessary. But because it was disagreeable, offending the pride of the one who wanted flattery instead, such a person was elbowed out of the self-lover's life long ago. For many, this is one of the hallmarks demarcating their childhood from adulthood. When we grow up and make new friends, forgetting our old ones, is it because we genuinely have made new ones, or is it because we have chosen instead to forget friendship altogether and to seek flattery instead? In any case, as for those in need of flattery, no matter the personal history that led them there, they take those who correct them "to be an enemy and an accuser," whereas whoever praises and extols what they have done is regarded as "kindly and friendly."[57] When it comes to listening, Plutarch's point is that the self-lover finds himself abandoned in the time of need. It is a lesson best avoided, that those we thought were friends were really not that at all, but flattering self-seekers.

What, then, is the hazard of living a kind of life that attracts false friends? True friendship must involve the shared goal of growing in virtue. If not, those we call friends will only encourage us to degenerate into vice. In making that point, Plutarch uses the metaphor of painters and their colors: "Others, like painters who set off bright and brilliant colours by laying on dark and somber tints close beside them, covertly raise and foster the vices to which their victims are addicted by condemning and abusing, or disparaging and ridiculing, the opposite qualities."[58] When fake friends are not busy trying to rationalize that our bad deeds are good (it helps them not feel so guilty about their own), they are busy dissuading us from changing for the better, by always denigrating the good. The inversion is apparent when we consider the flatterer's false advice. Internalizing his advice is to flirt with moral ruin. Let us take, for example, a young man whose reputation has been tarnished by a matter of some public attention. He is in possession of reliable evidence showing who the real culprits are, and it is evidence that will persuade anyone who sees it that what has been done to him is contrary to what people have been told and that it was unjust. Hoping to move on with things, he is disappointed upon arriving at his job when many pull him aside and, pretending to initiate him into their confidence, tell him that, contrary to all good sense, it would be in his best interest not to disclose the facts capable of exonerating him. As each of these various conversations progresses, it becomes clear what is going on. Because these men would themselves never be prepared to defend their honor when doing so could potentially lead to further damage to their careers, they have to justify their own cowardice by dissuading anyone else from risking what they would not. In a word, they do exactly what Plutarch says flatterers do. In the name of prudence, they counsel our young man not to come forward with the truth. If our young man responds by saying that others should themselves be prepared to point out the truth in difficult circumstances, he is condemned for arrogance or obstinance. Blessed, thus, is the one who walks not in the counsel of the flatterer.

Plutarch for his own part anticipates the above line of objection. The question, he sees, is this: are there instances when one is justified in presenting oneself as a moral exemplar? Plutarch answers affirmatively, observing that self-praise is not always in bad taste. As he notes in the fittingly titled essay "On Inoffensive Self-Praise," exhorting others to good action by presenting one's own example is "endued with life," in that "it arouses and spurs the hearer, and not only awakens his ardour and fixes his purpose, but also affords him hope that the end can be attained and is not impossible."[59] Quoting the Spartan chorus to underscore the point, Plutarch writes,

> "Time was when we were valiant youths";
> The boys sing:
> "So we shall be, and braver far";
> And the young men;
> "So now we are: you need but look."[60]

In some situations, Plutarch contends, self-praise is not a bad thing. For unlike the "demagogue or would-be sophist or of one who courts plaudits and cheers," someone who instead says, like our young man, what he does in sincere defense of the truth of his actions encourages others to do as well when they are called. In pointing to oneself, the aim is not to boast but to help others, by offering one's "virtue and understanding to his friends as security against despair."[61] In some situations doing so is hopeless. The coworkers in question have made up their minds and that means they will interpret however the young man responds in the worst possible light. Whether, then, our young man decides not to take his senior colleagues' advice ("arrogance"), defends his original actions ("stubbornness"), or tells them to follow his own example ("pride"), those giving him advice will take issue with it and characterize his response as bad, for they are looking for an excuse to be displeased. Reading Plutarch, we are reminded of the hard truth that those who hate us will persist in finding faults where there are none. If, as he says in another essay, "On Envy and Hate," the intention of the hater is to injure, hate here must be understood as "a certain disposition and intention awaiting the opportunity to injure."[62] Even where there is no actual wrong to condemn, those who hate us will set out to try to injure us by inventing wrongs we have not committed.

For this reason, Plutarch notes with Xenophon before him that we must "try to discover the system and art through which this admirable advantage is to be gained by those who find it impossible to live without an enemy."[63] In the edifying essay "How to Profit by One's Enemies," he observes how, by considering what those who hate us have to say about us, "wise men are able to make a fitting use even of their enmities."[64] As a first item of order, it is necessary to accept that with malicious characters, they are hyenas, emboldened by what they perceive to be weakness. Nothing stirs them to action as the prospect of a wounded foe. In a long passage on the subject, Plutarch begins by likening them, not to hyenas as we have, but vultures.

> And just as vultures are drawn to the smell of decomposed bodies, but have no power to discover those that are clean and healthy, so the infirmities, meannesses, and untoward experiences of life rouse the energies of the enemy, and it is such things as these that the malevolent pounce upon and seize and tear to pieces. Is this then profitable? Assuredly it is, to have to live circumspectly, to give heed to one's self, and not to do or say anything carelessly or inconsiderately, but always to keep one's life unassailable as though under an exact regimen. For the circumspection which thus represses the emotions and keeps the reasoning power within bounds gives practice and purpose in living a life that is fair and free from reproach.[65]

Hyenas rove in packs. And they must. They have reason to fear the lion, brave and strong. Due to their own weakness, the resentful people Plutarch has in view will look for any pretense to justify their bad opinion of the one they hate.

What better thing can we do, then, but to watch over ourselves, depriving slanderers of the least excuse to justify their hatred? This is what Plutarch advises. Whoever knows that he is being watched by a cloud of hateful witnesses "is more heedful of himself, and more circumspect about his actions, and brings his life into a more thorough harmony."[66] Taking precautions to ensure that we are walking in the right not only makes it more difficult for these others to lay any blame against us, it also provides the further advantage that, where necessary, it is possible without hypocrisy to call out the bad behavior of those who despise us. As he remarks, it is imperative to search ourselves: "Enter within the portals of your own soul, look about to see if there be any rottenness there, lest some vice lurking somewhere within whisper to you the words of the tragedian: 'Wouldst thou heal others, full of sores thyself?'"[67] In Matthew's Gospel, Christ is recorded as saying that we should not judge others lest we ourselves be judged. Contrary to a widespread misunderstanding of that statement, this is not admonishing judgment as such, but hypocritical judgment. Paul iterates the lesson in the letter to the Romans, observing that whoever judges others for doing the same things he does himself will not escape the judgment of God. Here again, the admonition is not against judging others at all, but for judging them for something we do too. If I am not a liar, there is nothing awry in telling a liar that lying is wrong; if I am not a thief, there is nothing scandalous in telling a thief not to steal. Irenaeus was to explain the point well where, in *Against Heresies*, he stresses that there is nothing wrong in finding fault with wrongdoing. On the topic of these verses from Matthew, he says, "[The meaning is] not certainly that we should not find fault with sinners, nor that we should pronounce an unfair judgment on the dispensations of God, inasmuch as He has Himself made out for the good, in a way consistent with justice."[68]

Avoiding hypocrisy is one good thing. But even better is taking what others have falsely said about us and using it as inspiration to improve ourselves, so that their accusations are rendered even more baseless. Claiming falsely that we have failed to meet a standard we in fact have, those who hate us without a cause remind us of the very ideal to which we should be continually striving. As Plutarch explains, "if anybody mentions things which are not really attributes of ours, we should nevertheless seek to learn the cause which has given rise to such slanderous assertions, and we must exercise vigilance, for fear that we unwittingly commit some error either approximating or resembling one mentioned."[69] Suppose I am down and out. My career has hit a hiccup. As I am struggling to come up for air, others take my misfortune as opportunity to taunt me. Relishing the financial and other hardships I endure, they take to claiming I am entitled. They know the suggestion is absurd, which is why they say it! The point is to provoke. The one who says so, cozy in his lavish mansion, living a pampered life of self-indulgent leisure, amuses himself by admonishing the one asking for his help. It is presumptuous to make demands of his time, he says. How better to put this spiteful talk to silence than to bear up under the ridicule and, doing what one can, resuscitate one's career without his help?

Contrary to what a common objection will predictably insist, the lesson is generalizable beyond that of the mocker who takes delight in taunting those who are suffering. It always is possible to learn something from others, even the vicious. Plutarch asks, what should prevent us "from taking his enemy as his teacher without fee, and profiting thereby, and thus learning, to some extent, the things of which he was unaware?"[70] Being unjustly accused of some vice by somebody who hates us might assist us in honing another virtue. To return to the present example, enduring the absurdity of being called entitled by the pampered rich man can deepen my commitment to living humbly. And in so doing, perhaps I truly am reminded of the importance of gratitude. Finally, choosing not to bother wasting my time cataloging all the subtleties of the other's malicious hypocrisy, I grow in self-control, learning in turn how to hold my tongue, even when the other deserves an admonition for spewing forth venom.[71] Having not returned evil for evil, the already existing gap between us grows. To whatever extent vengeance is a relevant consideration here, surely growing in the good, while he putrefies in his degradation, is the most excellent one.

Anticipating Rousseau in "On Tranquility of Mind," Plutarch observes how self-love often is the culprit behind so much trouble. It is folly to "have grown accustomed to live with eyes fixed on everyone else rather than on ourselves," since, as he continues, those who live in this kind of envy and malice are usually much uglier inside than they would like anyone to know: "draw aside the gaudy curtain of their repute and outward appearance, and get inside them, and you will see many disagreeable things and many things to vex them there."[72] What is occurring here is a problem traceable to self-love, as that is "which makes men eager to be first and to be victorious in everything and insatiably desirous of engaging in everything."[73] The desire to be admired by others leads to marginalizing others in competition. It is a reptilian attitude as shallow as it is petty. For what those in love with themselves are contending against one another is pointless. They are looking for a crowd of admirers whose very opinion is not worth obtaining. Better, contends Plutarch, to focus on ourselves and to seek after something abiding and good. Our task is to strive after what matters. The praise of others is excluded. If Plutarch admits that life is agonistic, the struggle is with oneself to continue to pursue what is good, not one with others to obtain what is not. "We know," he explains in an athletic analogy, "that runners are not discouraged because they do not carry off wrestlers' crowns, but they exult and rejoice in their own."[74] It was of course with another crown in mind that Paul mentioned what he does in his first letter to the Corinthians. He had in mind eternal life. And if we are going to have to struggle for something, let it be for what is eternal. For Paul, then, not unlike Plutarch, the only crown worth striving for is the one won by virtue. And for him it is an eternal prize: "And every man that striveth for the mastery is temperate in all things. Now they *do it* to obtain a corruptible crown; but we an incorruptible" (1 Cor 9:25).

It is in this context of evaluating what it takes to achieve what is worth achieving in life that Plutarch is led to consider more closely hate and envy. Both, he notes, hinder our progress. To grow in doing good is to want what is good for others. When others achieve some good, it is contrary to goodness itself to resent them for it. Rather, we should be glad. Plutarch in the essay "On Curiosity" cautions against various bad attitudes toward others we must guard against, defining envy specifically in these terms. It is "pain at another's good."[75] For whom except the morally depraved will be angry at another's discovering for himself the good? Plutarch expounds on the point, noting that such an attitude is bestial, one of a "vicious nature."[76] As bad as envy is, it is a particular form of malignance arising from the more basic attitude that, paying too much attention to others, has already gone wrong to begin with. Only an eye that is too focused on what others think and have is vulnerable to envy. Well aware, Plutarch tells us not even to read the scribblings on the city's walls: though there may appear to be no danger in doing it, there is. "It may seem," he comments, "that no harm will come from reading these, but harm you it does by imperceptibly instilling the practice of searching out matters which not concern you."[77] The danger is brought to a head in the consumption of mass political propaganda. Like the graffiti worrying Plutarch, it tries to convince us that what it says should concern us. And if we make up our minds that it does, it will be only because we have first lost ourselves in a world of concerns that do not matter.

In what initially appears to be a tangential comment, it is worth noting that because our being-in-the-world is indelibly one of being-with-others, we are beings for whom being exiled is possible. But is exile a punishment? It was commonly treated as one in ancient times. Not only does Plutarch insist that by "nature there is no such thing as a native land,"[78] he goes so far as to say that exile, contrary to common sense's opinion, can be a great good. He writes,

> "Well done, Fortune! Thus to confine me to a threadbare cloak and a philosopher's life"; while a man not wholly infatuated or mad for the mob would not, I think, on being confined to an island, reproach Fortune, but would commend her for taking away from him all his restlessness and aimless roving, wanderings in foreign lands and perils at sea and tumults in the market place, and giving him a life that was settled, leisurely, undistracted, and truly his own, describing with centre and radius a circle containing the necessities that meet his needs.[79]

If, as he says, "the exclusion from one city is the freedom to choose from all,"[80] it is because we are not as the plants. A plant in inhospitable ground and without adequate rain or sun will die. But with us things are different, he contends. Whereas "for a plant one region is more favorable than another for thriving and growth," not so for us, since "no place can take away happiness, as none can take away virtue or wisdom."[81] Society does not offer us nourishment. Nor, for that matter, does the propaganda world of news and other mass media. But neither can they uproot us. Plutarch's perceptive remarks concerning exile, it seems, have returned us to a consideration of Rousseau, for whom persecution led to the realization that salvation is not to be found anywhere outside ourselves. And no wonder. The "Citizen of Geneva" spent a good deal of his own life in exile. If there is to be serenity, it will not be found in society, for it must be found within. Here, it is possible to make the banal comment that Rousseau the man was liable to the charge of false moral superiority. And many have further noted that, despite his condemnations of *amour-propre*, he was himself something of a narcissist. But these comments, even were they true, are somewhat superficial. If it is fair in this context to speak of any performative inconsistency in Rousseau, it was not so much that he saw society as corrosive while he embodied too much of what he criticized about it. Criticisms to that effect, if anything, are overstated. The real trouble lies elsewhere. While he was correct to see us as naturally good and compassionate, he never availed himself of the only way truly to overcome the bitter loneliness of having to deal with those virtues being so scorned by the world. Correctly, he saw that the individual is more than what society wants him to be, rejecting the notion that human existence should be dedicated to chasing success and glory. But for all that, he lacked, so far as anyone can reasonably know, a commitment to man as made in the *imago Dei*.

In one of his later essays, "From Sincerity to Authenticity," Bernard Williams takes up the question of Rousseau's belief that beneath the social self lies a real one. Characterizing *amour-propre* as "competitive self-assertion,"[82] Williams says that for Rousseau a just polity would accordingly be one that allows for and encourages the expression of goodwill. But that vision of political organization, so he continues, implies that the real self "will be virtuous."[83] Here, Williams has his misgivings. He asks, "If there is such a thing as the 'real self' of an individual, what reason is there to think that it must coincide with an underlying character of honour, considerateness, and compassion?"[84] The implication is clear. Rousseau, according to Williams, never went the distance to convince us that this is the case.

Williams was not the first to doubt man's natural benevolence. Setting out what he will later in that same text term its "enquiry into happiness," Freud in *Civilization and Its Discontents* observes how *amour-propre* governs so much of our failed everyday pursuit of happiness. As he notes, "It is impossible to escape the impression that people commonly use false standards of measurement—that they seek power, success and wealth for themselves and admire them in others, and that they underestimate what is of true value in life."[85] In life, we "strive after happiness," because we "want to become happy and to remain so."[86] This is the program of the pleasure principle, the pursuit of experiencing strong feelings of pleasure with the avoidance of pain. And yet it is hard to be happy, when so understood. Freud identifies the sources of unhappiness as these: "the superior powers of nature, the feebleness of our own bodies and the inadequacy of the regulations which adjust the mutual relationships of human beings in the family, the state and society."[87] As for the third source of suffering, others can be cruel, Freud observes. The source of interpersonal conflict, he says, is our psychic condition. Lurking in us all, he claims, is an instinctive aggressiveness, a subterranean drive to destruction and death. Alongside Eros "there [is] an instinct to death."[88] If we want to be happy with the avoidance of suffering, yet suffering at the hands of others inevitably comes because there is a "piece of our own psychical constitution"[89] that is inherently aggressive, what is to be done? The possibility of isolation comes to mind: "Against the suffering which may come upon one from human relationships the readiest safeguard is voluntary isolation, keeping oneself aloof from other people."[90] This is one apparent method of protection against suffering. "The hermit," says Freud, "turns his back on the world and will have no truck with it."[91] But isolation will not for that bring peace. Nor joy. For as he notes, it cannot protect against the other causes of human suffering. There always is Fate to contend with.

Freud's assessment of human suffering returns us to the criticism of Rousseau. Is the nature of man benevolent? One might propose bracketing the question by suggesting that it is, from a practical standpoint, beside the point. After all, whether antagonism is seen as an instinctual feature of the psyche (Freud) or as a mere consequence of society's having perverted our true benevolence (Rousseau), the fact remains, as bad as society may be, and no matter how greatly we suffer from others, humans still need contact. That is true. The question of man's nature, however, is not unrelated to the matter of how we choose to deal with the pain of coexistence. And while it is not something Williams himself would find congenial, the beginning of an answer to that dilemma, it seems, comes into view by recognizing that, in diagnosing the ills associated with *amour-propre* as he did, Rousseau was right to see man as inherently good. The problem was not in his saying so, but that in saying it, he never appealed to a sufficiently theological view of man. Rousseau's anthropology views us as to some extent made in the image of God, but for him God remains largely a heuristic who in the last analysis falls out of the picture. What is needed to answer Williams's concern is a more robust view of ourselves existing in the image of God.

And here, where better to turn than to Kierkegaard, to whom we owe just such an account? With Rousseau, Kierkegaard will agree that a life of true individuality is free from the vicissitudes of self-love. Competition and comparison, as he emphasizes in *Works of Love*, are ticking time bombs for disaffection and emptiness. What is needed, as he notes elsewhere in the edifying discourse "The Lily of the Field and the Bird of the Air," is a return to nature (just as Rousseau also suggests), but one genuinely overseen and blessed by God. One must learn to exist nakedly, without artifice, pride, and cunning, and thus simply before God. As he says in a section of that text called "Contentment with Our Common Humanity," we must ask ourselves the question the lily of the field puts to us. "[W]hat does the concerned individual learn from the lilies? He learns to be satisfied with the fact of being human, and not to be disturbed about the distinctions between man and man."[92] To be as the lily and thus content with oneself is to stop comparing oneself with others and to stop letting their comparisons with us matter. Contentment, which is impossible with *amour-propre*, is hence not to be reached by looking to others or by being concerned with how they see us. But if doing as Kierkegaard recommends is itself sufficient for avoiding one kind of suffering that otherwise will afflict us, there is the suffering that overtakes us when others oppose us, trying to harm us even if we are doing our very best not to harm them.

The only escape from the suffering will be solitude. But what kind? To be sure, escape from the cruelty of others and a relief from being misunderstood is possible. But the road to travel to get there is not to flee the pain through the consumption of mass media. To become a mass man is to lose oneself. Nor, however, is the solution as Rousseau saw it, to retreat into private reverie, where there is nothing but the silent conversation of *soi de soi*. Only a God-relationship will do.

"To go alone!"[93] —here, in language evoking Rousseau's own figure of the solitary walker, Kierkegaard explains how suffering turns us back on ourselves. One walks alone. But in doing so, he suggests, one follows Christ. "To follow signifies, then, going entirely alone on the way the teacher went: to have no visible person with whom one can take counsel,"[94] since, without being left to oneself, no transformation would take place. As Kierkegaard explains, "To follow Christ, then, means denying one's self, and hence it means walking the same way as Christ walked in the humble form of a servant—needy, forsaken, mocked, not loving worldliness and not loved by the worldly minded. Consequently, it means to *walk alone*, for he who in self-abnegation renounces the world and all that is the world's, forsakes every relationship which otherwise tempts and holds captive."[95] Suffering often originates from without, and there is nothing we can do about it. The question is how to respond. If suffering is to profit us, we must hear what it says, learning that the peace we are looking for is not of the world. In the world, goodwill among men does not reign! Those who act in accord with man's true nature—honestly, compassionately, righteously—are without a home, having become pilgrims. It is because the world does not make existence easy but always brings suffering with it that Kierkegaard, likening suffering to a school, notes how following Christ demands obedience. Choosing to accept the suffering that comes from following Christ, we learn. It trains us for eternity: "When a man suffers and is willing to learn from what he suffers," says Kierkegaard, "*then he constantly learns only something about himself and about his relationship to God; this is the sign that he is being trained for eternity.*"[96] This is what he calls "the mystery of suffering," that in it there can be a profound joy. Not the joy of isolation's reveries as Rousseau thought, but of living-before-God.

Take again, as so many of the authors we have considered have, the phenomenon of suffering. In moments when it feels like we experience only the loneliness of a solitude without joy, why? I suffer, but at whose hands? Those of others, or my own because I grant them such power? Invariably, others can (and will) deny us what justice demands or kindness recommends. And in this, there is hurt. There is a relief from sorrow, if we wish to receive it. Stoicism is not totally mistaken when, comparing the inner man to a citadel, it insisted that peace is up to us. Others can make finding tranquility more difficult, but that decides how much exertion we must be prepared to expend in order to attain it, not whether we can reach it if we do. Pestered by the schemes of those who despise us, attacked with their darts of slander and false comfort, we discover that we are stronger than we had known. In being tested, we find ourselves able to cope where we had thought there could be no coping. We experience an unexpected calm, a balm of assurance and security. Having crossed a threshold we previously had thought marked the absolute limit of the endurable, what seemed impossible to bear becomes tolerable, even mundane. It is then that we find, here where we had been at our apparent weakest, handed over to the indifference and hypocrisy and cruelty of disingenuous men, that we were stronger than anyone, ourselves included, had estimated originally. Sometimes, we surprise even ourselves. And what a deep joy it is!

We look to those around us for aid when facing hardship. But given what past experience has taught us, before we ever go looking, we already know what we likely will find. Disappointment awaits us, for others too often prove incapable of interest or action. We are on our own. That suffering is solitary is not all bad. In it is opportunity. When rotten people attempt to deny us our daily felicity, their attempts to stir up strife merely remind us that, no matter what they try to do in animosity, serenity is within our own grasp. Whatever harm they aim to inflict is never an injury in itself, just the appearance of one. In order for some slight or other indignity to hit its mark, it depends on us laying down our armor. Such self-reliance is liberating, but not, to be sure, because it relieves us of any duty to others, turning us inwardly upon ourselves. Nothing selfish or dishonest is in it. Anyone still enrapt with the idea of seeking worldly gratification will not be ready to see others in their time of need. But the kind of independence we have in view has left that self-love behind. Where *amour-propre* blinds us to real contentment, which is to be sought within, rendering us indifferent to the plight of others, this is not so here. To recognize our isolation for what it is, if anything, makes us more attuned to the suffering of others. It is a matter of accepting humbly that suffering is an inevitability of life, all the more so when we try to do good, and that one of the common forms such suffering takes is not having our pain recognized by others. As for those who dish out that pain, there is no stopping them, but when we find ourselves worrying whether they have succeeded in their devices, we soon discover it only seems so because, in a spell of weakness, we have given their opinions and intentions more credence than they deserve. Rousseau was to note this in his *Reveries*. As he remarks in that work's Eighth Walk, serenity will be ours when we let go of social passions, leaving our wrongdoers to themselves, unconcerned with their intrigues. In such solitary reverie, it is possible to be content in spite of others. As he says, "I laugh at the incredible torments my persecutors constantly give themselves in vain, while I remain at peace, busied with flowers, stamens, and childish things and do not even think of them."[97] Others may bait us with their taunts or needle us with their scorn. For their manipulations and machinations, they are blameworthy. But it is we who have erred by allowing what they do to matter more than it does. To sum up, it is well known that tormenters all take delight in seeing their victim's distress. There is something vampiric about that sadistic lust. Dead to themselves, what sustains them is enjoying the pain they can suck out of their victim. From the perspective of this everyday sadist, there is no doubt as to who is in control: he is. Things, however, are the reverse of how he thinks. At bottom, whatever misery these hateful people induce is made possible only by their victim's decision to lend those efforts the power to have mattered. Just as any dart of torment hits its target when the one to whom it is directed allows it to, so it is possible to deflect it. Rousseau, for all his faults, knew this well when he observed that seeking approval from others in society is an invitation for disillusionment. Seeking recognition from corrupt men rather than from God, we may add, leads them to disappointing us. But whose fault is that? Theirs or ours? Too often we can be slow to accept it, yet the lesson of frustrated recognition or spurned concern is that solitude is preferable anyway.

The body speaks, above all, when it trembles under the strain of affliction. The experience, really, is not too uncommon. It calls to mind the experience of Paul, whose words recount that experience so well: "We are troubled on every side, yet not distressed; we are perplexed, but not in despair; persecuted, but not forsaken; cast down, but not destroyed" (2 Cor 4:8–9). When adversity strikes, then, and you are called to endure it, sigh if you must. Then catch your breath, look to God! Lift up your arms and knees, pressing on. Being at the apparent limits of our power to endure is cause to rejoice. Therein we find a purpose in the weakness that has borne it. Sustained by an infusion of divine assistance, the pain is overshadowed by the power of a hope received in having been emptied of ourselves. God's strength carries us on. These trials are not without their own distinctive joy, for there is a tranquility in them that your oppressors who nuisance you do not know. What a sweet imperviousness, to render those who hate you for seeking after good unable to rob you of the joy that has become your fortress.

As believers know, rejoicing in trials is not in vain. In the world, we would have been alone, but not *here*. God is with us. Tertullian articulates things nicely in chapter 8 of his treatise "On Patience." Patience, the root of so many other spiritual goods, is of God. And so, as he observes, it has its benefits. There are many, but chief among them is its ability to disappoint the sadistic desires of those who hate us. As Tertullian says, "No doubt the reason why anyone wants to hurt you is that you may be pained; because the hurter's enjoyment consists in the pain of the hurt. When, then, you have upset his enjoyment by not being pained, *he* must needs be pained by the loss of his enjoyment."[98] "Then," as he notes, "you not only go unhurt away, which even alone is enough for you; but gratified, into the bargain, by your adversary's disappointment, and revenged by his pain."[99] Such are the spoils that go to the patient one. Its accompanying victory, including equanimity of mind, Tertullian notes, contains a reversal sweet and complete. Since it really is the only concern of those who derive sick pleasure in injuring others, let us put the issue in terms they can understand. By that, we mean power. Who, we accordingly ask, knows real power? Not the impatient adversary, who, persisting in blind malice, rages in failed attempt after attempt at vengeance, but rather the one who perseveres in patience. Here, in one of God's many mercies, a transposition occurs. For what was your torment will have become theirs.

NOTES

1. This conclusion that the other's existence is indubitable runs contrary to the opposite one, typified by Descartes, who in the Second Meditation writes, "But then if I look out of the window and see men crossing the square, as I just happen to have done, I normally say that I see the men themselves, just as I say that I see the wax. Yet do I see any more than hats and coats which could conceal automatons? I *judge* that they are men. And so something which I thought I was seeing with my eyes is in fact grasped solely by the faculty of judgment which is in my mind." René Descartes, *Meditations on First Philosophy: With Selections from the Objections and Replies*, ed. John Cottingham (Cambridge: Cambridge University Press, 1996), 26.

2. Edith Stein, *On the Problem of Empathy*, trans. Waltraut Stein (The Hague: Martinus Nijhoff, 1970), 11.
3. Ibid., 13.
4. Ibid., 14.
5. Ibid., 15.
6. Ibid., 17.
7. Ibid.
8. Ibid., 60.
9. Michel Henry, *Incarnation: A Philosophy of the Flesh*, trans. Karl Hefty (Evanston, IL: Northwestern University Press, 2015), 241.
10. Henry articulates the sense in which this mode of existence, as a "transcendental illusion," distorts how we see others. See the chapters "Forgetting the Condition of Son" and "Paradoxes of Christianity" in *I Am the Truth: Toward a Philosophy of Christianity*, trans. Susan Emmanuel (Stanford, CA: Stanford University Press, 2003).
11. Claude Romano, "Solitude et secret. Prolégomènes à une phénoménologie du lien humain," *Annuario Filosofico* (2012): 28, 78.
12. Ibid., 81.
13. Ibid.
14. Ibid., 84.
15. Ibid., 97.
16. Ibid., 85.
17. Ibid., 84.
18. Ibid.
19. Ibid., 82.
20. Ibid., 100. Hannah Arendt had said the same as Romano in *The Human Condition* (Chicago: University of Chicago Press, 1958). She says therein, "The new always happens against the overwhelming odds of statistical laws and their probability, which for all practical, everyday purposes amounts to certainty; the new therefore always appears in the guise of a miracle. The fact that man is capable of action means that the unexpected can be expected from him, that he is able to perform what is infinite improbable. . . . If action as beginning corresponds to the fact of birth, if it is the actualization of the human condition of natality, then speech corresponds to the fact of distinctness and is the actualization of the human condition of plurality, that is, of living as a distinct and unique being among equals," 178.
21. Jean-Jacques Rousseau, *Discours sur l'origine et les fondements de l'inégalité parmi les hommes*, B. Bachofen et B. Bernardi (Paris: GF Flammarion, 2008), 190.
22. Rousseau, *Les Rêveries du promeneur solitaire* (Paris: GF Flammarion, 1997), 103.
23. Romano provides an exceptional study of how the notion of being oneself has developed across the history of philosophy. In recounting its evolution, he treats Rousseau directly in chapter 27, "Authenticité et alienation: Rousseau," 423–59. See *Être soi—même: une autre historie de la philosophie* (Paris: Gallimard, 2019).
24. Iris Murdoch, *The Sovereignty of Good* (London and New York: Routledge, 2014), 30.
25. Ibid., 82.
26. Ibid.
27. Ibid., 83.
28. Ibid., 89.
29. Ibid., 101.
30. While the theme recurs throughout Kierkegaard's works, *The Present Age* (New York: HarperCollins, 2010) deals with it most extensively.
31. Søren Kierkegaard, *The Sickness unto Death: A Christian Psychological Exposition for Upbuilding and Awakening*, ed. Edna Hong and Howard Hong (Princeton: Princeton University Press, 1980), 56.
32. Jacques Ellul, *Propaganda: The Formation of Men's Attitudes*, trans. Konrad Kellen and Jean Lerner (New York: Random House, 1973), 8.
33. Ibid., 6.
34. Ibid., 103.
35. Ibid., 121.

36. Ibid., 31.
37. Ibid.
38. Ibid., 42.
39. Ibid., 44.
40. Michel Henry, *Barbarism*, trans. Scott Davidson (London: Continuum International Publishing Group, 2002), 111.
41. Ibid., 140.
42. Ellul, *Propaganda*, 140.
43. Ibid., 41.
44. Ibid., 145.
45. Ibid., 147.
46. Ibid.
47. Ibid., 148.
48. Ibid., 106.
49. Ibid., 141.
50. Ibid., 169.
51. Ibid., 171.
52. Ibid., 214.
53. Jean-Jacques Rousseau, *The Reveries of the Solitary Walker*, trans. Charles E. Butterworth (New York: Harper Collins, 1979), 1.
54. Plutarch, "On Listening to Lectures," I, 39/215.
55. Plutarch, "How to Tell a Flatterer from a Friend," I, 49/265.
56. Ibid., I, 49/269.
57. Ibid., I, 55–56/301.
58. Ibid., I, 57/307.
59. Plutarch, "On Inoffensive Self-Praise," VII, 544/149.
60. Ibid.
61. Ibid., VII, 545/153.
62. Plutarch, "On Envy and Hate," VII, 538/107.
63. Plutarch, "How to Profit by One's Enemies," II, 86/7.
64. Ibid., II, 86–87/9.
65. Ibid., II, 87–88/13.
66. Ibid.
67. Ibid., II, 88/17.
68. Irenaeus, *Against Heresies,* in *The Ante-Nicene Fathers: The Writings of the Fathers Down to A.D. 325,* vol. 1, ed. Alexander Roberts and James Donaldson, 307–567 (Grand Rapids, MI: Wm. B. Eerdmans Publishing Company, 1950), IV. XXX. 504.
69. Plutarch, "How to Profit by One's Enemies," II, 89/23.
70. Ibid., 89–90/25.
71. Ibid.
72. Plutarch, "On Tranquility of Mind," VI, 470–71/203.
73. Ibid., 471/205.
74. Ibid., 472/211.
75. Plutarch, "On Curiosity," VI, 518/492.
76. Ibid., 518/491.
77. Ibid., 520–21/503.
78. Plutarch, "On Exile," VII, 600/527.
79. Ibid., 603–04/547.
80. Ibid.," 604/549.
81. Ibid., 607/571.
82. Bernard Williams, *Truth and Truthfulness: An Essay in Genealogy* (Princeton, NJ: Princeton University Press, 2002), 181.
83. Ibid.
84. Ibid., 182.
85. Sigmund Freud, *Civilization and Its Discontents*, trans. and ed. James Strachey (New York and London: W.W. Norton & Company, 2010), 23.

86. Ibid.
87. Ibid., 57.
88. Ibid., 106.
89. Ibid., 58.
90. Ibid., 45.
91. Ibid., 50.
92. Søren Kierkegaard, *The Gospel of Suffering and the Lilies of the Field*, trans. David F. Swenson and Lillian Marvin Swenson (Minneapolis, MN: Augsburg Publishing House, 1948), 183.
93. Ibid., 9.
94. Ibid., 8.
95. Ibid., 12.
96. Ibid., 56. Emphasis in the original.
97. Rousseau, *Reveries*, 112. It is well known that Rousseau believed himself to be the victim of a conspiracy (primarily on the Continent) to destroy him—suspects included Voltaire. But he also numbered David Hume among them. For fascinating accounts of Rousseau's personality and biography, with particular focus on his encounter with Hume, see David Edmonds, *Rousseau's Dog: Two Great Thinkers at War in the Age of Enlightenment* (New York: Harper, 2006) and Robert Zaretsky, *The Philosophers' Quarrel: Rousseau, Hume, and the Limits of Human Understanding* (Ann Arbor, MI: Sheridan Books, 2009).
98. Tertullian. "On Patience," in *The Ante-Nicene Fathers: The Writings of the Fathers down to A.D. 325*, vol. 3, ed. Alexander Roberts and James Donaldson, 707–17 (Grand Rapids, MI: Wm. B. Eerdmans Publishing Company, 1957), 712.
99. Ibid., 712–13.

Chapter Four

Forgiveness

To be true, forgiveness is an act that must be sustained. It takes our resolve. And when it is resolved honestly, which is to say firmly, then in a way, eventually, it begins almost to sustain itself. But at first it is not so, requiring a serious effort, one repeated, and thus affirmed, time and again. At its origin, there is as much a formal or even final cause as any efficient one. It is an act with a history, one for that matter with a promise. It therefore does not occur once and for all, but rather continues on, always only insofar as it unfolds through the ideal that incessantly solicits its resolve. When we forgive (and here we are considering the forgiveness that we show others, not yet the one we sometimes seek from ourselves), we do not make a decision that is thereby accomplished forever. Even when we pronounce it, whether explicitly to the other or simply to ourselves silently in our own hearts, any such declaration of forgiveness, though illocutionary, is not immediately and automatically successful. In reality, in every salient respect it is more like a commitment.

Hence, it is something akin to a promise. Whether something is a genuine act of forgiveness is initially contestable, it must be tried or tested. This is because its sincerity, or not, will determine whether it was authentic or an imposter. Its identity can only emerge across a span whose time of testing determines whether it was what it appeared to be when first announced. An act of forgiveness, or the statements we make to declare that we have initiated one, is not just a singular moment, as if it were a parousia. If it does not develop as expected, bearing the fruit true forgiveness would, this is because it was either never true to begin with, or else it has subsequently lapsed, receding back into a nothingness, revealed to be something less than what it had first aspired or pretended to be. It is a project, which is why there is such a thing as feigned (or scuttled) forgiveness.

All this reminds us that forgiveness is interwoven with time intimately. It shapes how we see our past, what we believe the future can bring. And so, whatever else it may be, or whatever it may produce, to forgive is to relinquish a way of having seen that past, or at the minimum how one (and maybe others too) chose to see that situation when it still was fully present. Assuming it is sincere, this decision to forgive someone will unfurl itself, as we have already said, in the form of a resolve altering how we see the future as well. No longer does the future control us from behind, propelling us forward along a fixed course, while we labor saddled with the freight of the past, beleaguered by the conviction that time will only hold more of the same. No longer do we feel ourselves projected forward by a past that, always ready to meet us, steers us in one direction. Instead, things are flexible and undetermined. Now originating from itself and coming toward us, the future is freed for possibilities that would have otherwise been closed off or obscured by our worries, regrets, and memories. As anyone who has lived too long without forgiveness comes to experience, fretting about the past screens what might have otherwise come to meet us. When we are being forgiving, the future, which is made ours, is no longer a projection of care and so the past, but *new*. In this space of action (Kierkegaard in his edifying discourses calls it the "today") we are liberated from yesterday. With an expansive horizon so revealed, and not through worries and regrets over the past but by the commitment to cease languishing in old ruts, we turn our back on bad habits. Maybe it is the drive to seek revenge that we have seen destroy so many others, or maybe the remorse of a frustrated desire. Whatever it is (and only oneself really knows), we leave behind what would have kept us frozen in a past that once was, or one we wish had been but never materialized. Forgiveness, then, reminds us to beware of what happens if we should choose to live without it, haunted by the frustration of something that never was, or no longer is. For each of us, there always is a danger of becoming what we laugh at in Al Bundy.

Initiating a kind of forgetting, forgiveness reorganizes how time encounters us. In some instances, that means letting go entirely. The one we have forgiven, whether it be a true friend who has uncharacteristically disappointed us or a false one who has undermined us, recedes from our consciousness. No more the focus of recurring thoughts, the object of imagined conversations, or the cause of late-night sulking, the other shows up instead as another in an entirely new light—expelled from the shadow of our concern; he is restored to himself rather than remaining a figure seen in the reflected image of our own disaffection. To see the other in this way (as he is) means adopting a posture toward him that puts first, or at least more prominently than before, what objectively is best for him. He is, we decide, not someone solely deserving of our resentment or animosity, but one whose dignity as a person transcends whatever situation he had come to figure in relation to us. In this letting-go, we are released from the shackles of egoism, recognizing that the other who had mattered until then primarily just to the extent that he had wronged us matters much more than that. It could be objected that this is a rather insignificant result, too obvious to need stating. But that objection is unfair. For even if the point is obvious from an intellectual stance, accomplishing it can be difficult practically. It is one thing to say the other transcends our concerns (or that the other should), and quite another to meet that realization. Too often, what we consider a slight, even if it genuinely was, is a small thing. Lingering over it becomes petty too.

For this reason, the forgiveness that makes the other recede from the foreground of our consciousness to the periphery makes it possible that the other be left to himself instead of remaining someone experienced as a player in our own life, or as a participant in some episode that matters more to us than it ever did to him. Such forgiving is not an act of forgetting only. It also is a work of love. A work because it requires effort. Of love because it is concern for the good that at once initiates and energizes it. When we grow little in love, we stagnate, and our vision grows narrow. Things get stuffy, and we feel ourselves constricted.

It is an undeniable fact that in coming into contact with others, sometimes we feel they are enclosed within themselves in this way. And probably others have at some point had that impression of us when we were not at our best. The real trouble sets in with those who learn to love this misery. Bad memories of hard times can become a source of perverse satisfaction. Who has not known someone, who, no matter what they say to the contrary, basically enjoys being upset, always hunting for the negative in all situations? Inevitably, when we succumb to the temptation of dwelling on past pain, whoever has done us the wrong can become an idol, a phantom who, ever with us, haunts how we get on, or rather fail to get on, with our lives. Better then not only for the other, but for ourselves too (and for all those who come into contact with us!) that we bracket whatever wrong was done to us and let the past truly *be* past. No longer letting it torment us is a start. What has happened cannot be erased. And nor for that matter should its having happened be denied. But it need not take the precedence it once did.

This act of love responsible for restoring another to his objective status in the world, rather than as someone consigned to be pigeonholed into our understanding of what he has done to us, sometimes takes on even altruistic proportions. Who has not had the experience of turning away, if need be indefinitely, from a friendship because the other no longer has the time for us, or no longer sees the value in it? It can be a very hard thing to see someone we love hurt themselves by squandering their time with others who do not care for them genuinely, but unless we want such a situation to deteriorate into little more than a slight to our pride, or an occasion for jealousy, better to let the other learn for himself that the true friend is the one who is willing to go unappreciated. Not every act of love must be known.

The solemnity of this experience is one we learn in childhood, but it stays with us, because probably it is one of the first times where we experience how love, by its very nature, must necessarily not always be requited. As we come to discover, sometimes the truest works of love are those we commit knowing they will be ignored. Sometimes, letting a friend drift away brings him closer to us in that it allows a relationship room to breathe—in the other's absence, his presence is more formidable than when it had been taken for granted. Here, forgiveness becomes a kind of vigil, where the future is awaited in the hope for what we acknowledge might well never happen. Bitterness does not overtake us. Loving the other for his own sake and wishing what is best for him means doing so even when he does not know that we do. What more may love do? To hold the other in love is to contend with the freedom of another, with all the attendant uncertainty that brings with it. Simply to know that what has been torn asunder might one day be restored will have to be enough.

If we find ourselves capable of such acts of relinquishment, of abandoning the past for the good of the other who has wronged us, of letting go of someone who is unwilling to reciprocate our affection, is this not because, in a way, even when it is not noticed consciously, we do to the other what we would want to be done for us? In these works of forgiveness, the other who was the lover or the friend figures above all as our neighbor. The other begins to matter to us insofar as that mattering transcends our own personal concerns, projects, or needs. It is not so much that those connections cease, just that they no longer loom as large. They are subordinated to a new relation, whereby the other comes to be seen, not exclusively in terms of our own perspective, but from a perspective that puts his own good first. Here, we are approaching what is meant by seeing the other as a child of God.

It is this same aspect of the other's independence that partly explains the origin of the ethical duty we bear toward others. Is forgiveness one obligation among them? Seen as an act of mercy, forgiveness might appear to be supererogatory. Strictly speaking, others cannot demand our forgiveness, as they have no right to it. When others ask us to forgive them, that is exactly the point: they *ask*. And what they ask closer resembles a favor of generosity, less so something that is owed. Seeking forgiveness from someone, indeed, is far from a formality or pleasantry. When we seek it genuinely, we do so often with apprehension and at our own peril, because when the outcome is in doubt, whether we will receive it hangs in the balance—the matter is undecided until the one we are asking decides it, choosing to extend us that forgiveness or not. That we might in some sense have a duty to forgive others suggests itself because others are free to refuse it to us, when we are the ones asking for it. If we have a duty to do as we would have others do unto us, and no one likes not to be forgiven, what right do we have not to forgive?

It would be premature, then, to conclude, as we might ordinarily think, that extending forgiveness is entirely removed from the dimension of duty or obligation. In a way, there is a command or an imperative of sorts at play when we are asked to forgive someone. The plea claims us by issuing an appeal cutting to our heart. Calling upon us to summon the strength to overcome the inertia to leave things be, it challenges us to override the disinclination to show mercy and to see instead that the one we believe does not deserve our forgiveness has (perhaps for that very reason!) made his plea most felt. And when we feel that desperation stir our heart, then, if only for a moment, the forgiveness that once seemed supererogatory appears that way now owing only to our former egocentrism. What we thought were the limits of obligation prove not to have been a matter of fact but of our perception. Just one such moment in life is enough to raise a hard question more generally: is what I experience as the bounds of duty a reflection of obligation's true geography, or are those apparent limits not too often a reflection of my own desire to see things that way?

As audacious as a duty to forgive may seem, there are at least two reasons for concluding it is so. To begin with, when we are seeking forgiveness, the desperation is an experience born of weakness. At the mercy of the other, in need of what only they can give us, we have no power to give it ourselves. There is something mortifying, even terrific, about it. Absolution must come from the one alone who is able to grant it, and here that prerogative rests solely with the one we have wronged. It can be hard to live with ourselves until we know whoever we have hurt has forgiven us. In a way, we are held hostage till that happens. This is not to suggest we are the victim. Nor is it to deny that our predicament is just. For when it is right to see ourselves in need of forgiveness, indisputably that situation was brought about by ourselves. Were we not to blame, we would not so desperately be seeking relief for what has occurred. It is I to blame and no one else. Here, the other's forgiveness will free me from my plight, as it alone has the ability to lift me up so that, no longer languishing in the shame, or guilt, or regret of what has happened, things can change. And while experiencing the other's mercy may not straightaway deliver me from the prison of past wrongs, it at least makes it possible. In assigning things to the past, they no longer must linger.

To seek forgiveness from the one we seek it, then, is to find ourselves in a position like the prisoner to his jailer. The other alone holds the key to our freedom, since only he can pull us up from the pit in which we have plunged ourselves. Such forgiveness is the life preserver we need. Though no one denies that it is we who have brought ourselves to where we are, paradoxically, it is for that very reason why it will take the hand of the other to save us. To seek forgiveness is to admit being out to sea. Desperation contains a recognized dependence, which is why sometimes even admitting we need someone's forgiveness can require a painful act of humility or courage. And it is from a perspective that acknowledges the plight one has felt when seeking an other's forgiveness that we can see why, when we are the ones being asked by another for forgiveness, duty encounters us in an inchoate form. If it is in someone's power to deliver somebody else from suffering, to relieve someone of his burden, to help him be freed from the weight of guilt, ought it be done?

An objection must be addressed, one originating in a natural worry. For by forgiving, are we not subverting justice, by coddling bad behavior, or rewarding evil? But this objection, which rests on a concern that things will fail to find their proper balance, still thinks in juridical terms, from within the mindset of a regime of exchange that the logic of forgiveness supersedes. Though it might not seem it, to forgive is not to condone or excuse what we forgive, to in effect pronounce that it was okay. To forgive whatever has been done is not to say the one who has done it is not accountable for what was done, that the repercussions of his action are suddenly eliminated. It is just to decide that, inasmuch as those actions do have consequences, we are going to do what we can to alleviate one of them and, in solidarity with the dictates of mercy, do what we can to assuage the other's pain by assuring them we do not harbor any overzealous animosity toward them, or are nursing a pathological grudge. We take what may have felt like a judgment that was written in stone and, without denying what has happened, stop letting it serve as the foundation from which everything must subsequently be built. Extending forgiveness, we break new ground. For in forgiving the other, we give him hope, a reason to believe that the other has a future that need not be determined strictly by past actions that would otherwise engulf him. We douse the flames of hopelessness.

Here, the second reason for thinking forgiveness can be a duty presents itself, one already alluded to. If being-with-others is seen exclusively as concerning oneself and another (or others), forgiveness seems capricious or unmotivated. But is there not a third party to consider? We have in mind God.

It is in appreciating our relation to others as one overseen by God that the power of forgiveness comes squarely into view, not just as something we can be compelled to exercise (the idea of it as a command will otherwise remain oxymoronic), but as what, once situated in the dimension of transcendent duty, works to our benefit as much it does for whom we are commanded to extend it. Truly, God knows better than ourselves what is best for us. The suggestion that forgiveness may be commanded, that it is commanded because it is right to forgive and that it is good to do so, is highlighted by the consequences of disregarding these facts. Who has not seen what becomes of the vicious and cruel man, who, ignoring that imperative, went through life never forgiving to his own ruin? Whatever fleeting satisfaction there is in withholding forgiveness from someone we dislike, the hurt we do ourselves is always just as great (or greater) than whatever harm we think we do them. The redemption that the other is looking to receive from us is that which, in our very denying it to them, leads us into our own form of bondage. It consigns us to a sad existence. The heart hardens, the eye darkens. Intentions become more self-interested, pride inflates. Not to forgive is to refuse what the other needs. But it also is to contort ourselves into someone who becomes incapable of other noble acts of character that would otherwise spring from a heart that still knew mercy. God, then, does not command us to forgive others for no reason, but because, as a searcher of the secrets of the heart, he knows what the heart needs. Where there is little forgiveness, there is little love, and where there is little of the latter, there can be no joy—in the last analysis, a life unable to show others mercy is a life unfit to give it, for it becomes a life that needs forgiveness from God for having become so unforgiving.

As Kierkegaard never ceased to emphasize in *Works of Love*, when I have something to do with the other, then, whether I realize it, I already have something to do with God. Nowhere is this more apparent than in the intersubjective space opened up through situations calling for forgiveness. As it happens, we sometimes find ourselves seeking God's forgiveness when we realize that we have not yet forgiven somebody else as we should have already. Maybe there is unhealthy resentment that is not fully extinguished. Or maybe bitter emotions formerly put to bed resurface. If forgiveness is to be complete, it has to withstand temptation. Everything about our being-with-others suggests that we are meant to forgive. To live in peace and harmony with others demands it. And in showing forgiveness ourselves, we come to see the truth, that if everyone were to show some too, the world as a whole would be a place where increasingly it would be less necessary. Very often, unjust actions originate in a callousness enflamed by pain. When others feel themselves unforgiven, they internalize it and take it out on others. More wrongdoing is the result, and now others are drawn into the spiral of pain. If I am feeling wronged and in a nasty mood I wrong someone else, what will be his response? Perhaps he will in turn wrong someone else, miffed by how I have wronged him. To forgive, then, is not only to attempt to reconcile a fracture between me and one particular other. It is to take action that guards against other ills that might be set off if that forgiveness is not shown. To observe so is not to cheapen moral obligation, or to encourage others not to hold themselves to a strict moral standard. On the contrary; it simply is to observe that, in expecting the best from others, we must first be ready to exercise what is perhaps the most daunting of duties, to forgive those who have wronged us.

Reconciliation is a potential fruit of forgiveness. Nowhere is that more evident than when, haunted by shame or regret or guilt, we seek after forgiveness, and not from another but from our very selves. Self-forgiveness is not a figure of speech. It is real. And it can profoundly haunt whomever has not yet found it. Were it not one face of forgiveness, it would be impossible to explain why then, even after someone we have hurt has forgiven us, we may still feel the situation is somehow unsettled. The exoneration is not complete. Let us take, for instance, the adulterer who sleeps with a woman he knows from work. Let us suppose that, when the affair is discovered, he eventually is forgiven by the woman's husband. This settles one aspect of the matter, but not entirely. If the adulterer has any conscience, he might still be deeply troubled by what he has done. Being forgiven by the husband does resolve a considerable element of the situation, but not fully the adulterer's own self-standing. The other man's act of forgiveness puts him in bearable standing in the eyes of the husband. But the adulterer has not yet been reconciled to himself. The adulterer who knows himself to be forgiven must nevertheless learn to live with himself. However, even when we are forgiven by somebody, it can take us time to accept it. In situations as these, often the last stage of acceptance is self-acceptance. The litmus test for knowing whether everything has been reconciled back to its former state is whether we can come before ourselves and live with what looks back at us in the mirror. For the one who cares about others, sometimes the self is one's harshest critic.

It is the search for forgiveness from ourselves that explains the catharsis of finding it. And yet even that assurance is not always enough. Though the adulterer may be forgiven by the other party he has wronged, and though he may have forgiven himself, there remains a lingering sense that this is all a bit too easy. It is too much a matter of psyche and social convention. The other has said he forgives me. And I might accept that forgiveness, to the point of being able to be reconciled to myself. From that standpoint, it seems, all has been forgiven. Or has it?

It is characteristically human situations as these, both quotidian and more extreme, that prompted the twentieth-century French philosopher Vladimir Jankélévitch to ruminate deeply over the question of what successful forgiveness takes, and hence what forgiveness is. In *Forgiveness*, a powerful work that is often neglected,[1] Jankélévitch begins by noting that it is most promising to take an apophatic approach, specifying first what forgiveness is not. For him, there accordingly is the question of its origin. How does forgiveness happen? In the pages of brilliant analyses that follow, he will emphasize how forgiveness exhibits no ordinary etiology—it escapes the quotidian regime of "the because"—true forgiveness, as he notes, must be distinguished from clemency, magnanimity, or forgetting. Likening it to a "grace" or "gift,"[2] it erupts as an event without reason, suddenly and wholly gratuitously. It is a spontaneous act—Jankélévitch will not hesitate to describe it as "supernatural"—of human freedom. To acknowledge that it requires effort, and even that it perhaps must be sustained across an interval, is not to deny its *sui generis* origin, but just to state that its subsequent history, whatever that proves to be, begins when it happens originally without cause, since it happens instantaneously, as an interruption and contravention of the definitively typical course of what precedes it: "to forgive is an effort to begin again continually, and no one will be astonished if we say that in certain cases the ordeal is at the limits of our strength."[3] There is some ambiguity plaguing this aspect of his account, but Jankélévitch stresses that the act of forgiveness, while it is not an act of will in the Kantian sense, like a decision "is an event that is initial, sudden, and spontaneous."[4] Were it not entirely free and up to us, if etiologically it happened as a necessary result of causes that antedated it, or if juridically it could be demanded as a right, it would not emerge starting from itself and as a superabundance. In short, it would not be what it is. There could not be forgiveness: "a forgiving machine or something that automatically doles out graces and indulgences has undoubtedly only a distant relation to true forgiveness!"[5] And just as automatons cannot forgive, so those who are unforgiving become inhuman.

If forgiveness is both free and extraordinary, it is because it has responded to another person. It is wounded, and it feels it. Someone who feels as though he is above others is capable of clemency, but not forgiveness. Enthroned in the citadel of indifferent superiority, he views others as gnats, as mere furniture incapable of harming him. As Jankélévitch explains, "Clemency is forgiveness that has no interlocuter."[6] For Aristotle and the Stoics (these are his examples), if the magnanimous one shows clemency, this is because it is tinged by a subtext of detached superiority, since the one who shows it does not feel capable of having his honor legitimately insulted by anyone. Clemency is detached and impersonal, but also amorphous, since it originates from a general attitude toward everyone and hence no one in particular. Enclosed within a solitary indifference, others become virtual nonexistents to such an extent that magnanimity in effect is incapable of offense. And thus, indifferent to the insults and offenses of others, this attitude, insensitive to the very presence of others, and which "has never abandoned this armor of sublime indifference,"[7] never enters into vulnerable relations with others. Consequently, forgiveness is not possible, for there is no relationship where wrongs (and hence resentment or hurt) can even occur.

Jankélévitch's analysis continues. Forgiveness becomes possible, so he suggests, only when an individual is susceptible to offense. Now, if someone is wronged and resents it, how should the rancor be addressed? This truly is where the problem of forgiveness comes in. To begin with, as he says, it will not suffice to claim that time alone will heal the injury, by consigning it to oblivion. Time corrodes memory, and so to that extent it leads to forgetting.

Forgetting, however, is not forgiving. To be sure, the "naturality of time," as he calls it, counsels forgetting, insofar as the passing of the years lessens the sting of a wrong, sometimes to the point that the resentment subsides entirely without any intervening decision or effort on our part. And assuming even if we do remember some past injury, it does not hurt as badly as it did when it happened. Almost without exception, time deadens the vitality of the rancor. As Jankélévitch says, this is why holding a grudge can be such hard work! "As is the case with old anger and old pain," he says, "nothing more will subsist of old rancor than a vague memory, which is a phantom rancor or a shadow of anger. For the offended person becomes tired of holding a grudge against his offender! Time that erodes mountain chains and makes the pebbles on the beach smooth, time that levels all harshness and consoles all pain, soothing and healing time, is this not the vocation of decay?"[8] Yet this again falls short of forgiveness. As the incisive metaphor he immediately uses next to explain the insight makes clear, such forgetfulness is more amnesia than amnesty. This naturality of time that tends to forgetting cannot be the basis for forgiveness. As he has shown, fatigue or indifference are not moral attitudes.

Rather, true forgiveness "is an event, a gratuitous gift, and a personal relation with the other,"[9] a suddenness of the instant that interrupts continuous time. The decay of time cannot absolutely erase what has happened, for it cannot make what came to pass not have come to pass. The deed has been done, and if forgiveness is to occur, it must be reckoned with. This is where what Jankélévitch calls intellectualism comes in. Such a view, most associated with Socrates and Platonism, classifies wrongdoing as a species of ignorance. Here, its motto is that "To understand is to forgive."[10] Where there is no wrong, there is nothing to forgive. Thus, what is to be done, when, because time alone is unable to banish the source of the problem and the wrong cannot be forgotten, all that remains is the option between forgiving and rancor? Jankélévitch starts by noting how intellectualism, which is unwilling to endure the trial of forgiveness, seeks instead an excuse for the deed in question, in the hollow attempt to show that, all things considered, there really is nothing to forgive. This is why it says that where there appeared to be an injury, it was mere appearance. The deed at issue, so this intellectualist thought continues, must be pardoned when it is understood properly, because there is an excuse for it. *Voilà!* Understanding has exempted us from the pain of forgiveness, by instead conjuring the misdeed out of existence.

Inevitably, the strategy of equating understanding to forgiveness—one Jankélévitch dedicates considerable space to combating in many ways—must fail, for it cannot successfully reduce forgiveness to understanding. Simply put, to forgive is not to understand, since, paradigmatically, we forgive when and only because it is impossible to understand what has been done. If we could understand it, that is because there would be reasons for it, which is to leave things in the realm of the excuse. Here, raising a theme to which he will return at the book's conclusion, he notes how the misdeed that requires forgiveness remains without any excuse, insofar as it cannot be understood. "But conversely, could we say yes or no that to understand is to forgive? To understand is either to exonerate an innocent person, recognizing that there was nothing to forgive, or to become sometimes more indulgent and sometimes more severe with respect to the accused depending on the circumstances."[11] Attempting to see the offense as a phantom, intellectualism treats wrongs as to be explained away by mitigating circumstances. Doing so, it shows the leniency of intellection. But the heart of forgiveness is not present.

It is here that another semblance of forgiveness threatens to intrude. If trying to evacuate the need for forgiveness by excusing the wrongdoing as not being an actual wrong is a strategy that fails, there next is the risk of overcompensating. As Jankélévitch explains, the risk is indulging the wrongdoing with a kind of "liquidation," a shallow decree mimicking heartfelt sincerity, which on the contrary superficially and thoughtlessly "[agrees] to pass over the misdeed and not to hold it against the guilty person."[12] This may sound just like what forgiveness does, but internally, there is a marked difference. Though the wrong is treated as never having happened as with forgiveness, it is a mere "simili-forgiveness," a merely exterior movement that "does not have any heart."[13] Thus, what should have been the initial, sudden, and gratuitous event of forgiveness is "tarnished by the excusability of the misdeed."[14] It sweeps things under the rug, instituting a disingenuous silence, without ever facing up to the evil of the misdeed. In a passage that occurs toward the very end of the book, Jankélévitch elaborates more on this attitude of liquidation. He says of it:

> Before there can even be a question of forgiveness, it is necessary that the guilty person, instead of protesting, recognize himself as guilty without pleas or mitigating circumstances, and especially without accusing his own victims; not at all! In order for us to forgive, it is first necessary, is it not? No, the criminals do not ask us for anything, nor do they owe us anything, and what's more, they have nothing for which to reproach themselves. The criminals have nothing to say; this matter does not concern them. Why would we forgive those who regret their monstrous crimes so little and so seldom? This is not all. When on the day after the massacre frivolity and convenient indulgences were discreetly covering over the crime in silence and forgetfulness, forgiveness became derisory; henceforth, forgiveness is a farce. This eagerness to fraternize with the hangmen, this hasty reconciliation is a grave indecency and an insult with regard to the victims. . . . By excusing crimes almost immediately, repugnant and cowardly indulgence has rendered forgiveness not only useless and premature but also impossible.[15]

As Jankélévitch stresses, whether by the glib indulgence of liquidation or the shrewdness of intellection, the wrong is denied, and so there is no room for forgiveness. It seems there is an aporia. On the one hand, forgiveness is neither clemency nor pardon. On the other, neither is it excuse nor indulgence. What, then, is it? Jankélévitch concedes that it is a mystery, a phenomenon whose reality cannot be discounted, yet one that remains impossible to characterize fully. He is happy to define it accordingly: "Let us call it the I-know-not-what."[16] With language anticipating Claude Romano's and Jean-Luc Marion's work on the event, he explains the manner in which forgiveness is without reasons, without a cause.[17] First, it is without reasons because, contrary to either the naturality of time's decay or the superficial act of liquidation, it must confront the inexcusable. It must waive rendering reasons, since it admits what stands in need of forgiveness has no excuse. It is possible to pardon someone in light of mitigating circumstances or other motivations or considerations. When confronted by a misdeed that has no such excuse, however, what then? It will be impossible to render any reasons attenuating or exonerating it; pardon or clemency, concepts that belong to the juridical realm of the "tit for tat" and the arbitrary sovereign, do not apply. And if the guilty cannot be exonerated on grounds that what has been done is excusable, without denying the act is worthy of condemnation, and without trying to coddle or excuse it by sanitizing or rationalizing it, forgiveness will have to do so gratuitously, without reasons. Suddenly in an instant and hence without reasons, cause, or ulterior motive, forgiveness like the act of love with which it is so deeply connected will have to set its gaze upon the naked face of the guilty party and, seeing what is to be seen, nevertheless somehow open a new order by deciding to once and for all make "a tabula rasa of the past."[18]

Nearing his magisterial work's conclusion, it is here that Jankélévitch must confront the issue lurking in the background throughout: is there the unforgivable? To ask the question is to struggle with the nature of wickedness and evil. It is to stretch thought to its limit. Justice, we know, functions in accord with what can always in principle be understood. A wrong takes place, we consider the guilty who has done it, why it was done, and the various relevant extenuating or exacerbating circumstances. Once the judgment is passed, either guilt or innocence, it is decided what kind of punishment is appropriate, if any. With the evilest of things, the situation is otherwise. We are left in a state of incomprehension. A twisted thing about evil is that the more we think about it, trying to make sense of it, the more apparent it becomes that there is nothing there to understand. According to Jankélévitch, then, forgiveness therefore is faced with the limits of what our understanding understands. In forgiving what it cannot entirely understand, it learns something deep about the nature of itself, and hence evil too. As he explains in a profound passage: "What exactly did it understand or learn by forgiving? To tell the truth, it did not understand wicked freedom (for no one understands the incomprehensible) . . . it understands *that* there is in the end nothing to understand! It *understands that*, but it does not know how to say *what* it understands; it understands without knowing *what*."[19] A few pages over, in the book's final lines, he suggests in a very gentle but haunting sequence that what forgiveness here understands is its own weakness. Love is strong, yes. So, though, are death and evil. Jankélévitch concludes with the frank admission that he finds it difficult to believe love decisively wins: "The mystery of irreducible and inconceivable wickedness is, at the same time, stronger and weaker, weaker and stronger than love."[20] Human forgiveness sheds light on darkness, but maybe not enough.

In response to this agonizing worry that forgiveness might not possess the last word over evil, it is necessary to call on God's forgiveness, whose own powers in this regard, as ever, infinitely surpass ours. Concerns regarding the limits of our own forgiveness are understandable, as are those regarding its various shortcomings and weaknesses. Not so with God, who is stronger than death and evil. In thinking seriously on the notion of whether there exists anything unforgivable, and thus in turn ruminating over the kind of vulnerability incurred by a forgiveness that exposes itself to such overwhelming evil, it can seem as if evil and death possibly have the last word on existence. The consequences for interpersonal forgiveness, if so, would be devastating. Nothing would be secure truly. Everything in the end would be a ruse, destined to be annihilated by personal death and forgotten in the inhospitable sands of time. It would be as if all the evils had never happened, for all the bad things that were done would be buried by the past, forgotten without resolution due to the passing of the years. Our lives would be as nothing. Even if all of the living decided together that justice had been served to their satisfaction (and who could ever say so?), there still would be no cosmic justice, for the entire situation, including everyone's resentments, memories, thoughts, hopes, desires, and loves, will have been no more. Gone! Thus, unless the act of forgiveness springs from a more fundamentally inexhaustible eternal source, it would succumb to death and time. Evil would triumph. Does this not explain why wickedness strains to convince itself that there is no eternal judgment, that the only reality is its brief sojourn under the sun? The hope that time will wash away the least trace of its stain is evil's most secret, and for it, consoling thought. The Machiavellian will that wills the evil to humiliate and dominate others delights itself in the hope that it can enjoy what it does voluptuously, thinking that what it does now will be forgotten with its departure in death. To think forgiveness to the extreme, to accordingly reject the idea of the unforgivable, is to understand why the love of God is hardly superfluous. To the contrary, it is inexorable. True forgiveness presupposes it, since otherwise evil is stronger, and we are evil's dupe.

Paul Ricœur in the epilogue to *Memory, History, Forgetting* explores the paradox of forgiveness—"Difficult Forgiveness," he calls it. But however difficult forgiveness is to understand or enact, it is not impossible. Difficult even to conceptualize, says Ricœur, because of the fundamental disproportion that exists "between the poles of fault and forgiveness," a "vertical disparity" between the depth of the fault and the height of the forgiveness. The language here operates as an allusion to the way the Apostle Paul speaks of Christ's love. Later in the study, Ricœur will invoke that debt explicitly, mentioning the hymn of 1 Corinthians to love. But with the thought of that distance in mind, one might also recall not just Paul's words on love's expansiveness to the Corinthians, but to the Ephesians as well: "That you, being rooted and grounded in love, may be able to comprehend with all the saints what *is* the width and length and depth and height—to know the love of Christ which passes knowledge; that you may be filled with all the fullness of God" (Eph 3:17–20). To recognize the polarity between fault and forgiveness, and hence in turn the wide distance between them, initiates us into a struggle to cope with this great divide. The struggle is evident in our everyday language. Asking for and showing forgiveness is something with which everyone has some experience. And for Ricœur, the polarity between the depth of fault and the height of forgiveness is epitomized in the two speech acts defining them: "below, the avowal of fault; above, the hymn to forgiveness."[21] For Ricœur, if forgiveness is difficult but never impossible, it is because, through the love of God which makes anything possible, forgiveness can be received and given as a gift, as an act of superabundant grace transcending the economy of reciprocal exchange.[22]

However, it was Dostoevsky who a century before Jankélévitch and Ricœur had already been sensitive to the problem of how love can be stronger than evil. In *Notes from Underground*, he attempts to meet the challenge directly. As he was to tell his brother, for the undertaking to succeed, it would be necessary to deduce "the need for faith and Christ."[23] To do so, he takes in turn the phenomenon of forgiveness as a focus, showing how if it is to be understood in its possibility, it must be seen in terms of God's love. It is surprising then, that for a work that has been studied extensively, little accentuation has been placed on how in many ways it is a study in forgiveness, or better, one in the horrendous consequences attending unforgiveness. To begin with, the underground man, who openly confesses to being sick and wicked ("I am a sick man. . . . I am a wicked man."[24]), fears magnanimity; or more exactly, he fears being "tormented by the consciousness of its utter futility."[25] The "heightened consciousness" he mentions so many times, turned in on itself and constantly ruminating on how he is seen by others and feels about them, thereby becomes an isolated consciousness. The more one compares oneself to others and takes umbrage at their perceived slights, the more one departs into a world of dark fantasy. It is clear how, in certain notable ways, Dostoevsky's underground man is a parody of Rousseau, the solitary one who confides his thoughts to a public audience of readers. In a clear allusion to the Citizen of Geneva, the underground man at one point even admits to his "terrible amour propre."[26] This disordered self-regard leads him, in the gall of bitterness, to protect a fragile pride by shutting out others. And thus unsurprisingly, when he perceives himself to be wronged, the only course is to "forgive nothing."[27]

In considering the root of the underground man's wickedness (or spite), it is no small thing that the first time God is mentioned (and routinely afterward as well), it appears cavalierly under the underground man's pen in blasphemy.[28] From the outset, this is not a man with a sound relationship to God. Clearly, he is someone who does not yet accept his own need for forgiveness from God. He instead has a view to nothing but human affairs: how he sees others, how he thinks others see him, and so on. Everything is about social perception. He is, in the biblical sense, a respecter of persons, someone who seeks to please men, and to seek their esteem, which is why he becomes so disconsolate when he feels it is refused to him. The obsessive thinking about others, wherein he plots various revenge scenarios, is a psychological coping mechanism for an extreme spiritual void. Cut off from God, wallowing in his own sin, overcome with arrogance and pride, he refuses to humble himself before God and seek the forgiveness that would lay the basis for a change in himself and hence toward others. The underground man, anyone cannot help but notice, recoils from forgiving others because, from his egoistic standpoint, to forgive would be to show weakness, which in turn would be to let others dominate and possibly triumph over him. Forgiveness to him is seen as becoming somebody's dupe.

Thus, Dostoevsky's underground man lacks the conviction that forgiveness is stronger than evil, and it is because of that distrust that he has become so evil himself. His cynicism and callous self-involvement cover over an inner weakness, a lack of fortitude to be made vulnerable to the actions of others. Secretly terrified that forgiveness will fail him and make him the fool, he becomes bitter, angry with himself for his weakness, resentful toward those he suspects are too strong for him. Suspended in a fantasy world of derisive memories and petty grudges, he murders concocted enemies in his mind. As the underground man's twisted confessions make plain, a life without God's forgiveness can become a very small, mean, and spiteful one, a world with no room for anyone but oneself.

The novella's well-known saga regarding the bumped officer is most illustrative. Not incidentally, it begins with a moment of unforgiveness. The underground man has been walking the streets at night, when after witnessing a brawl he wanders into the tavern in question, fantasizing about getting into a fight himself. Upon walking in, he stands by the billiards table, where he has a brief encounter with a man who will come to dominate years of his attentive scorn: "I was standing beside the billiard table, blocking the way unwittingly, and he wanted to pass; he took me by the shoulders and silently—with no warning or explanation—moved me from where I stood to another place, and then passed by as if without noticing. I could even have forgiven a beating, but I simply could not forgive his moving me and in the end just not noticing me."[29] The underground man cannot muster a word, and for that, he cannot live with himself. The resentment and shame lead to a pathological obsession: stalking, late-night sulking, and fantastical plotting. Finally, after trying to work up the courage for years, in a pathetic act of revenge, the underground man deliberately bumps into the officer on the Nevsky Prospect. If he were not so delusional, he would see how anticlimactic it is: "Suddenly, within three steps of my enemy, I unexpectedly decided, closed my eyes, and—we bumped solidly shoulder against shoulder! I did not yield an inch and passed by on a perfectly equal footing! He did not even look back and pretended not to notice: but he only pretended, I'm sure of that. To this day I'm sure of it! Of course, I got the worst of it; he was stronger, but that was not the point. The point was that I had achieved my purpose, preserved my dignity, yielded not a step, and placed myself publicly on an equal social footing with him. I returned home perfectly avenged for everything. I was in ecstasy. I exulted and sang Italian arias."[30] No further comment is necessary than to say the situation is mortifyingly cringeworthy. Without doubt, these are years that could have been better spent.[31]

Tolstoy, too, for this reason championed the indispensability of God's forgiveness. It alone, he said, makes possible a compassion whose lucidity allows us to see others as they are in God's image, not merely through the lens of bitter self-interest or the thirst for vengeance. To make the point evident, he in the short story "God Sees the Truth, and Waits" tells the odyssey of a husband and father, Iván Dmítrich Aksenov, who encounters life's adversities in a way that embodies the reverse image of Dostoevsky's underground man. By way of contrast to the life apart from God, Tolstoy shows the extraordinary possibilities that define the life that is open to God uniquely. And as with Dostoevsky, so for Tolstoy forgiveness is the key. It is necessary to recount the plot. The action begins with Aksenov planning a trip, which his wife warns him not to take. She has had a dream the night before of her husband with gray hair. The implication is that if he leaves as planned, he will be gone for a very long time. He discounts her worry and departs anyway. On his journey, he stays a night at an inn, sharing a room with a merchant. In the morning, he rises early for a tea with the merchant and then continues on with his journey. Later in the day he stops, and soon he is approached and questioned by policemen traveling from the direction of the inn: "'Where did you spend last night? Were you alone, or with a fellow-merchant? Did you see the other merchant this morning? Why did you leave the inn at dawn?"[32] After Aksenov answers the questions, he asks why he is being questioned. The answer is shocking: "I am the police-officer of this district, and I question you because the merchant with whom you spent last night has been found with his throat cut."[33] The officers search his belongings, and in his bag they find a knife with blood. Despite his declaration of innocence, the officers arrest him, since the facts seems to suggest no way Aksenov is not the murderer. In jail, his wife and children come to visit him, and eventually even his own wife suspects him of the crime. Crushed with grief, he is left alone to be sentenced for a murder he has not committed.

Of interest is what happens next, how Aksenov spends his twenty-six years in Siberia. As Tolstoy describes, he loses his mirth, but he does not sulk. He does not harden his heart to the point of bitterness. He is meek with the other prisoners and guards, and he earns a reputation for being a just and fair man. What happens next, Tolstoy relates as follows: "One day a fresh gang of convicts came to the prison. In the evening the old prisoners collected round the new ones and asked them what towns or villages they came from, and what they were sentenced for. Among the rest Aksenov sat down near the near-comers, and listened with downcast air to what was said."[34] One of the new convicts, an older man Semenich, is from Aksenov's own hometown of Vladmir. He complains about having been wrongly convicted for stealing, and it becomes clear that this well may be the man who murdered the merchant. After asking Semenich directly about the incident, his evasions and odd humor increase the suspicion, until finally Aksenov is convinced that this is the one who has framed him. That night Aksenov is in agony thinking about what could have been; the time he lost with his family and the suffering he has endured in Siberia both haunt him. Overcome with grief, his heart is filled with a lust for revenge: "And his anger was so great against Makár Semenich that he longed for vengeance, even if he should perish for it. He kept saying prayers all night but could get no peace. During the day he did not go near Makár Semenich nor even look at him."[35] Two weeks like this pass, until one night Aksenov is met with a night visitor who has dug through the walls. It is Semenich. They have a brief exchange, and Semenich flees before he is discovered by the guards. When the tunnel is discovered the next day, the prisoners are questioned as to who is responsible. Knowing that Aksenov is an honest man, the guards finally ask him. He is put on trial: what to do? As Tolstoy writes, "Aksenov's lips and hands trembled, and for a long time he could not utter a word. He thought, 'Why should I screen him who ruined my life? Let him pay for what I have suffered. But if I tell, they will probably flog the life out of him, and maybe I suspect him wrongly. And, after all, what good would it be to me?'"[36] Aksenov answers, saying it is not God's will that he say anything, and he tells the guards to do with him as they wish. Eventually, the guards leave off questioning. Aksenov has spared Semenich, the man who framed him for murder.

The next sequence is even more powerful. "That night when Aksenov was lying on his bed and just beginning to doze, someone came quietly and sat down on his bed. He peered through the darkness and recognized Makár. 'What more do you want of me?' asked Aksenov. 'Why have you come here?"'[37] Makár has come to beg forgiveness: "Iván Dmítrich, forgive me!"[38] Then comes the confession: "'It was I who killed the merchant and hid the knife among your things. I meant to kill you too, but I heard a noise outside; so I hid the knife in your bag and escaped through the window.'"[39] The plea continues, "'Iván Dmítrich,' he said, 'forgive me! For the love of God, forgive me! I will confess that it was I who killed the merchant, and you will be released and can go to your home.'"[40] Aksenov is stunned, but not yet entirely moved. The extraordinary turn of events cannot alter the past; it cannot restore him lost time. "'It is easy for you to talk,' said Aksenov, 'but I have suffered for you these twenty-six years. Where could I go to now? My wife is dead, and my children have forgotten me. I have nowhere to go.'"[41] Tolstoy's scene builds to a crescendo: "Makár Semenich did not rise but beat his head on the floor. 'Iván Dmítrich, forgive me!' he cried. 'When they flogged me with the knout it was not so hard to bear as it is to see you now . . . yet you had pity on me and did not tell. For Christ's sake forgive me, wretch that I am!' And he began to sob."[42] Aksenov too starts to weep: "'God will forgive you!' said he. 'Maybe I am a hundred times worse than you.' And at these words his heart grew light and the longing for home left him. He no longer had any desire to leave the prison but only hoped for his last hour to come."[43] Semenich soon after confesses his guilt as promised. Aksenov, however, is already dead. His life complete, he has returned home to the Father.

As Tolstoy shows, it is God's forgiveness that has made human forgiveness possible. Mercy even in the most apparently impossible of situations is not futile; love is never weaker than evil. If it seems so, it is only because we are leaning too heavily on our own strength, neglecting God's love. Semenich's redemption, triggered by Aksenov's forgiveness, demonstrates how God's forgiveness ignites compassion that otherwise would not be, for it assures the one who has opened himself to God's love that forgiveness is worthy of our trust. With God, forgiveness has the capacity to overcome evil, precisely because the love of God is stronger than anything else. There no longer is merely a dyadic relation between the guilty and the wronged. Despite the misdeed, each now stands in a way equal to the other, transfigured by their mutual subordination to God. This provides room to breathe. Tolstoy shows it well. Aksenov, who knows the love of God, experiences the forgiveness of God, which thereby enables him to show forgiveness to the guilty one who has wronged him. He has done exactly what Dostoevsky takes such pains to show the underground will not. Though he has been genuinely wronged, though he was separated from his family, though his life has not unfolded as he would have envisioned, Aksenov's heart did not ice over. Having kept his heart open to God, his life ends with a supreme act of forgiveness that, inspired and sustained by God, gives his life a transcendent meaning that would otherwise never had been thinkable. Aksenov comes to see that he has not actually lost his life, but that the purpose was to do something he could not understand until the time had come to do it. Being placed into the situation he was, his act of forgiveness leads Semenich to Christ. Unlike, then, the underground man who lives for himself and ends away from God and alone from others, Aksenov accepts that his life was never about himself as he originally had conceived it; he embraces his role as an instrument in God's providence, coming to see Semenich as a fellow brother also created in the image of God. Tolstoy suggests that we would all be better off also if we did as Aksenov.

It would be too easy for someone here to dismiss the lesson by saying it is contrived. Is Tolstoy's ending contrived? Only the one who actually has lived a life with the love of Christ and shown the kind of forgiveness it enflames, it seems, is in a position to determine whether it is unrealistic to claim such forgiveness has the power Tolstoy says it possesses to transform others. How would one whose own existence is much closer to the underground man's than to Aksenov's know the thresholds of love's power? One aspect of Dostoevsky's and Tolstoy's point is that those who do not yet know Christ are in no position to judge. Completing Dostoevsky's deduction, then, Tolstoy suggests that God's forgiveness is at the heart of all forgiveness. It is what makes it possible, always assuring us that love is stronger than evil. It is what likewise energizes it, moving us with compassion for others, when our own strength would have been insufficient. In sympathizing with God, by seeing others as God wants us to see them, a seeing whose own realization begins with the admission of our own need for forgiveness, God's superabundant love transfigures whatever situation it touches, even the most seemingly hopeless and broken of them. Why is forgiveness commanded by God? We now have something of an answer. More awaits us than we could ever imagine, when forgiveness makes things new. And, so, it is not too difficult to see why we should obey. For who are we to refuse forgiveness to another, to possibly stifle a miracle?

Returning to the case of our adulterer who has sought forgiveness from others, and even himself, this is why the situation so described is only partial. In one important sense, only God forgives. While the forgiveness I receive from others (or which I extend them) makes amends and allows for healing, it does not in any absolute sense blot out what has happened; it changes how everyone feels about it, or what its having happened means. Reshaping how we view or feel about the past, it alters how, or to what extent, the forgiven deed will shape the future. But this human forgiveness does not erase what has happened. Only a divine act is sufficient for this, a kind of forgiveness that reaches beyond human forgetting. That divine forgiveness is available is a great good. Take again for example our remorseful adulterer. Suppose he remains unforgiven by the woman's husband. Should he have to live the rest of his life tormented, just because the man he has wronged has never forgiven him? Even if the husband never forgives the indiscretion, God will potentially. The divine arms are always extended. Were that not so, were forgiveness exclusively an interpersonal affair between others and ourselves, it would usually regress (as too often it does) into a power struggle. A presumed authority not to forgive someone can be a powerful drug. And one form of vengeance it takes is abusing that power for the sake simply of enjoying the decision not to extend forgiveness. By refusing to forgive someone, the one originally wronged ends up being in the wrong. Without God to intervene, it would be impossible for us to negotiate mercy and judgment successfully. We would be left to ourselves, ever at war.

At the same time, it is mistaken to think that because God commands us to forgive others, this means we should be lax, as if there will always be easy divine absolution from God for whatever we do, no matter if we obtain it from others. Divine forgiveness is not a license to be selfish or wanton. Nor is it reason to condone the injustice of others, as Jankélévitch's notion of liquidation highlights. We can forgive without simultaneously approving that which we have forgiven. But forgiveness without any element of disapproval is illogical. If we did not see a given thing as wrong, even inexcusably so, we would not see it as standing in need of forgiveness. Forgiveness, then, does not abandon a standard of judgment. It presupposes one.

Neither does forgiveness eliminate personal moral uprightness. Just as there is a role for accountability with others, so it in no way absolves us of personal responsibility, for forgiveness acknowledges that, when it comes to ourselves, holding a grudge in pride, harboring animosity in jealousy, or wishing someone who has wronged us ill, does nothing to bring about justice. Punishing someone with our resentments does not reform them. To the contrary, an icy heart snuffs out a radical transformation that might take place in the other when, in being shown forgiveness, those who have wronged us experience the same mercy we have received from God. To do so is not to coddle evil. It shows whomever has gone astray that God, who is willing to forgive, has assured us that there is no excuse for that bad behavior—it is because there is forgiveness waiting for anyone who is willing to make amends that not breaking off with the bad is so inexcusable. If there were no divine mercy capable of rectifying what we had done, there truly would be no turning back. But this is not so, and so there is hope. The act of forgiveness we show to others exemplifies it.

Forgiveness, which is inexhaustible, is something of which there always remains more to be said. It calls incessantly on our speech, which is why the act of forgiveness consummates itself paradigmatically in the broken or tender voice that utters it: "Don't worry," "It is okay," "Forget about it"—"I forgive you." To conclude, we note again that forgiveness is multiform. First, sometimes the task is showing it, other times finding it. And it comes in many ways. It may come in the form of a deep yearning, as when in making amends we seek it from others. Other times it comes in the form of a duty, when as an imperative we extend it to the one who has hurt us. Then there is the form of the paradox it takes when one seeks it from one's own self. Above all, there is its supreme form, God's forgiveness, which is a blessing that both assures and sustains. In sketching these intentionalities of forgiveness, it is apparent how necessarily we either expand through enacting it, or else contract in rebuffing it. We are marked most personally by what we have forgiven, and what we have been forgiven.

NOTES

1. I owe thanks to Michael Kim for having drawn my attention to it.
2. There is an etymological connection in French between forgiveness (*pardon*) and gift (*don*) that Janékévitch exploits continually.
3. Vladimir Jankélévitch, *Forgiveness*, trans. Andrew Kelley (Chicago, IL: University of Chicago Press, 2005), 1.
4. Ibid., 3.
5. Ibid.
6. Ibid., 6.
7. Ibid., 8.
8. Ibid., 23–24.
9. Ibid., 36.
10. Ibid., 65.
11. Ibid., 88.
12. Ibid., 99–100.
13. Ibid., 104.
14. Ibid., 113.
15. Ibid., 158–59.
16. Ibid., 116.
17. See, for example, Jean-Luc Marion's recent account of the phenomenon of revelation in "Thinking Elsewhere," *Journal for Continental Philosophy of Religion* 1, no. 1 (2019): 5–26. There he sketches what provides a way of accounting for the phenomenality of forgiveness, which, as Jankévélivitch says, happens as an event. As Marion says, "The phenomenon of revelation always remains on reserve. It does not simply repeat itself endlessly, nor occur with predictable regularity, since it manifests itself only when and as much as it wants. But most importantly, at the unexpected and unforeseen moment when it commences, it maintains a reserve of the *unseen* within what manifests itself. Far from this reserve and my incomprehension of it rendering it opaque and negligible to me, it is precisely *because* I will never be able to render the phenomenon completely intelligible to myself, nor reduce it to its essential components and final conditions, nor master it and thereby reproduce it, that I will be unable to forget a phenomenon of revelation—it does not pass away because it *happens* of itself from itself," 12. He says on the next page over, "the phenomenon of revelation on the contrary imposes its remoteness and irreducibility on every classification with another—it always appears without genealogy, as an original rupture, as inaugurating itself, as a new beginning that none foretold and that will never be summarized or repeated," 13. Hence, as an event, like the erotic phenomenon exemplifying it so well, we may say of forgiveness what Marion says of the revealed phenomenon more generally: "surging among the phenomena that our world does not tire from opening up to, a phenomenon coming from *elsewhere* than the world," 25. And if Marion emphasizes love's evential status, so Jean-Louis Chrétien makes a similar observation about eternity. And no wonder! The two phenomena are related. As Chrétien observes, "Now, to press forth toward eternity is not to flee from time, but to transfigure it. It is to respond to the urgent call that eternity issues to us when it gives itself to us as though in advance, summoning

us to itself in the form of a future wholly distinct from the future that we plan for ourselves by means of our own calculations and controlling strategies," *Spacious Joy: An Essay in Phenomenology and Literature* (London: Rowman & Littlefield, 2019), 28.

18. Ibid., 153.
19. Ibid., 159–60.
20. Ibid., 165.
21. Paul Ricœur, *Memory, History, Forgetting*, trans. Kathleen Blamey and David Pellauer (Chicago: University of Chicago Press, 2004), 457.
22. As Richard Kearney says in an article analyzing among other things the debate between Ricœur and Derrida, forgiveness "involves moving beyond a reciprocity of exchange to a difficult, almost impossible, order of charity—a leap which transcends the rules and laws of justice in the name of something 'more,'" *Journal for Continental Philosophy of Religion* 1, no. 1 (2019): 71–89.
23. Fyodor Dostoevsky, *Notes from Underground*, trans. Richard Pevear and Larissa Volokhonsky (New York: Vintage Books, 1994), 3. In the foreword to his co-translation of the text with Larissa Volokhonsky, Richard Pevear mentions how the censors cut material Dostoevsky felt essential on the subject. The text was never restored, so we may only guess at what was lost.
24. Ibid.
25. Ibid., 9.
26. Ibid.
27. Ibid., 12.
28. He writes, "My God, but what do I care about the laws of nature and arithmetic if for some reason these laws and two times two is four are not to my liking?" (*Notes from Underground*, 1978, 13). It could be argued that things are not so simple, since later in the text the underground man reports praying to God right before bumping into the officer. Is it, then, fair to say he has no God-relationship when he prays? But the prayers are immaterial. As Dostoevsky well understood, God does not hear the prayers of the wicked (Prov 28:9; Prov 15:29; 1 Pet 3:12; John 9: 31). It becomes clear why Dostoevsky, who was a close reader of the Bible, has chosen to begin the novella as he has. The underground man, who admits to his own wickedness, later prays to God for bad things! Even his prayers are blasphemous. Here again, Dostoevsky ironically highlights how the underground man's thoughts, which sometimes misfire as phony prayers, are infected with a repellant selfishness and maliciousness.
29. Ibid., 49.
30. Ibid., 55.
31. There are other unspeakably embarrassing scenes too, of course. For example, the meltdown at his old schoolboy acquaintance Zverkov's going-away party, where he paces the room in sullen silence for three hours, only to eventually challenge everyone to a duel before being left behind when the party moves on without him. When he asks for Zverkov's forgiveness, it is a ploy—his earlier Rousseauian remark during the bizarre dinner speech, "Third point: I love truth, sincerity, and honesty" (77), had already fallen flat for good reason. The same double-mindedness is apparent later that same night, when he asks for Liza the prostitute's forgiveness after having tried to humiliate her. Clearly, his motives in asking are just part of his "game." It happens again, three days later, during an episode with the caretaker, Apollon, who, fed up with his antics regarding the pay, rejects his demand for forgiveness; as Apollon rightly notes, he has done nothing wrong to the underground man. And it happens again, finally, when Liza turns up at his apartment where he excoriates her, concluding with a bit about how he'll never forgive her. In the wake of his spree of callous debauchery, it becomes clear that his forgiveness problems stem from a demonic urge to humiliate and destroy others. At the bottom of his destructive outbursts and self-sabotage is a twisted inability to love, consisting in a compulsion to control and subdue others: "For without power and tyranny over someone, I really cannot live" (124).
32. Leo Tolstoy, "God Sees the Truth, and Waits," in *The Portable Tolstoy*, ed. John Bayley, 475–83 (New York: Penguin Books, 1978), 476.
33. Ibid.
34. Ibid., 479.

35. Ibid., 480–81.
36. Ibid., 481–82.
37. Ibid.
38. Ibid.
39. Ibid.
40. Ibid.
41. Ibid.
42. Ibid.
43. Ibid.

Chapter Five

Making Peace

Following a distinction he borrows from the sixteenth-century Spanish spiritualist Luis de León, the philosopher Jean-Louis Chrétien, in a brief but supple chapter of *Pour reprendre et perde haleine* titled "Paix," distinguishes three forms of peace: "la paix avec Dieu, la paix avec soi, la paix avec les autres."[1] Far from separable, notes Chrétien, they are intimately entwined, standing as they do in a relationship of "mutuel engendrement ou renforcement."[2] This same image of triangulation is what guides Donald Davidson's 1991 essay, "Three Varieties of Knowledge," where each of self-knowledge, interpersonal knowledge, and knowledge of the objective world is described as structurally implying the others.[3] Though Davidson's purpose is the theoretical task of defeating skepticism in its various forms, not the practical quest of finding peace all its own, the structural parallel seems salient. No one who is not at peace with himself will be capable of peace with others. And if it is a thesis that many will initially be prone to view unfavorably, stating it as a hypothesis is nevertheless worth the risk: the peace that we are all seeking, both in ourselves and with others, will elude us so long as we have not first made our peace with God. Chrétien's source may be old, yet the reference is pertinent, because it concerns a matter that was not only personal to León but remains ours also. How can we expect tranquility in our affairs with others when we are tossed to and fro by a turbulence from within? Bring to a still the deep waters of strife roaring within ourselves, and then, but only then, will there be a calm without. These remarks regarding peace co-implicate violence. And if it is to the tradition of phenomenological philosophy's great credit to have posed the problem of the world as a question, such an analysis must come to terms with violence. The world, perhaps essentially, is a place of violence. What sense can be made of that statement?

In the first proposition of the *Tractatus,* Wittgenstein says, "The world is all that is the case."[4] The world is irreducible to things, because fundamentally it comprises states of affairs. In taking the world as a totality of facts, such a definition follows a tradition that previously had defined that totality in terms of things or objects. There is a progress in the shift. But the early Wittgenstein, no less than the metaphysical tradition to which his own work creatively reworks but still epitomizes, never passes on to the question of *how* the world is totalized. The question of the world's totality is left shrouded in indeterminateness.

Such an approach—here we can call it metaphysical, in the sense someone like Jean-Luc Marion has given to the term—fails to pose the problem of the world as a problem. "How is the world given?" is the unasked question. In a chapter in *Reprise du donné* explicating the various weaknesses attending the metaphysical concept of the world as a totality, Marion observes that whether the totality said to constitute it is taken as a collection of objects, things, or facts, the world remains in a state of indefinition. The attempt to represent the world as a whole, in its totality, overlooks that, strictly by virtue of its mode of unique givenness, the phenomenon escapes any such totalization. As he comments in §25 "La dispense et la reserve" of that same work, "Totalité toujours encore possible et donc intotalisable, le monde ne peut se définir que comme indéfini, comme la totalité intotalisable des possibles. En bref, comme ce qui dispense."[5] Wittgenstein's characterization of the world as a collection of states of affairs marks a radicalization of a tradition that had theretofore seen the world as an ensemble of entities or things, and yet, despite the development his view represents, the advancement it accomplishes remains beholden to a perspective that neglects to appreciate that the givenness of the world—its mode of phenomenalization—means it must necessarily defy any totalization. Thus, for a phenomenological philosophy that thinks the world aright, the task no longer would be one of determining in what the world's totality consists, but instead in thinking it otherwise than as a totality.

Approaching the world as a phenomenon is, perhaps above all else, the chief goal of the classical phenomenologists. Though the issue usually is most associated with the name of Heidegger, it is Husserl who first formulated it. For him, the world is not the world as it is described by the natural sciences. As he will insist throughout his career all the way up to the *Krisis,* the world is a human place always already inflected by the concerns of history, art, politics, religion, work, and leisure. The world is an everyday world of personal and communal meaning, a *life world.* That our rapport with the world involves a more expansive domain of meaning than what a solely scientific description of it would leave room for is something Husserl emphasizes as early as *Ideas I.* The world is a human place, he says. In the natural attitude, what we encounter far exceeds what the scientific or metaphysical definitions of the world capture. He comments,

> Therefore this world is not there for me as a mere *world of facts and affairs*, but, with the same immediacy, as a *world of values*, a *world of goods*, a *practical world*. Without further effort on my part I find the things before me furnished not only with the qualities that befit their positive nature, but with the value-characters such as beautiful or ugly, agreeable or disagreeable, pleasant or unpleasant, and so forth. Things in their immediacy stand there as objects to be used, the "table" with its "books," the "glass to drink from," and the "vase," the "piano," and so forth. These values and practicalities, they too belong to *the constitution of the "actually present" objects as such*, irrespective of my turning or not turning to consider them or indeed any other objects. The same considerations apply of course just as well to the men and beasts in my surroundings to "mere things." They are my "friends" or my "foes," my "servants" or "superiors," "strangers," or "relatives," and so forth.[6]

In taking account of this conception of the world as a practical place of value, the concern is not whether Husserl deserves to be assigned credit for a discovery generally attributed to Heidegger, nor even that the attribution might go back further since it was something known to antiquity, particularly Aristotle.[7] Nor is there any immediate need to deny whatever differences do separate the two. Regardless of how exactly one negotiates the similarities and differences marking the Husserlian and Heideggerian conceptions of the world, crucial to both is a shared understanding that sees the world as defined by human action and thought. To borrow the language of Jeff Malpas, we might say the world is not so much a space as it is a place.[8]

Being and Time's famous analysis of the "worldhood of the world" in terms of the "ready-to-hand" highlights that lesson. To the extent that it makes sense to speak of the world as a totality, it is precisely to the extent that there is a holistic context in which things, when taken together, each has a role to play. It is possible to count the number of ordinary objects in my room. When of that mind, once collected they can even be assigned a set. But whatever logical, abstract, or numerical structural order we might assign to them, this cannot account for the way in which we originally encounter them in our intercourse with the everyday world. When I twirl my pen, reach for a book to retrieve a passage I wish to quote, or lean forward to open the window for a breeze, I do not interact with a collective that is best understood as the set comprising the members pen, book, and window. No doubt there is a coalescence at work in organizing what preoccupies me, but the principle of collection by which the things are gathered into a cohesive whole is one that resists, at least at the level of practical relevance to my ordinary purposes, any logical formalization. The pen and book are on the desk, and the latter sits against the wall below the window, which all lie in the study in the corner of my apartment's living room. There is a context—that is, a place—not so much a space.⁹ For as §18 of *Being and Time* notes, the spatiality of the world at issue is not one of impersonal, geometric extension. It is one place whose significance is that of involvement. Everything about my environment assumes the sense it does insofar as the surrounding things appear against an underlying situation itself determined by human goals, purposes, needs, and actions. And of course, the concerns are not mine alone. Others contribute to the situation's constitution, too. Because the things concerning us involve others constitutively, the world is a social world. Before anything such as the writing corner is thinkably equivalent to a space of bare particulars arrayed neutrally in pure geometric space, it is always first the field for a human word or deed.¹⁰

Now, to this mode of being-in-the-world belongs what Heidegger calls "being-with" (*Mitsein*). To be the kind of being I am is to find myself located among others in a world as much theirs as mine. It is ours because it is shared. One central takeaway of Heidegger's proposed destruction of the history of philosophy in 1927 is that the problem of whether there exist minds other than my own is only a purported problem. To be the one I am is to be intermeshed with others. There can be no skeptical worry concerning the reality of the world or others. Ontologically, the very idea of an existence without a world would not *be* the existence we know as ours. The same applies to others, without whom our existence would not only be unrecognizable from what it now is, but perhaps not an existence at all. As Heidegger states in §25 of *Being and Time*, "In clarifying Being-in-the-world we have shown that a bare subject without a world never 'is' proximally, nor is it ever given. And so in the end an isolated 'I' without Others is just as far from being proximally given."¹¹

If we encounter the things around us in the availability of the "ready-to-hand," that we encounter others in the mode of concern (*Fürsorge*) further underscores that the world is not something totalizable. That the face of the other resists any intentional signification (*Bedeutung*), producing instead a counterintentionality whereby I experience myself as the one constituted by him, is a lesson we owe to Levinas and one Marion has done well to develop with his analysis of the saturated phenomenon. This ineliminable transcendence of the other was already in a way known to Husserl, which is why he struggled so mightily in the Fifth Meditation to account for it within the resources available to a theory of transcendental subjectivity. One may remain agnostic about whether Husserl's account of intersubjectivity succeeds, or how exactly to improve upon it assuming it stands in need of revision. Without having to address such questions again here, the lesson is that the other's appearing entails that the world resists any totalization. And if the world as a phenomenon defies any finite conceptualization that would gather it into a whole, acknowledging the other's mode of appearing introduces an additional distinguishing feature about it. The other puts a demand on me that is not my own. Not only then is the world something that eludes collectivization, but its own face is altered by the face of the other. The other's appearing constitutes the world as a fundamentally intersubjective space—henceforth, the world becomes a place subject to contention, and, as history too often attests, a battleground.

Hegel recounts in the *Phenomenology of Spirit* how the struggle for mutual recognition at stake in this interpersonal context initially is one of conflict. In that work's account of the evolution of self-consciousness, there is said to be a moment in which two independent subjectivities meet one another. Someone must yield. As Hegel explains, if true self-consciousness can exist only inasmuch as it is acknowledged by another consciousness, the ensuing battle for recognition is a struggle for mastery over the other. The stakes are nothing less than total submission. Of the two, who will be the one, having compelled the other to recognize himself as lord, who reduces the opponent to the status of an object—the bondsman? Yet as he shows, the initial logic of submission staging this encounter harbors a fundamental contradiction. Ultimately, the means must annul the desired end. For in subjugating the consciousness of the other to the role of the bondsman, the latter becomes an object, and hence someone (or better: *something*) unfit to recognize the lord's subjectivity. In negating the freedom of the other's own self-consciousness, the lord eliminates the very condition necessary for securing the affirmation he sought. Accordingly, the lord realizes that his victory has been pyrrhic. For what reward is there in receiving the recognition of another subject who has already been robbed of all his dignity, by having been negated into an object? Hegel summarizes the impasse facing the lord in §192, "The object in which the lord has achieved his lordship has in reality turned out to be something quite different from an independent consciousness. What now really confronts him is not an independent consciousness, but a dependent one. He is, therefore, not certain of *being-for-itself* as the truth of himself. On the contrary, his truth is in reality the unessential consciousness and its unessential action."[12] The struggle for recognition between these two subjectivities leads where all sadism does. Here stand two subjectivities dehumanized, who, deprived equally of dignity, have been denied whatever good they initially thought they stood to gain by entering into this dangerous game.

Our mention of Hegel might be forgiven that his closest readers would refine elements of its presentation here, for the account still serves its purpose. When we think about our personal situation in light of the dialectic it describes, do we not recognize our own situation with others? The Hegelian account does not directly concern violence, much less that of war, for it remains merely an analysis of the relation between two consciousnesses, and yet it describes a situation whose egoism naturally leads to it. Too frequently, that situation is one of incipient combat rather than cooperation. Returning to

Husserl's sketch of the natural attitude, it is worth remembering that in the world, as he noted, others do not show up in neutral terms. They appear always with an axiological salience: as a friend or enemy, as an ally or rival, as a stranger or friend. In appreciating the world as an intersubjective space, and thus on the way to a phenomenological analysis of the ground of violence, it is necessary to raise, as Hegel's reconstruction of the dialectic for recognition between self and other had, the question of the enemy. Who is the enemy?

Without committing ourselves to any claim of priority or reciprocity, we can safely say that the enemy is the one to whom we are opposed. It may be that we oppose him (whether he knows so is another issue), or it may be that he opposes us (where again that does not decide whether we know of his adversarial intentions). Sometimes, of course, the situation is one of open hostility. Neither conceals that the other is his foe, as in the case of rivalries or feuds. But this latter possibility, as we have just remarked, is merely one form interpersonal opposition may take. For it is entirely possible to have enemies who keep their enmity a secret from us, as in the case of the false friend, the betrayer, the collaborator, or the spy. And though we are right to be ashamed of it, who has not at some point chosen to appear supportive of someone whose cause or person we inwardly wish far from the best? The successful conspirator is one who keeps his true feelings hidden, which is why the most dangerous and pernicious of all enemies is the one who comes in the pretense of friendship.

Whether we are enemies is a matter of our relationship, and the relation is not necessarily reciprocal. Even then, when it is not mutual, it may nonetheless obtain. Someone may count me as an enemy when I do not see him as one. And the point only expands. Sometimes there can be an adversarial relation (in the strictest sense of an opposition) without either party having been motivated by animus or ill will. That the other can count as an enemy without our necessarily sharing a mutual hatred for one another sometimes proves to be the case owing only to the fundamental divergence in our respective aims and intentions. We do in some sense stand opposed, but that is beside the point, since the opposition is the result of what Anscombe identified in the principle of double effect. That you oppose me (or I you) was foreseen, yet the outcome was not willed for that sake. The consequence may be unavoidable and unfortunate but neither pernicious nor morally repugnant. It does not suffice, then, to ensure we will not in that sense be enemies simply by agreeing that I shall go my way, while you simultaneously shall go yours. For what if each of us desires to arrive at a destination that necessarily only has room for the one of us? Or what of the case when I see the situation as one calling for drastic reform while you see it is as one demanding no action, or even protection? This is made manifest with regard to territorial disputes. Scarcity alone can set us at odds. But even plentitude offers no sure inoculation against strife. Competing visions of what we wish to do with the land we share can produce dispute. If you hope to alter what I hope to safeguard as it is, we may become enemies, even when there is no malice, simply to the extent that we are set against each other by the competing causes that we have joined. The region of Palestine is probably the most striking example, but, as a matter of phenomenological essence, the depressingly trivial proceedings of the local city council meeting on housing development policy provide no less a case in point.

In a way, that we can be put into conflict without any personal history causing it, and without the least trace of personal animosity perpetuating it, is what brands certain acts of violence with an indelible inhuman mark. No matter what precisely occasions it, ruin and misery result from the violent conflict with another. And though eventually violence is almost always accompanied by rancor, resentment, hatred, or even wrath, whatever negative dispositions come to define our relations with others, it is first because, in having become my enemy, he simply stood in the way of my desires. Before he assumes the figure of the enemy, often he saw himself as my competitor. Thus, interpersonal conflict—which can sometimes explode into physical violence—is the eventual bad fruit of egoism. The struggles of strife do not originate in a primal malevolence. Conflict is already nascent simply in selfishness itself, in the self-regarding desire that sees everything first and ultimately in terms of what it wants or what it thinks should be its own. Should it, then, come as a surprise that lust incites violence?

That sometimes the myopia of egoism is to blame for even the greatest atrocities is what, in part, makes the tragedy of war so striking. We are shocked by the colossal incongruity between the pettiness of the perceived slight or the vanity of the initial yearning that triggered it, on the one hand, and the utter devastation that follows, on the other. For those who have seen it themselves, looking upon the fields of the dead can produce that disorienting effect. In the immediate aftermath of the battle's carnage, could the survivors of Cannae, Gettysburg, or Verdun perceive the suffering as worthy of the dust or mud beneath their feet? Sometimes years after a war, veterans of a bloody campaign will be haunted by visions whose remembrance calls into question whether what they did, and what was done to them, has been worth the price. Regardless of how much others may try to console them that the cost was not too high, they are plagued by a gnawing worry (and often guilt) of which they cannot be rid: was this land, which has soaked up the blood it has, along with the very cause itself, however reputedly great, unworthy of its liquid sacrifice? And if the tradition of pacifism has long contended that the reality of war's frivolity is most perspicuously revealed not so much immediately in the carnage of the battlefield itself, but rather in the later disillusionment frequent among even those who had originally supported it (World War I and Vietnam both come to mind), the truth is that the very nature of violence ensures not everyone will be satisfied with the victory, nor will find the sacrifice just.

Certainly, disillusionment is sure to be the case with those on the side history calls the losers. The vanquished are broken, something reflected often by seeing their cities ruined and their accompanying way of life humiliated when it is not outright destroyed. Something in the spirit of the vanquished dies, which is why the act of razing their homes is as much a symbolic gesture as it is material. Yet the victors are not exempt from loss, though the form it takes may be subtler. When Dresden had finished burning, it was not only the city that was left in ashes with those who had survived the inferno, but also the humanity of those who had dropped the bombs. In these extreme moments, to do violence to others is also to have done harm to ourselves. Phenomenologically, it is worth considering: when the phenomenon concerns war, perhaps it belongs to the very essence of victory that it be hollow.[13]

Because of this harm that one must do to oneself when inflicting violence on others very often even the eyes of the victors see the outcome as one not worth its effort. Against the sense of regret that might otherwise grow among the people if everyone is sent to his own house, the victors flee into collective abstractions for comfort. On May 8, 1945, thousands filled the streets of Manhattan to celebrate V-Day in Europe. Later, on September 2 of that same year, everyone celebrated V-J Day when the Imperial Japanese forces surrendered to the Allies aboard the USS *Missouri*. Despite these victory spectacles and the memorials that continue to commemorate them to this day, we must ask: was it worth it? On Tarawa, at the conclusion of the first day of the marine assault the lagoon turned blood red for nearly a mile from the shore where men laid torn to pieces, eaten by sea crabs that emerged from the ocean to gorge on the flesh of the corpses. Years later, the scene was still ugly albeit in a different way. Reduced to a trash heap for the local island inhabitants, no one nearby had the slightest thought for the events that had taken place, or the mortal remains of the men who lay fallen there. The war may as well have never happened. A crewman of a Higgins landing craft, Leon Cooper, was to discover this when he returned to Tarawa. Haunted by nightmares and the knowledge that he took many young marines to their deaths, Cooper decided to clean the beach and repatriate the remains of the fallen. The restoration on Red Beach became, in a way, an exercise in washing away the blood he felt was still on his hands. So long after almost everyone else had forgotten those lying in unmarked graves, it was fitting that he would be the one to bring them home. And if Cooper himself was haunted by that past until the day of his death at ninety-eight in autumn 2017, he was not alone. If the soldiers and their families must seek closure, wondering whether what has exacted its toll is worthy of being deemed noble, is that not because, while peace outwardly can be restored with a treaty, interior peace will elude those who endured the violence? It is one thing for a people to declare peace, but it is quite another for everyone involved to find it.

Here, a powerful objection that appears even decisive must be addressed. No matter how senseless the objectives of specific battles like Tarawa proved (the airstrip later taken at Iwo Jima would also be largely useless to the bombing campaign against Tokyo), if our issue concerns whether a war was truly worth it, would not a better-advised example be World War I rather than World War II? It seems impossible to raise any such doubts regarding the latter, which is why it has been an exceptionally well-maintained consensus as much among historians as the public that the destruction of Nazism and Japanese imperialism, given their extensive and violent genocidal projects, was one of the most obvious necessities in history. Granting the assumption that there was no nonmilitary way to stop the spread of tyranny and genocide, is not the issue accordingly settled? Here, war was indeed just.

The choice to highlight World War II as an instance of a war that did not justify its bloodshed is not designed simply to be provocative. Everyone is prepared to concede that the "War to End All Wars" was a foolhardy tragedy. But are there not factors that provide equal reason for seeing the second war as essentially flawed, too? Let us recount just a few of the most obvious. To begin, it is necessary only to look to the end of the war in the Pacific, where the campaign against the Japanese was brought to a cataclysmic halt with the horrifying use of two atomic weapons on Hiroshima and Nagasaki. Not only is it possible to see the total annihilation of two civilian cities as a war crime rivaling the notorious barbarism the Japanese inflicted on their victims during the rape of Nanking, in addition to touching off decades of hostilities between the Soviets and the West (beginning with the debacle of the Forgotten War), everyone must now live under the constant threat of potential thermonuclear destruction. And though it is customary to see the situation in Europe as far less ambiguous, the impression perhaps is more the consequence of how we have come to treat the relevant history and less so anything about what truly shaped it. It is possible, for instance, to detect a deep incoherence between the stated effort and the outcome itself. The goal of liberating Europe from tyranny was no doubt a noble one, but if that were truly the goal, then the war might well be judged a failure by that very standard. The facts are beyond dispute, though they remain widely undiscussed. In 1939, the Soviet Union invades Poland from the east two weeks after Germany had already done so from the west. Shortly after, war is declared among Germany and Britain and France. After the relative interlude of inactivity marking the period of years dubbed the "Phony War," the inaction comes to a sudden halt, as Hitler attacks the Soviets in Operation Barbarossa, violating the nonaggression pact he has with Stalin and the communists. And yet by 1945, when the Soviets are first to Berlin, just shortly after Roosevelt and Churchill had enjoyed the company of Stalin amid the decadence of champagne and ice sculptures at Yalta, it is no longer possible for anyone to deny that Stalin's regime is as murderous as Hitler's. According to the logic that was said to have governed the Allied effort against the Axis powers, the contention seems to be clear. And for what it matters, it is one the American General Patton was making himself right up to his death from the complications of a car crash: if the goal is the liberation of Europe, the destruction of tyranny, and the cessation of genocide, why not take the war to the Soviets having now finished off Hitler? And yet that does not happen. Half of Europe is handed over to Stalin, and the rest is history.

But perhaps one need not look to the war's aftermath to doubt whether the noble reputation history has assigned it is deserved. That positive assessment has in part to do with many of the events themselves having been forgotten because they were suppressed from the moment they were occurring. We might mention just the most egregious example. Right while the Allies were waging a campaign of liberation in Europe, millions in India were dying directly from the results of an artificially induced rice famine by Churchill and the British. Essentially whitewashed from the history books, the 1943–1944 Bengal Famine claimed the lives of nearly four million people in a forgotten holocaust. Admittedly, to insist a war was unjust because of the bad things that took place during it is, without further substantiation, a non sequitur. But when evaluating the question of a war's justness, is it really so easy to disassociate, as the doctrine of just war does, the causes of a war from its subsequent events and consequences? Nothing could be less obvious. The separation depends on the commitment that there is no necessary connection between a war's true causes and its eventual consequences, as if the latter do not retrospectively shed light on the former. We can know whether the tree is good or bad by its fruits. Is war any exception?

Thus, the empirical reality concerning the historic facts confirms the original claim of phenomenological essence. The result of war will be confusion and disappointment. A purely philosophical justification for unconditional pacificism is admittedly elusive. But that such a truth remains without a deduction is not to say it is baseless, but instead to recognize that, in this case, the evidence consists in *seeing*, in the sense Husserl highlights when discussing the intuiting of a thing's *eidos*. To grasp that it was essentially flawed is to see why it must be practically unnecessary. The conventional wisdom, which claims that military violence was practically necessary despite the logic behind its use perhaps being essentially flawed, overlooks the very essence of modern war, that it is incapable of bringing about the peace and security it seeks because it is fraught with an underlying instability within. Here, this hard fact is made all the more disheartening since the configuration brought about in Europe manifestly failed to live up to the war's original stated ideal and purpose of liberation. In 1948 and in answer to Roosevelt's private question as to what the war should be called, even

Churchill, who originally had been a warmonger, took a dim opinion of the situation: "I said at once 'The Unnecessary War.' There never was a war easier to stop than that which has just wrecked what was left of the world from the previous struggle. The human tragedy reaches its climax in the fact that after all the exertions and sacrifices of hundreds of millions of people and of the victories of the Righteous Cause, we have still not found Peace or Security, and that we lie in the grip of even worse perils than those we have surmounted."[14] It is true that Churchill's comment was intended to say why the Allies should have attacked Hitler sooner than they had (he was never a pacifist), but his disillusionment in the face of the war's aftermath aligns with the more general claim of phenomenological essence we take to underlie it. Not only as a matter of contingent circumstance (as Churchill assumes), but rather of essence as such, a modern just war, being necessarily contradictory, will leave only ruin. For in the end, even the "Good War" betrayed itself.

Here it is necessary to note what until now has remained only a presupposition: is it truly the case, as we have thus far simply assumed, that relations between individuals and those between peoples (as with nations or tribes) obey the same laws? A consideration in favor of doubting such an equivalence would consist in highlighting a second but related concern. Noting the varying types of war (civil, colonial, world, revolutionary, preemptive, or these days perpetual) and the different kinds of laws governing them, does it not become clear, so the thought might continue, that while interpersonal conflicts are rooted in the absence of interior peace, such is not always the case with wars among states or between peoples? Unlike in personal conflict with other individuals, might there essentially be more at work than mere selfishness or strife? While never welcome, might they sometimes be both unavoidable and just. For is it not necessary to recognize, with Chrétien, what can be designated as a "typology of wars," and thus in turn the possibility of a war that is just?[15] Perhaps the worst is the civil war, whose often unparalleled violence makes it, as the American Civil War attested, the evilest of all. And though the issues regarding the various types of war are so vast as to exclude an exhaustive treatment of them here, it is worth noting one reason for thinking that the relations between individuals and between peoples may, after all, be the same. Appreciating a distinguishing feature of what makes the civil war the worst of wars is the key. The civil war is a struggle in which a people is turned against itself, where the enemy is within, and where the conflict thereby strikes to the heart of the people involved. It is, really, an instance of a house divided. The associations with Plato's analogy in the *Republic* regarding the unjust soul and unjust city are not only inevitable, but apt. The unjust city is characterized by a disorder (and hence disharmony) within its internal elements—as Plato says, similarly in the case of the unjust soul, the appetitive principle (or the spirited part) oversteps its limits, assuming a role of unchecked operation thwarting the harmony that would otherwise result were reason to govern as justice demands. Injustice is thus a phenomenon of disharmony lying within the one who does not yet know peace, and thus instead commits violence. And if Plato has Socrates tell Glaucon that "a man is just in the same way as a city," and that the city itself is just "because each of the three classes in it" is consigned only to its own work, the fundamental operative law is one establishing a common basis for the relations ruling both individuals and peoples.[16] Though Plato no doubt approaches the matter from the perspective of one whose moral psychology differs in key respects, his central insight that violence emanates from within the disordered soul highlights a law the Apostle James later reached, too. It is a spiritual law. Condemning the violence that results from the inner strife of unbridled lust, James admonishes the mentality responsible for the brutality of war and the injustice of violence as one originating with selfish desire: "From whence come wars and fightings among you? Come they not hence, even of your lusts that war in your members? You lust, and have not: you kill, and desire to have, and cannot obtain: you fight and war, yet you have not, because you ask not. You ask, and receive not, because you ask amiss, that you may consume it upon your lusts" (James 4:1–3). Where there are warring peoples, whether among separate nations or strictly from within, we can be sure that there are individuals who do not yet know peace, because they are still ruled by a passion that inevitably sows violence instead. Just as for Plato the unjust city is a macrocosm for the disharmony of the soul at war within itself, so for James wars between both individuals and peoples are the reflection of the interior, personal strife responsible for having inflamed them.

Probably here a more general objection may be raised against the drift of our present analysis. The criticism takes the form of alleging that the preceding analysis of violence, and perhaps specifically the critical remarks regarding the justness of war, implies a form of quietism, apathy, or even cowardice. Is not to claim that peace with others is only possible when there is peace within ourselves, so the thought continues, to downplay the contribution of institutional, systematic, historical, and sociological forces at work in producing violence? By claiming that the power to make peace lies solely within the discretion of living single individuals, are we not giving quarter to violence, by denying its true mechanisms? Since at least Marx, there has been a tendency to dismiss as false consciousness any account of the human condition that sees society's problems—including violence—as attributable to anything besides class or systematic injustice. We owe it to Michel Henry's phenomenology of life to have demolished this commonplace. If there is a threat of illusion here, as he has noted in works such as *Barbarism*, it does not reside in concluding that the responsibility for change always rests in the actions and attitudes of free individuals. Individualism does not breed false consciousness or moral complacency. As Henry explains, the true peril is valorizing the political. The danger is subordinating the individual to technology, state, class, or other depersonalized collectivities, all of which attempt, but fail, to render the events of human experience intelligible in terms of power relations and forces beyond the ken of individuals. In doing so, such positions do not diagnose the root of violence as they take themselves to, but actually refuse to face up to the one way any of us might do something to seriously curb it. In a trenchant but largely unknown study concerning the dangers of such political abstractionism, Henry, in a spirit reminiscent of Kierkegaard's own critique of the present age, summarizes the danger associated with substituting political abstractions for the individual. He remarks,

> This phenomenological meaning of the political—its ability to be shown to everyone—is the basis of what I call its hypostasis. It is considered as an autonomous reality and as the only true reality in which individuals can participate. Individuals draw their own being from it, to the extent that they have any being at all. This phenomenological valorization of the political—whose immediate consequence is the ontological inflation of the political essence—expresses the great deficiency of Western thought. This is really a phenomenological deficiency. It is the operative belief that, when it comes to phenomenality, there is nothing but the phenomenality of the world.[17]

The danger before us is not so much an unjust *polis*, but a society that wants to believe the *polis* could ever be humanity's salvation. The equal preposterousness of the "safe space" or "Trump tweet" reflects a political illusion brought about by a phenomenological delusion. In self-forgetting, we have made politics the scene of humanity's salvation. Following Henry's phenomenological critique of modern mass politics and media, we see that those who are fond of quoting Marx's refrain that religion is the opiate of the masses neglect to realize that the very same thing could be said—as events today have made particularly clear—of politics. It would only be rational to visit the theater when the goal is the diversion of entertainment, not salvation. As for the political arena, is it any different?

This phenomenological assessment of violence that sees the outward turn to the political and the ceaseless debate regarding societal ills and injustices it provokes consequently allows an appreciation for why the latter perspective does not curtail violence, but only exacerbates it. It worsens the violence it hopes to ameliorate by ignoring the depths of the problem's source. Violence, when it concerns the lack of peace with others, originates in the strife produced by the desire to get what we want, sometimes at any cost, even should the cost mean the horrific suffering of others. It is rooted in the attitude of a transcendental egoism that sees things only in light of what seems good for itself, or at most those who happen to share its opinion of what is good. And without meaning to erase the distinguishing differences between the respective forms self-violence and violence against others take, the dynamic of strife is still at play. Is it coincidental that, sometimes, the one who hates himself because he cannot find peace within ultimately does violence—to himself, as in the case of the suicide? To thus emphasize, as we have here, that peace with others is never possible unless we have first found peace in ourselves is not to coddle or excuse violence by refusing to see its systemic or institutionalized faces, nor is it to sanction quietism, or to advise escapism. To admit the phenomenological validity of the thesis that peace with others presupposes interior peace is to register a truth about the world as a phenomenon inherently prone to violence. There can be no peace unless we learn to live without enemies.[18] Thus, if the violence we witness in the world ultimately is due to individuals who have chosen to commit it, we have no right to bemoan the injustices and suffering accompanying that violence until we have made peace—beginning with ourselves, and then with the others in our lives. It is very easy to watch the television news or surf the internet, scolding imaginary others for the absurd condition of the present political, social, and economic world. It is much harder to make peace with the enemies in our own lives.

The preceding remarks have limited themselves to the peace with ourselves and the peace with others, as well as the relation between them. What about the peace with God we mentioned originally?

A return to Hegel's dialectic of our being-with-others here proves necessary. According to that account, conflict is the reality of the interpersonal encounter. Can the dialectic be disrupted? In what may initially have seemed to be a mere misdescription of Hegel's characterization of the master-slave dialectic, the consciousness who becomes the bondsman was said to be the product of compulsion. He is dominated by the one who becomes lord. Yet that is not quite right, for as Hegel's text makes clear, this is not because he is compelled by the other to relinquish his subjectivity, but because of his failure to risk his life in the struggle for recognition—it is not that the lord-to-be conquers him by the power of the former's own strength. Rather, it is the bondsman-to-be who flinches, falling victim to a metaphysical cowardice or lack of insight. Mistakenly understanding himself as a mere object, he fears to risk his objectivity for the higher reward the lord himself thereby seizes. But if even this polished account entails there must be a victor and a vanquished, is that not precisely because, in describing the texture of our interactions with others as it has, it omits the crucial third party, that of God? Hegel, who sees our encounter with others as inherently competitive, sees interpersonal life as fraught with incipient violence, because he neglects the essential third term responsible for mediating all access we have, first, to ourselves and thus in turn to others—God, the one and true Lord of all. If for Hegel (or Sartre) violence is a transcendental feature of our interaction with others, it is because, in ignoring the essential role of God, the only hope for any genuine peace, first with ourselves, but then in turn others too, is eliminated. There will be violence with others where there is no peace with God.

Just as conflict with others in our daily lives results when the presence of God is excluded from that encounter, so it is impacted at the political and societal levels. In his *Authority and the Common Good*, the twentieth-century French thinker Gaston Fessard analyzes dialectically the relationship between the title's two concepts, situating our individual role in political life in terms that define the person as a son of God, one whose task is a moral one of embodying the tie between the historical present and eternity. Fessard's account of politics functions as an exercise designed to direct our conscience, to induce the spiritual epiphany (and accompanying resolution) that a choice is required of us to incarnate God's love by loving our neighbor. For Fessard, all purely human efforts to universalize the good become idolatry. Politics alone is not enough. That is why communism, Nazism, and liberalism, whatever their stated intentions to the contrary, end up distorting the common good in how they aim to implement it. An idolatry of the "good of the community" leads to Nazism, where a master race of people is wrongly taken for the common good. The idolatry of the "community of the good" becomes communism, where the classless and stateless society seeks refuge in a chimerical Universal. Liberalism vacillates between these two extremes, beset by party politics, ever without resolution. Only the adoption as a son of God establishes a universal bond of brotherhood. What is impossible with man alone, notes Fessard, is thus possible with God—true peace with others. This does not mean that theocracy is the solution. It merely means that those who know the true basis explaining the equal dignity of all men—their paternity in God—let that realization inform all they do in the time that leads to death. It is an earthly vocation whose activity takes on an eternal purpose.[19]

When withdrawn from the horizon whose hope is the *eschaton*, the idea of progress loses all sense. There is no goal to time. The "cult of progress" is thus revealed for what it is: myth. When reduced to what political and social mechanism—both present or even unforeseen—can promise, there is no satisfying end in sight. The contents of the magazine rack in the checkout line of the grocery store are not incidental, for they evince the fundamental confusion at work in a society that does not have any sense of what it should desire. In line, we read taglines telling us about some exercise routine or diet meant to assuage our fear of impending death, and yet we lack any sense of why life is something worth clinging so desperately to anyway. We are told of exotic places to vacation, as though we shall find happiness at our destination, but we know we will not, for we are victims of the very same anxiety, depression, and stress that the magazine right next to it is telling us how to overcome through meditation or medication. We are told of various ways to spend our leisure, yet we all increasingly have less time away from work. We are told of what the politicians are saying, yet we know more undeniably than ever that we have no say. Not only is contemporary technological society one that fails to provide a framework from within which we are able to settle disputes regarding the course of our future, it leaves us wholly bereft of any sense of what the aim of that striving should be. There is no sense of what Aristotle called the common good. We disagree not only about the means of political, social, and economic progress, but, more foundationally, we lack any real vision of what that progress would even involve.

Thus, in the face of revolutionary political rhetoric about liberation, we must be honest, recognizing that such discourse is itself complicit with the very violence it thoughtlessly denounces. At bottom, the struggle for power is at work. It is possible then to diagnose the social and political reforms prevailing today as Kierkegaard did those associated with the Hegelianism of his day. Disregarding the eternal, the essence of the individual has been erased. Now there is only a crowd, transfixed by the media and entertainment, a spectacle where politics has become the stuff of gossip and intrigue and an engine for malignant narcissism and vapid self-identity. It is hard to see how any of that might ever serve as an instrument of justice. Such was the lesson Dostoevsky was to learn in frequenting the revolutionary circles of 1830s and 1840s Russia. Among the utopian socialists of the Beketov Circle where the teachings of Fourier were on the lips of everyone, Dostoevsky imbibed an intellectual atmosphere in which, as biographer Joseph Frank reports, he said, "everywhere one could hear indignant, noble outbursts against oppression and injustice."[20] Nothing is new under the sun. Rubbing shoulders with the intelligentsia of the parlor rooms, eventually Dostoevsky came to learn what he did: because true change would require everyone first beginning by revolutionizing themselves (a kind of self-transformation his work would contend was possible only by bringing oneself to first have to do with Christ), no matter how outwardly noble or good-intentioned, merely social and political revolution will lead to bloodshed. The history of the twentieth century in Russia (but elsewhere too of course) brought home that truth. True revolution begins from within: before Paul was Paul, he was just Saul. The prescience of Dostoevsky's vision, then, is remarkable not so much because it was prophetic, but for the spiritual realism that guided it. Unless those who are calling for justice have themselves already been transformed into the image of God's love, there still is just a slavery to self, and so there will only be more of the same.

A Twitter headquarters stands on Market Street in San Francisco. Outside the complex, the streets of the Tenderloin district are littered with the refuse of suffering and poverty. Trash, human waste, and used syringes are everywhere. Employees coming to and from work dodge the injustice lying, literally, at their feet. To the list of forms injustice can take that we have alluded to, one might also note economic injustice, and of course the ecological harms that arise because of consumeristic society. How is one to reconcile the discrepancy between two very different worlds existing side by side, between the technological glitz and rapacious greed exemplified by Twitter and the despair and sorrow of the homeless on Market Street? The situation we have described is perhaps extreme, but neither is it totally unique, for it generalizes.

Accordingly, those who see what is given to be seen find themselves confronted with an almost unbearable tension. One sees that the world's injustice and violence cannot be eliminated, yet one cannot accept the world as it presently is. What is such a one to do? The metanarratives of human progress here are of no assistance, for they give an abstract answer to a concrete question. It is from this state, from the political illusion of a technological society that reduces us to directed leisure, shallow spectacles, and empty rhetoric—in short, from what Jacques Ellul called the "perpetual dream"—that one must awake. The basic plight of our culture remains precisely unchanged from what it was when diagnosed in the 1940s at the advent of the atomic age. It is perennial: "Our contemporaries only see the presentations which are given them by the press, the radio, propaganda, and publicity. The man of the present day does not believe in his own experiences, in his own judgment, in his own thought: he leaves all that to what he sees in print or hears on the wireless. In his eyes, a fact becomes true when he has read an account of it in the paper, and he measures its importance by the size of the headlines!"[21] Violence demoralizes community and shrouds individual destiny; it ejects us into the abyss of a cruel world where it can appear as though there is only the fruitless striving of unending, senseless suffering. No political solution is possible.

Must, then, we understand our condition as one of despair? The world is violent. No one will deny it. Nor will anyone deny that the prospects for a full and permanent peace must remain but a hope. Thus, peace takes the form of a promise. For not only do we know that the world to come will be otherwise than this one, we ourselves can be different, too, as we await its coming. "Blessed are the peacemakers, for they shall be called the sons of God" (Matt 5:9).

NOTES

1. Jean-Louis Chrétien, *Pour reprendre et pedre haleine: dix brèves meditations* (Paris: Bayard, 2009), 72.
2. Ibid.
3. See Donald Davidson, "Three Varieties of Knowledge," in *Royal Institute of Philosophy Supplement*, ed. A. Phillips Griffiths, 153–66 (New York: Cambridge University Press). I owe thanks to David Liakos for drawing my attention to this most surprising, but interesting, connection.
4. Ludwig Wittgenstein, *Tractatus Logico-Philosophicus*, trans. C. K. Ogden (London: Routledge, 1922/1955), 29.
5. Jean-Luc Marion, *Reprise du donné* (Paris: PUF, 2016), 144–45.

6. Edmund Husserl, *Ideas I: General Introduction to Pure Phenomenology*. trans. W. R. Boyce Gibson (New York: Macmillan Publishing Company, 1962), 93.

7. The relation between the phenomenological conception of the world and its ancient pedigree is examined by Rémi Brague in *Aristote et la question du monde: Essais sur le context cosmologique et anthropologique du l'ontologie* (Paris: PUF, 1988).

8. See Malpas, *Place and Experience: A Philosophical Topography* (Abingdon, Oxon and New York: Routledge, 2018).

9. Maurice Blondel makes the point in *The Starting Point of Philosophical Research*. His example is a piece of paper, which, as he says, hovers in a context of *ad usum* itself calling upon the writer's action and being: "There is therefore an initial type of knowledge which, perfect in its own sphere, is direct, at the service of our real and actual intentions, linked to our life in its entirety, turned towards the future, which it anticipates, as if to lean on it by foreseeing it and calling it to mind, capable of growing in clarity and precision without losing anything of its synthetic and practical character . . . a knowledge *ad usum* which has no need of doubling back on itself in order to be valid, which is sure and useful, but which, within sight of its goal, only implies the means in so far as they are adapted to the concrete end it particularly sets for itself; a knowledge *ad summum* which, looking along the course of the action it prepares, accompanies, and continually passes beyond, continually maintains unease and makes us live always beyond the point where we are, in the expectation and the realization of a future equilibrium" (*The Idealist Illusion and Other Essays*, trans. Fiachra Long (Dordrecht/Boston/London: Kluwer, 2000), 116–17.

10. One might register an objection against the idea that the phenomenological conception of the world makes impossible the attempt of totalizing the world. Is it so impossible to characterize the world as a totality? Take the following trivial example that potentially succeeds: *the world consists of all those things I have experienced, together with all those things I have not experienced*. Why think, as has been suggested, that accounts of the world offered by modern particle physics, for example, are foreclosed on phenomenological considerations? Assuming such a description of the world entails that beings like us exist in it and have the experiences we do in it, why should anything about those human experiences themselves entail anything about whether such a totalization is possible? This line of thought is attractive. There is a response, however. Any totalizing view of the world depends on reducing reality to a collection of entities and the relations among them. This notion of world is what Husserl calls the "formal" concept. But this is not the phenomenological concept, and it is only the phenomenological concept that is at issue: is *it* fully determined? The question turns on the essential finitude of human knowing. Is the world that we experience—the "never fully determinable" horizon of all our determinable indeterminacies—fully determinate or not? The formal concept of world does not answer that question. Hence, to assume that the world in the phenomenological sense is also determinate like the natural scientific one is unfounded reductionism. Another way to put the point is to say this reductionism overlooks the finitude of human knowing. As Marion notes, scientific reductionism is incoherent because it depends, first, on a tacit appeal to the epistemic criterion of certainty (the scientific object is that which can be known with exactitude and certitude), and, second, this epistemic formalization itself depends on a dubious dematerialization of nature. For a review of how the formalization and dematerialization of the world have contributed to a "crisis of objectivity" whereby the technical object reigns supreme in a consumer culture that downgrades other modes of truth, see §26–§30 of chapter 4, "Les Limites de la phénoménalité," in Marion's *Reprise du donné* (Paris: Paris Universitaires France, 2016). For an analysis of the world's indeterminateness that explores the phenomenon by emphasizing the notion of horizon in Husserl and Heidegger, see Steven Crowell, "Determinable Indeterminacy: A Note on the Phenomenology of Horizons," in *The Significance of Indeterminacy: Perspectives in Asian and Continental Philosophy*, ed. Robert H. Scott and Gregory S. Moss, 127–47 (New York and London: Routledge, 2019).

11. Martin Heidegger, *Being and Time*, trans. J. Macquarrie and E. Robinson (San Francisco: Harper & Row, 1962), 152.

12. G. W. F. Hegel, *Phenomenology of Spirit*, trans. A. V. Miller (Oxford: Oxford University Press, 1977), 116–17.

13. Harris Bechtol has reminded me of a similar phenomenon from a different context. Not far outside Houston in Huntsville is the Texas Prison Museum. Huntsville is the location of the state Death Row Unit. In the town's museum, there are very poignant and raw statements from family members of the murder victims. In some of these accounts, the families describe how seeing the guilty executed never brought them the resolution they had hoped for—the wound is still there. They recognized that what they truly wanted, to see their loved one again, is something the execution cannot address. Here it is worth noting that this feature about human mourning opens naturally unto a theological horizon: our desire for a healing justice must in certain ways remain unmet in the time that leads to death. Only a resurrection where we are reunited with the dead will satisfy us.

14. Winston Churchill, *The Gathering Storm: The Second World War*, vol 1. (London: Houghton Mifflin Company, 1953), preface.

15. Chrétien's most developed account of the laws regarding the destruction of a people and its ways is chapter 4, "Ruines," *Fragilité* (Paris: Minuit, 2017), 77–107.

16. Plato, *Republic*, in *Plato: Complete Works*, ed. J. M. Cooper and trans. G. M. A. Grube and C. D. C. Reeve (Indianapolis/Cambridge: Hackett Publishing Company, 1997), 441d.

17. Michel Henry, *From Communism to Capitalism: Theory of a Catastrophe*, trans. S. Davidson (London: Bloomsbury, 2014), 102.

18. Jean-Yves Lacoste has examined such a theme expressly, not only as a phenomenological possibility, but also as an empirical imperative, in a recent study. See Jean-Yves Lacoste, "Existing without Enemies," in *Phenomenologies of Scripture*, ed. Adam Wells (New York: Fordham University, 2017), 65–87. To observe that we may live without enemies is not to say that there will not be those who hold us as theirs. Living without enemies is an ideal of personal holiness, so even when we meet it, that will not necessarily guarantee enmity is altogether eliminated, since, while it may not be reciprocal, it remains relational: that I love others cannot force someone to quit hating me. In such cases, the one who is an enemy is so only insofar as he counts me as his. It is possible to influence, but not coerce, others to let go of a grudge, or to cease from envy, or to forgive us, or to have a change of heart. To lay down one's arms—or not—is a decision that falls individually to each of us.

19. I am indebted to Stephen Lewis for telling me of Fessard, and for sharing a paper whose analysis of *Autorité et bien commun: Aux fondements de la société*, ed. Frédéric Louzeau (Paris: Ad Solem, 2015; first published 1944) guided my summary of that work's central idea here.

20. Joseph Frank, *Dostoevsky: A Writer in His Time* (Princeton, NJ: Princeton University Press, 2010), 129.

21. Jacques Ellul, *The Presence of the Kingdom*, trans. O. Wyon (New York: The Seasbury Press, 1967), 100.

Chapter Six

A Sketch of Silence and Evil

Is it not an experiential fact, perhaps even a phenomenological necessity, that evil, together with the one who commits it, eventually retreats into silence? But why? Why does the one caught in wrongdoing, like Meletus before Socrates, invariably fall silent? What is this essential connection, if any, between silence and evil? To lay aside initially the question of this connection's distinctive necessity does not forbid us from observing confidently that such is the way of things, as evident in the fate of four figures without whom no analysis of the intentionalities of silence would be complete: the liar, the conspirator, the mocker, and the hypocrite. Recognizing these silent types in daily experience is an easy thing, but deciding how to conceptualize the eidetic laws governing their behavior presents a methodological issue. For by what method shall an analysis of the phenomena proceed? Here, the best we can do is try to describe what we see. In a fashion characteristic of Merleau-Ponty's account of the anorexic or Sartre's of the voyeur, so our approach will be descriptive. Beginning with broad strokes, a composite sketch of our four figures of silence will gradually emerge, stitched together from everyday experiences familiar to us all, thereby bringing the evil of these silences (and thus the various connections between silence and evil) to light.

The description begins with an observation: when the winds of fate have turned back against such an individual (henceforth the "silent one"), when such a one has been stripped of both the initiative and advantage, what else is to be done but to fall silent and to build a barricade against the truth, hoping for the best? As an example, let us imagine the case of an absent father. Considering our specific silent figure more (and here we have in view a type), we are struck by the immense form of contradiction between his rhetoric and conduct. Our dad says that he loves his daughter, yet does he? The facts surrounding his disappearance speak otherwise. Had he perhaps rendered some credible reason as to why he has broken off contact, he may have made something of a pathetic figure. But that is not so, for here there is nothing noble about his intentions that begin to explain the break. There is no room for pity, for although we might find his plight unenviable (it is, after all, embarrassing), anyone looking on it finds nothing moving about it. And while no one will dare say it aloud, everyone (friends, family, and colleagues alike) know the unspeakable: this father's silence contains some secret that, were it to be disclosed, would only further underscore the justness of his predicament. Hence, a fog of evasions and obscurities rolls in. Phone calls are left unmade, birthday cards are unsent. Nor will he attend holidays or family gatherings. What once were—and what should be—ordinary occasions are no longer. Something clearly is broken. But the banalities just rehearsed only skim the surface. For the silence is not only uncomfortable because of the embarrassment it produces. There is a darker subtext here. In dereliction of his duty, the dad has abandoned his daughter over to a cruel world from which he should be protecting her. Not only, then, does he refuse to come to her aid in the time of need, he tries to justify his forsaking her as if doing so were a right. Around the daughter's family lingers the haunting absence of what should instead be a reassuring presence. He is failure personified. For he has brought that judgment upon himself, as everybody sees. Denying his daughter, he consequently has denied himself, for in doing so he admits that he is not what he wanted everyone to think he was. Now, he manifestly is what he is. Nothing more, nothing less: a father who has failed to *be* one. And if here the silence is the Alamo of the rightly accused, it is because the decision to flee to the fortress of silence is to accept, simply by readying to make a last stand, that everything is already all over. Finally, in a moment, the years of insolent silence erupts in a pathetic spasm of violence, and then the embarrassing saga is concluded. The dad is a dad in name only.

Sometimes, therefore, denial is the heart of a guilty silence. In the first lines of that work's opening Canto, for instance, the *Inferno* recounts Dante's terrifying epiphany that what he has followed to this point is really the path of no return: "Midway upon the journey of our life I found myself in a dark wood, For the straight way was lost."[1] As he recognizes before meeting the shades who will confirm that premonition, all those who ultimately find themselves condemned to this road's bitter end are tormented knowing there is no one to blame for that fate but themselves and their own stubborn denial. When there still was time, they did not turn back. If the path leading to the gates of hell is surrounded by a wood, "savage, dense and harsh," Dante's impression of that wood is fitting, for it is a decision ground where each must choose whether to change and turn back, or whether instead to press farther on, to the place where, once there, there is no turning back, for as it is written: "Abandon all hope, you who enter here."[2]

Just as Dante's doomed endure a punishment they know was avoidable before it became inescapable, so our silent one suffers the pangs of anxious regret, the price to pay for having decided not to abandon whatever wayward deeds he now must consequently oversee. On unflagging alert, the silent one exhibits a peculiar vigilance as incriminating as it is unmistakable. Careful to pretend as though he has not heard a comment which if acknowledged might lead the conversation in a direction he cannot allow, he neither confirms nor denies anything that could require of him a response he is unprepared to make, which is why, if necessary, he takes entirely to avoiding settings, however otherwise banal, that may jeopardize his ability to keep up the appearance he maintains. In time, a pattern of avoidance emerges. Like the waiter who is playing at being a waiter, our silent one is playing at being nonchalant. But the effort is too calculated. As with the adulterer, the con-man, or the spy, the silence required to conceal the double life eventually becomes bizarre; in turn, it only arouses the suspicion of guile it was meant to dispel. Though it is true that not discussing an issue is a way to avoid it, sometimes that very avoidance only emphasizes it. The unsaid sticks out like a sore thumb. That is why, when a silence has been held intensely enough, it no longer can be dismissed as normal. And when the surface veneer of the silent one's persona becomes this unbelievable, to continue holding his peace is the greatest liability of all. Experienced actors performing in the heat of a comedic sketch will know when they can no longer stay in character, double agents will know when their cover is possibly blown, and so the silent one in general knows when he has become his own worst enemy. His silence has betrayed him.

In his 1843 short story "The Tell-Tale Heart," Edgar Allen Poe describes this confederacy of silence, conscience, and confession, showing how the unnamed narrator, after the murder, comes to learn the same hard lesson Dostoevsky's Raskolnikov will in *Crime and Punishment*. If at first Poe's narrator smugly invites the policemen in, "In the enthusiasm of my confidence, I brought chairs into the room, and desired them *here* to rest from their fatigues, while I myself, in the wild audacity of my perfect triumph, placed my own seat upon the very spot beneath which reposed the corpse of the victim,"[3] as the reader might expect, the plan soon backfires. For a time "the officers were satisfied. My *manner* had convinced them,"[4] but shortly he becomes agitated and uneasy, wishing they would leave. Convinced they hear the steady pounding in his chest and believing that they already know of his guilt and are feigning ignorance just to toy with him, he can no longer endure it, blurting out his confession: "'Villains!' I shrieked, 'dissemble no more! I admit the deed!—tear up the planks!—here, here!—it is the beating of his hideous heart!'"[5] At stake in Poe's psychological study is a phenomenological law we have been provisionally tracing. At its extremities, silence no longer functions as an instrument of concealment, but instead morphs into one of disclosure that speaks for itself. Silence speaks! This, it is clear, is the strained silence of a figure who must worry that at any moment the truth will be discovered. This is the thick silence of one become a sentinel of shame.

An unintentionally confessional silence is a variety of the more general kind of silence that guards what it conceals. It is easy to call examples of it to mind. They are familiar, because we encounter them often throughout the day. Whether in the preoccupied stare of the stranger passing by us on the street, the rueful look in a friend's eyes, or the cagey tone of someone's voice whom we had thought would never disappoint us, these withholding silences intimate *we-know-not-quite-what*. The motivations, feelings, and thoughts of the other are mysterious. To experience such silence is to encounter an appearance we have all learned to recognize and whose impression we have come to fear when we do. The phenomenon is a hybrid between, on the one hand, the indicative phenomena Husserl and Heidegger observed as belonging to the domain of the sign and, on the other, expressive phenomena Scheler and Merleau-Ponty highlighted in the intersubjective and emotional life of human incarnate existence. These silences appear in person (they are not intended emptily), yet in appearing, they indicate something beyond themselves, pointing to something else which for its own part is present, albeit not fully. Their presence effectuates a felt absence, making something that is as yet unidentifiable manifest in outline. Appearing, guarded silence is the harbinger of what we know we do not want to see or hear; too often it portends bad news.

Similarly, the silence of our original figure arouses the very suspicion it was intended to avoid; it too indicates something beyond itself. But perhaps the most notable feature about it is its guardedness, that in its refusal to speak it expresses something distinctively protective, even defiant. The silence is like a "no trespassing" sign. Encountering it, we feel ourselves up against a boundary we cannot penetrate. We know the one deploying it is hoping to delay sentencing for whatever matter this silence concerns. And though we cannot know its specific cause, we do know ourselves to be wrestling with a silence that is withholding *something* it desires not to divulge. Very often, such silence may never be broken. There are those who take a secret to the grave. But that is not to say it necessarily remains forever impenetrable. Sometimes these most persistent of silences are the ones for that very reason prove to have been kept in vain. As the protagonists of Poe's and Dostoevsky's crime stories realize after it is too late, despite their intentions, silence induces the very confession it had been designed to forestall. Inevitably, those party to the situation find themselves curious, befuddled even to the point of intrigue. Thus, they end up asking the questions their subject would have preferred to remain unasked. Why is the silent one silent? What explains this silence? To the chagrin of the suspect, it does not take a Porfiry Petrovich to see the obvious: if anyone truly with nothing to hide would have by now spoken forthrightly, why then does the silent one not? Why has the subtext gone from something initially innocuous, to something so tense? What is lurking beneath it? Those previously who had put these questions out of their mind, attempting to rationalize the silent one's actions as unremarkable, come finally to admit what they had been unwilling to see. The silent one, everyone sees, does not want us to know what his pattern of deflection indicates, that there is a deep secret lurking in the shadows. Undermining itself, the silence not only has failed to hide what it hoped it would. It has disclosed that it has something to hide.

Thus, in hiding behind a wall of silence, the silent one suppresses that the intention behind remaining silent, on the one hand, and the situation occasioning and shaping it, on the other hand, fundamentally conflict. If it is a luxury we have all indulged in despite denying it to others, is the hope ever justified that we can evade the truth merely by ignoring it? To state the intention that way underscores its futility, yet that is what the silent one attempts. Given the absurdity of it, no wonder pressing headlong into such denial never leaves the one who does so completely unaware of how embarrassing he looks. And according to a piece of everyday wisdom, time reveals all things. Is the one who tells a lie any exception? Far from it: the silence that attempts to shield the exposed liar must fail, for it is ill-equipped to quench every fiery dart coming against it. That would require perfection. And though it takes some time, inevitably, an arrow of truth finds its mark. In the face of the situation's recognized futility, wishful thinking sets in, acting as the driving motivation behind the silence that hopes in vain to block the truth from coming out. What this silence aims to accomplish, or better, that which it really craves, would be the utter annihilation of what it can instead only refuse to address. It hopes for the impossible, by trying to destroy the truth it cannot bear to tell. But has what anyone decided simply to ignore ever thereby disappeared? No! Keeping something from the spotlight conceals it for a time, but it does not banish it to nothingness. The truth *is*.

Thus the silent one's deepest wish is frustrated. When something has been flooded in the light of truth, it no longer is possible to conceal in the shadows what has been shown. What is apparent is so. And when what was occluded is laid bare, perhaps there is forgetting, but here there is no thing as unseeing. The manifest is manifest. The silent one knows this as well as anyone, which is why when he senses that everyone is noticing what was never supposed to be on display, but now is, or at least at any possible moment could be, there is nothing left to say. Try as one may, what would be the point? The ruse over, the attending silence itself says it all: "I am not as I had wanted to appear, for I am merely what I am, guilty."

How does this verdict, which once had seemed so slim a possibility that its mere mention could elicit jeers in those who were told it would come, as if it were too incomprehensible or even delusional, suddenly arrive? Coincidence, luck, or happenstance do not explain it. Seen retrospectively, from beginning to end, the sequence of events leading to the verdict always exhibited the arc of justice. Few saw it. In a path that charted a steady course leading to the exposure of the silent one, events have unfolded, everyone now recognizes, in a way that promised the exposure of the silent one was inevitable, even when the idea of such an exposure had appeared to most impossible, maybe even inconsequential. That for a considerable time where things stand now was taken to be impossible is, above all else, what confirms that its arrival was all along an inevitable *fait accompli*. To be sure, there were very few who would accept this inevitability for what it was, which is why it came as such a shock to those who did not see it coming. As for the silent one, he was the most stunned of all. The chink in his armor was pride, and so, following the path he did, he never discerned where it must lead until it was too late. Blinded with self-assurance, hauteur proved to be the fatal weakness. Thinking at each stage that there would be a way to evade the impending judgment, the noose only tightened. This is why, after a prolonged silence (context determines what that means: it could be just seconds, or instead days, weeks, or maybe even years) designed to conceal whatever it desired to conceal, suspicion eventually is raised. Uncomfortable questions the silent one had hoped would never arise begin to: *Is something wrong? Is everything okay? Is there something you want to tell me? Are you not telling me something?* Thus, even if the original deed he hoped to hide is not a lie (the details need not concern us), there is now the lie of having pretended that the silence was not what it was, that it was not a ploy designed to deflect and conceal. Offer whatever excuse he may, the one now put in question (whether by a spouse, a friend, or a business partner) knows he at the minimum is guilty of a deceit by silence.

Therefore, what holds true of mortals does not of lies. No lie dies with dignity. When exposed, the silence designed to direct our attention away from the lie's discovery (and thus demise) only exhumes the ugly truth it was meant to bury—here, the deflection acts not as an eraser but a boomerang. That the lie returns transfigured in the light of truth for what it is explains why sometimes the truth gives no warning before it arrives, leaving no one any time to duck. Essential to truth's revelation is its sudden judgment, the truth that no one ever saw the revelation, and hence the judgment, coming. The truth comes as a thief in the night, in the form of the event (as Claude Romano or Jean-Luc Marion mean it), when everyone had least expected it—sometimes when everyone had assumed it would not only not arrive when it has, but never at all. The shock, then, results not so much as a consequence of the revelation's arrival defying our expectations concerning when it could or would specifically arrive, either sooner or later than we had believed plausible, but instead consists in its simply having arrived. It occasions a silence taut with tension, a cloud as thick with shame as it is surprise.

For when what was thought never to be mentioned suddenly addresses itself directly to those who assumed they would never be so addressed, when what was presumed always to be unmentionable no longer is, it predictably elicits the response it does: awkward silence.

But why awkwardness? Discomfort, after all, is not the sole conceivable reaction to the unexpected. Sometimes a thing's unanticipated arrival brings exclamations of joy, as with a letter from a friend or a kind comment from a stranger. No one has ever bemoaned good tidings as these even when (or because) they were unexpected. The unpredictability, rather, only intensifies the relief, enthusiasm, or satisfaction they bring. But as for the lie that was thought to be long ago buried but is now revealed, it is different. To the eyes of those who had initiated it, shaped it, and sustained it, its unforeseen return is the most unwelcome of developments. Truth raises from the dead what was taken to be well behind those it now implicates. Those who would have liked it to have stayed that way, out of sight and thereby out of mind, in learning that it now is back, seeing that it has been resuscitated, recognized finally by everyone for what it always was, respond predictably: with stunned silence. Snared by what they thought could never see the light of day, they know there is no use trying to feign excitement in the face of the situation, as though pretending would possibly convince others that they did not know what everyone now knows they must have known. It is an embarrassing thing to be caught having tried to deceive others, which is why, far from counting the lie's unmasking as a cause for celebration, for them, its resurfacing is a calamity.

In a situation like this, the intense duress produced can lead to a state of almost feverish disbelief: *Is this really happening? Why did I not see it coming?* What originally had seemed inapparent is obvious. It is all too clear that things were bound to end as they have, because a path of self-destruction belongs to the case in question as a matter of its very nature. The essence of the lie is to destroy everything and anyone that gets in its way, including eventually (and perhaps above all) the one who told it.

Upon weighing these truisms, it might be tempting to dismiss them as little else than that. But this reaction, however natural, overlooks that such indifference should instead motivate us to interrogate the question it indicates, one that does matter: if the risk of backfiring associated with lying is so great, what explains the decision to lie? What explains the leap into deceit? This is the mystery animating Kierkegaard's own analysis of the explanation of the origin of the act of sin in *The Concept of Anxiety*, which inspires the analyses of Michel Henry's account in *Incarnation* of sensuality and seduction. In both, the task is to explain why the transition from the possibility of the act of evil to its actual commission resists any understanding by the objective sciences like psychology, psychiatry, biology, sociology, or history. Here, in the realm of the spirit where a human being is most qualified as himself, there is bound to be a fundamental remainder that escapes the intruding gaze of theoretical inquiry. For though the heart has its reasons just as Pascal was to note (love is not irrational), the fact remains, as Jean-Louis Chrétien's analyses dedicated to the question in *Conscience et roman* have explored, those reasons are secrets that are veiled to others, and hence inaccessible to the sciences that presuppose everything about us can be laid bare.

To reach the view that human moral action is irreducible to objective explanation, Kierkegaard trains his focus on the theological idea of hereditary sin and that dogma's implications for each individual's own relation to sin's possibility. "Through the first sin," he notes with the Genesis account, "sin came into the world."[6] Once this originary act of evil is committed, the world changes. Now, sin becomes an active influence in a creation that formerly had been pristine. What was pure is marred. Things are broken, a fact arguably made most perspicuous in our own mortality and of those we love. The reality of death is a permanent reminder that how things are is not the way God had originally intended. While the world can be beautiful, we sense the glory is somehow faint, a mere shimmer of what we can only imagine it was meant to be. The Fall is the immemorial event that has left us forever wrestling with an absolute past it renders irretrievable. Truly, we are all now east of Eden. And yet even so, none of that is to say, as Kierkegaard hastens to emphasize, that sin is a necessity. Merely because Adam sinned, it does not follow that everyone is fated to walk perpetually in his footsteps. That we all have done so remains strictly our own doing, pointing to the freedom that marks the humanity of man as higher than the animals yet lower than the angels. We are most defined by our capacity to decide whether we will live an existence of being-in-the-world, or one instead of being-before-God. Kierkegaard will thus insist that, while Adam is numerically the first sinner, each of us experiences our own fall from innocence. At some distinct point in life, we stumble into evil as Adam had. For each of us, there is a time where we become the original sinner: "Precisely in the same way it is true of every subsequent man's first sin, that through it sin comes into the world."[7] What accounts for this loss of innocence?

Appeal to the Augustinian dogma of hereditary sin can be of no help, for by attempting to explain the individual's original sin in terms of humanity's supposed intrinsic sinfulness, we are led inevitably back to the figure of Adam, who was innocent before sinning. But how, then, are we to explain his sin? Even if we somehow could explain our own sin in reference to sinfulness, that would not explain Adam's sin. Sinfulness presupposes sin, and not the other way around. In response to the problem of explaining sin's origin, the doctrine of original sin fails.

In light of this paradox Kierkegaard will accept that Adam's sin came about as ours does too, by a leap that by its nature must remain inexplicable: "Thus sin comes into the world as the sudden, i.e., by a leap; but this leap also posits the quality, and since the quality is posited, the leap in that very moment is turned into the quality and is presupposed by the quality and the quality by the leap."[8] We are free to act (without freedom there can be no love), and it is this fundamental capacity to act, one Husserl will call in *Ideas II* the *I can*, that accounts for the underlying anxiety at the heart of that condition. Commenting on Adam's condition before the Fall, Kierkegaard notes: "The prohibition induces in him anxiety, for the prohibition awakens in him freedom's possibility. What passed by innocence as the nothing of anxiety has now entered Adam, and here again it is a nothing—the anxious possibility of *being able*."[9] To be free is to be anxious, to be anxious about whether (or rather how) I will act. To be free is always already to be responsible before-God. Now, if "sinfulness moves in quantitative categories, whereas sin constantly enters by the qualitative leap of the individual," it is the latter that ineradicably makes me the single individual I am, since it is up to me as to how I will exercise my powers before God, either in service of innocence or instead in service of sin. What I do in turn gives me a personality and history uniquely mine. It is a serious responsibility to be human. And we feel it. As Kierkegaard remarks, "Anxiety may be compared with dizziness. . . . Freedom succumbs to this dizziness. Further than this, psychology cannot and will not go. In that very moment everything is changed, and freedom, when it again rises, sees that it is guilty. Between these two moments lies the leap, which no science has explained and which no science can explain."[10] With the introduction of sin into the world, the world becomes sinful. Following Adam's example to eject ourselves from the garden of innocence, the leap into sin alters the experience of our embodied power to act. With the advent of a sensuousness that no longer is innocence, things change. Temptation has become an essential feature of life in the world: "By sin, sensuousness became sinfulness. . . . That sensuousness at one time became sinfulness is the history of the generation, but that sensuousness becomes sinfulness is the qualitative leap of the individual."[11]

Lest there be any lingering concern that Kierkegaard's account of the leap into sin and its results imply a kind of gnostic deprecation of the human body, it becomes clear this is not so when turning to Henry, whose phenomenology of the flesh takes up the same themes, and whose line of questioning reaches the same conclusions. The goal is not to denigrate the body as evil, but to understand how the possibility of evil is linked fundamentally to a set of powers whose exercise presupposes an anxiety that, for its own part, is inherently embodied. The body (Henry will say the "flesh") is not bad per se; it can be used for good or for bad. In the third chapter of *Incarnation* titled "Phenomenology of Incarnation: Salvation in the Christian Sense," the analysis begins by observing that our power to act is so without our having done anything to bring it about. I do not put myself into possession of this ability; I simply find myself already in possession of it. As Henry emphasizes, to be an

I can indicates a power above us making possible this ability. No one, as he says also in *I Am the Truth*, has the power to have given himself the powers associated with life. That we have such powers points to a higher authority than ourselves: "From above, the Christ says. And this means first that no man actually holds any kind of power since he never gets this power from himself."[12] The history of the individual's leap into sin implicates the question of how one's original condition as a son of God is lost. Becoming instead a man of the world, the one who exercises his powers of life without the awareness that they have come from God takes on the figure of the idolater, the one who experiences himself as the source of his own ability to do what God alone enables. He takes for granted what is a gift.

The ingratitude is not without its severe consequences. They are felt above all in the course of our everyday lives, where we must confront a world where callousness, selfishness, and a general indifference to the needs and dignity of others is the norm. But these same inhuman consequences take shape in the world of ideas, as the history of philosophy well attests. The effect is most plain in the menagerie of moral fatalisms surrounding nineteenth-century Romanticism, whereby the early Schelling, Schopenhauer, and Herder took the individual "I can" to be an illusion, and hence something to be escaped. What emerged was a program advocating the dissolution of individuality as the solution to existence. An existence turned against itself!

In his 1809 *Philosophical Investigations into the Essence of Human Freedom*, Schelling will note that the "correct concept of freedom" is one that affirms the positive value of evil (it is not a mere privation as Augustine or Leibniz hold) and acknowledges freedom "is the capacity for good and evil."[13] While he denies that pantheism entails the abolition of individual freedom (those like Jacobi draw that inference too hastily, Schelling will say), he does maintain that it is incorrect to attribute the cause of evil to sheer weakness of will or a failure of reason. To characterize evil as the result of sensuality overcoming the rational understanding is to imply that we are in some sense passive to evil actions. If that were so, choosing evil would not be a performance of our freedom, but a lapse in it. For Schelling, then, evil must arise from the volition of man, not in a weakness. Against views like those of Spinoza and Leibniz, Schelling insists that seeing freedom as the "mere rule of the intelligent principle over sensuality and desires" is inadequate. Ultimately, his *Naturphilosophie* will aim to strike a balance between two extremes, affirming the individual freedom of human personality to choose evil, while simultaneously doing so from a perspective in which things, we included, are subject to cosmic principles that in some sense determine individual personality. Thus, Schelling from the start rejects the mechanistic conception of nature popularized by the French materialists Baron d'Holbach and La Mettrie, a view Dostoevsky would later parody in the character of his underground man, who equates the natural necessity of the

Newtonian world to a "stone wall": "Impossibility—meaning a stone wall? What stone wall? Well, of course, the law of nature, the conclusions of natural science, mathematics. Once it's proved to you, for example, that you descended from an ape, there's no use making a wry face, just take it for what it is. Once it's proved to you that, essentially speaking, one little drop of your own fat should be dearer to you than a hundred thousand of your fellow men, and that in this result all so-called virtues and obligations and other ravings and prejudices will be finally resolved, go ahead and accept it, there's nothing to be done, because two times two is—mathematics. Try objecting to that."[14]

Though Schelling with Dostoevsky rejects the mechanistic view of things, his pantheism still subordinates human personality to cosmic principles transcending individual freedom. There follows a kind of moral determinism reminiscent of Calvin's supralapsarianism. He mentions the formal similarity himself: "We too assert a predestination but in a completely different sense, namely in this: as man acts here so has acted from eternity and already in the beginning of creation. His action does not become, just as he does not become as a moral being, but rather is eternal by nature."[15] Rather than God choosing from all eternity who will be the saints and who the sinners, man himself does. That each decides in an eternal act that "does not itself belong to time but rather to eternity," is an idea which, though at first seemingly incomprehensible, Schelling attempts to support by noting how "there is indeed in each man a feeling in accord with it as if he had been what he is already from all eternity and had by no means becomes so in time."[16] No one, he claims, is arbitrarily good or evil, but by an absolute necessity. "How frequently does it occur that," Schelling notes, "from childhood on, from a time when, considered empirically, we can hardly attribute to him freedom and self-reflection, an individual shows a propensity to evil from which it can be anticipated that he will bend neither to discipline nor doctrine, and which consequently brings to ripeness the wicked fruit that we had foreseen in the earliest sprout."[17] Some have an innate propensity to evil, others to good. Individual human freedom does not involve the choice of choosing our deepest personal character. For Schelling, all choice starts from it. Ultimately, the most intimate form of moral character and disposition is not personally up to us.

As prevalent as is this Romantic trend to see the freedom of individual agency and personality to be a metaphysical illusion, a trend repeated by the scientism of today's popular media, it betrays the life with which we are familiar, the life from which it hopes to flee. It is with an eye to this intellectual history's devastating effects on culture that Henry, reminiscent of his similar work in *Barbarism*, will in §37 of *Incarnation* recount how the encounter with others, particularly so the erotic encounter between man and woman, is shot through with a sensuousness that constantly implicates the presence of genuine personal freedom and responsibility. Each of us decides whether and in what way he will yield the body in reply to the summons of desire. In that same work's section "Forgetting Life and Recalling It with Pathos in Anxiety" directly inspired by Kierkegaard's own treatment of anxiety, we are provided with a vignette of a man and a woman who have slipped out from the ballroom onto a secluded balcony. There is nothing serendipitous about finding each other there alone, where the possibility of the man's grasping the woman's hand takes on the dizzying intrigue it does. They are both there, notes Henry, precisely because they were so drawn, sucked in by the allure of tantalizing possibility. On the basis of following Kierkegaard's observation that sin "is characterized in the first place by the loss of innocence,"[18] Henry goes on to explain the inexplicability of the leap. In the face of the possibility that desire may lead to transgression, there is anxiety. And when that threshold is crossed, the experience of our body changes.

Henceforth, it has become a potential servant of evil.

> Thus Kierkegaard's synthesis of the soul and the body in the spirit takes place, such that the latter is present in the former, invisible life in our objective body. So that our objective body is not a thingly body whose living character would be reducible to a field of intentional significations that confer on it the ideal capacity to sense and to move; but rather, this what it is in truth—it really carries within it this real ability and these real powers.[19]

Henry's review of the erotic encounter between the man and the woman on the starlit balcony accordingly returns us to the original mystery. How, it is necessary to ask, is the leap into sin possible? If for Henry the answer regards the anxiety underlaying human desire, that observation does not explain how we succumb to temptation in each individual act of sin. Henry does not deny the opacity at play: "How desire, not content to be desire, can want to and be able to satisfy itself—how, in other terms, anxiety succumbs to sin—is, according to Kierkegaard, something that can never be explained. At the very least, the fulfillment of desire, the leap into sin, must be possible. And the phenomenology of life, without claiming to give account in any way for each particular act in which sin happens, is able to bring to light this possibility."[20] In its taking place, the leap opens a field of action wherein it becomes possible to deploy life's powers apart and away from the God who originally bestowed them. They become instruments directed toward our own pleasure and purely for the sake of that pleasure. The *I can* no longer acknowledges its dependence on the One who has brought it into this condition of power. "It is this leap into Apostasy," Henry consequently notes, "that has destroyed our original nature and, being unceasingly reproduced by it, unceasingly destroys it."[21] Concluding his analysis, Henry notes that the resulting consciousness and the form of bodily style marking it assumes the form of idolatry. Intoxicated with the ability to deploy the powers of life, one marshals them simply for the sake of satisfying what they seek. Phenomenologically, this is what it means to be a lover of self. "It is this love of self," he explains, "that leads to death because what is loved—this pretend power or the sensations it procures—precisely does not have the power to give itself to itself, to give itself life. And thus by loving them, it is his own powerlessness that man loves, and it is to his own finitude and death that he entrusts himself."[22] The leap into sin is the leap into death.

Though the case certainly may be subtler than in the case of acts of sexual immorality, the same antilaw of inexplicability is at work with the lie. Here once again the significance is not so much that the lie resists reductionism—that is true of all sin in general, as we have just noted with Kierkegaard and Henry. What matters is not that the lie's reasons are unknown insofar as they are inaccessible. *Rather, they are inaccessible because there are none.* With the lie, it is not that we are looking for an explanation that merely eludes us. That would already be to presuppose there *is* an explanation. Explanation eludes us, instead, because there is no explanation. The act of lying is inscrutable because of the fundamental inexplicability Kierkegaard and Henry observe of the phenomenon of sin in general. Strictly speaking, *nothing* explains the leap into evil. In the very opening section of Poe's aforementioned "The Tell-Tale Heart," the narrator confides to us that his reasons for murder are inscrutable because they are inexplicable, fundamentally without and beyond all reason: "It is impossible to say how the idea first entered my head. There was no reason for what I did. I did not hate the old man; I even loved him."[23] Where a predominant philosophical tradition since at least the Middle Ages, inherited by moderns like Leibniz, maintains that everything existent has a reason, lies exempt themselves from the ontological domain of *ratio*. They are what they are precisely because they have no reason. They are ontologically inexplicable. It is not that they admit of a reason we cannot comprehend. Here there is no reason to comprehend, for to lie is lunacy. Nothing in the last analysis explains the leap into a lie.

An objection at this point must be addressed. Understandably, someone will be prepared to concede that the present analysis regarding deceitful kinds of silence are illuminating so far as it goes, and yet still insist the matter for all that remains hazy. In a word, is there here only the appearance of essential necessity? For even if we are ready to concede the phenomenological validity of the foregoing analysis, admitting that it captures experiential truths that are essential in their own way, is it not entirely right, so the objection continues, to dismiss it, along with the entire domain to which these truths belong, as the characteristically hyperbolic rhetoric of existentialism and thus as an analysis lacking the legitimate rigor reserved exclusively to the domain of formal truth in logic and mathematics? It is an objection whose central line of thought stretches back to Carnap's confrontation with Heidegger.

The *liar paradox* is a statement in which the said is both true and false (or really neither), for it is true only when it is false, and vice versa. As mathematical logic has observed since Russell's discovery of these statements (we note only in passing they were known already to Zermelo), the self-contradiction at work in them hangs on a fundamental irreconcilability between the said and the conditions that would make it true. This suggests a clue. Is not there a parallel inconsistency at play within the liar's personality? In this case, however, the paradox is not the semantic one involving a statement that is true only when it is false, but rather a deeper kind, one whereby the liar assumes erroneously to be in possession of an authority over what has already usurped that power, mastering him. The paradox in question, then, does not involve a lie that is *stated*, but one that is *lived*. A lie is something one assumes will not be identified for what it is (or whose risk of being found out is sufficiently tolerable), yet what makes it what it is (a lie!) is precisely that it deceives, first and above all else, the one that it has assured it cannot (or probably will not) be discovered. From the beginning, the lie thus is pregnant with instability and volatility. It thrives on the misguided assumption that, in speaking it, the one who does so knows it for what it is (an untruth) and thereby is free to mold and guide it (either by revision, diversion, or disavowal), and yet, at the same time, that misplaced assurance is what accounts for the situation's ultimate incoherence. For to know what is false and to speak it anyway is *ipso facto* to subvert the authority of the one who conjures it. No one deceives expecting or hoping to be caught, which is why the deceiver takes precautions against it, and yet, in lying, one assumes to be in control over what in essence defies anyone's control, and hence any precautions one judges will be sufficient to guard against its unmasking: the essential unpredictability of a lie's future. Just as the semantic *liar's paradox* involves self-contradiction, so the existential variety involves self-delusion. To lie is to see predictability where there is none.

The liar is under a strong delusion. Inherent to the moment of every lie's inception is the necessarily mistaken presupposition that it will be (absolutely if not in every detail) controllable by the one who brings it to be. If one were not so reasonably assured, one would not take the risk. Hence, the lie harbors within itself a certain distinctive, yet misplaced, self-assurance. The lie thereby claims its first victim, the one who chooses to tell it thinking it will remain suitably under his thumb. Its primordial act of deception is first to triumph over the one who succumbs to giving birth to it, for no one (certainly not the liar who tells it) can know, with the least confidence or certainty, where the lie will lead, much less that where it will is a matter of the liar's own foresight or command. Every lie has a journey, and the ground it covers necessarily is unknown, and indeed unknowable. Before it can deceive anyone else, it must have already deceived the liar in an originary respect. Assuring the liar that there is assurance where there really is none, the lie takes the liar in. One lies because one takes oneself to be its master, yet the lie by its essence defies any such mastery. Hence, in telling it, I do so on the false premise that the relation in which I take myself to stand to it is the opposite of the reality. To lie is to trust that I, and not it, am in control. But I am not, and so to breathe it into being is to make myself its dupe.

Should it then be considered a wonder that, having decided to indulge its stakes, there is only silence when, completing its circuit, the lie descends on the head of its author turned victim, along the way having revealed it to everyone that this liar—the now silent one—is its estranged source? There is something at once deeply instructive and sobering about the itinerary. Not unlike the worst of all possible errant missiles that turns back to its launchpad, so the lie returns from whence it came, shutting the very mouth that told it. Its path of destruction run, the lie ends with an explosion of silence.

Shifting the metaphor for emphasis, it might be said the liar is as the overconfident lion tamer who steps into the cage without a whip. And if the liar locks himself in, part of the punishment to which he has sentenced himself involves enduring the haunting regret of knowing it would have been better never to have spoken, but to have kept silent. A haughty spirit, he learns, precedes a personal fall. Sartre's *Being and Nothingness* describes a species of this aggravated form of regret in an account whose multilayered series of vignettes progressively exemplifies being-amidst-others-in-the-world. As these relevant sections concerning our relation to others detail, to be the one I am is to be able to take up the others I perceive as objects. This mode of existence, earlier observed by Fichte, is associated with a freedom-denying mode of philosophical "dogmatism" (embodied best by Spinoza) that treats everything, including ourselves and others, as mere objects wholly subject to the causal forces of nature. Sartre's denial that we encounter others as objects is not just a denial of necessitarianism, however. There is more to it. For we are, he notes, able also to encounter them as fellow subjects. In a famous analysis of our relation to others that eventually culminates in a description of the look of the other, Sartre notes how being capable of encountering others *as* others depends on me being taken as the object of another. This reversal, which initiates a form of existential self-estrangement, involves my becoming the object of judgment for another subject, and is, as he thus notes, a matter first of my being-seen. For it is in the look of the other that I am constituted as someone whose mode of existence is being-for-others. As Sartre notes there, the truth of "seeing-the-other" is "being-seen-by-the-other," for the other is *"the one who looks at me."*[24] But what does it mean to be seen?

Occasionally, we almost in passing have used the term "situation." The term's use was not accidental, for to be seen is to find oneself in what the analyses of Sartre's own text is called "situation"—it is to be immersed in a tacitly self-involving awareness of the world in which all that appears does so in terms of the possibilities my project projects. It is this unreflective situation that is radically transformed from one referring exclusively to my immediate consciousness and what thereby was preoccupying me, to one instead whereby everything now shows up how another sees those same things. In the shift, my experience of myself shifts with it, since the other who sees me does not only see what I see, but sees who I am, given my role in the situation. To be encountered by the other therefore is to move from the consciousness of being-a-subject surrounded by objects, to the consciousness that itself has become the object of someone else's look. As Sartre states, "*I am no longer master of the situation.*"[25]

The text's ensuing analysis accounts for this primordial situation's change by the look of the other. The seminal passage regarding the metamorphosis in question is well known yet deserves quoting at length. Describing a voyeur on the stairs, Sartre writes:

> Let us imagine that moved by jealousy, curiosity, or vice I have just glued my ear to the door and looked through a keyhole. I am alone and on the level of a non-thetic self-consciousness. This means first of all that there is no self to inhabit my consciousness, nothing therefore to which I can refer my acts in order to qualify them. . . . I am pure consciousness of things, and things, caught up in the circuit of my selfness, offer to me their potentialities as the proof of my non-thetic consciousness (of) my own possibilities.[26]

Everything—the door, the keyhole, and indeed the spectacle in the room—are given in terms making ultimate reference to the voyeur's project. The door is "to be handled with care," the keyhole "to be looked through," and the scene in the room as "to be heard" or "to be seen." Losing oneself in the world, the situation takes over; things show up purely as instrumentalities of my aims. It makes final refence to the jealousy of the peeper: "Jealousy, as the possibility which *I am*, organizes this instrumental complex by transcending it toward itself. But *I am* this jealousy; I do not *know* it. . . . This ensemble with the world . . . we shall call *situation*."[27]

Then, in a moment, the situation changes: "I hear footsteps in the hall. Someone is looking at me!"[28] The voyeur no longer experiences the hall, the door, the keyhole, and the scenario in the room in an unreflective consciousness enrapt with the moment. Now the voyeur experiences himself in a mode of self-reflection, seeing himself in the reflection of the look of another. Frozen by the gaze of the other, he is laid bare and brought into judgment. As Sartre will insist, the texture of this mode of being-for-others is one of shame and pride. Apprehending his possibilities as from outside and through the other, even the most visceral and immediate of the voyeur's inclinations to run away ("too late!") or to hide in the dark corner ("too risky!") are made manifest in terms of another, who, now in charge, is watching: "My possibility of hiding in the corner becomes the fact that the Other can surpass it toward his possibility of pulling me out of concealment, of identifying me, or arresting me."[29] A shock, Sartre says, seizes our voyeur when discovered by the other's searching look. The shock is not merely psychological, but ontological, for the look strikes to the heart of the world itself, upturning all its possibilities. In it, there is the experience of a subtle alienation of all his possibilities, an existential estrangement where, "now associated with objects of the world," these possibilities are far from him, instead in the "midst of the world."[30] As its readers will know, if the immediately preceding stretch of that text's section dedicated to our being-with-others had already observed that an interpersonal encounter in a public park acts as a drain hole on the world, in such instances where the world is "perpetually flowing off through this hole" because I am no longer at its center, the "total disintegration" of the universe at issue does not yet involve the still further form of estrangement in the look. Being apprehended in the look of the other generates a deeper disturbance, for it is one thing to see someone who sees what I see, but it is another to experience oneself as what someone sees. When I see another, I experience the mere fact that the other sees the scene I see. But in being seen by the other, the scene not only shows up as something shared, but more to the point, the situation is experienced as one in which I and my actions are up for judgment. Rather than surveying the scene, I have become part of it.

The voyeur spotted in the hall, hence, no longer is master of the situation. Transported into a situation whose ensemble of possibilities refers not just to his own freedom, but to that of others, there is a fundamental unpredictability at work—an unpredictability Sartre calls the situation's "reverse side." Alienating me from a mode of pure unreflective consciousness where I had answered to no one because things had showed up solely in my terms, I pass in the look of the other into a situation where, suddenly estranged from the immediate realm of self-intoxication, I experience myself as I am seen by the other. In an instant marking the dividing line between this unreflective consciousness and its reflective double, I register that I must reckon with possibility in terms of others.

This unpredictability, notes Sartre, is what our unsuspecting peeper "did not wish." Is it then coincidental that it entails a deeply painful self-recognition? By being seen by the other, the voyeur not only knows what he has done is exposed, but also is subjected to the horrifying realization that the world does not accord exclusively with his desires or actions and hence his anticipations—in the eyes of the other who has passed judgment, he has become what he is: a voyeur. The true meaning of his actions therefore exceeds the meaning he was free to give them. Because they necessarily involve others, it is a verdict that escapes him. Others will have a say in the matter, including what the consequences of his actions will be and how he will be judged for having committed them.

A situation like the one characterizing our discovered voyeur's shame converges with the earlier description of the liar's own paradoxical position. Fundamentally, the liar was the first one deceived because by taking the lie to be opening a horizon that was his own, he was deceived into thinking he was the master of a situation that on the contrary transcends his control and hence his anticipation. For just as the voyeur apprehends in the look of the other that he was never fully master of the situation now revealing him for what he is, so too the liar caught in the net of his own lie undergoes a similar experience of self-estrangement. Just as the voyeur experiences the shame of the other's judgment precisely because there is no escaping it, so too does the liar snared in his own devices. However, in a way the judgment for the liar is worse than for the voyeur. Whereas the voyeur can resort to consolations ("The other misunderstands me, for this was a one-off," "Everyone else really wants to do the same," "It is only the petty prejudices of common morality that say what I've done is wrong"), the liar cannot, because the ordinary rationalizations of bad faith are unavailable to him. One simply is a liar, nothing more, a just sentence rendered as a result of one's own unambiguous choosing, not somebody's flip judgment, or moral interpretation, or uninformed opinion. The judgment is final, because it is indisputable.

It would be mistaken to think that the arc beginning with self-delusion and ending in the shame of judgment is limited to the single liar. Is not the same law at work in the more intricate, and accordingly egregious, lie told by many? Take the example of the conspiracy, where those who lend themselves to the cause act together to achieve a deception the results of which transcend the sum of their individual efforts. With the conspiracy, the goal is to produce what otherwise would be unattainable were those who are working together not to cooperate. Always, such a conspiracy involves deception, at least in its tactics, if not the ultimate objective. This is most evident in the smear campaign, where the conspirators plot to produce an impression of its target that comes to *be* merely because it has been *said*. In this way, the slanderous speech-act behaves as Austin had noted the perlocutionary act does generally: merely by virtue of saying what is said, a certain impression in the listener is produced. This is different than in illocutionary acts, as when the officiant actually brings about holy matrimony simply in saying "I pronounce you husband and wife," or the judge renders one a criminal by pronouncing "Guilty!" What makes the act of slander's linguistic context so disturbing is the presupposition failure defining it. Because most listeners would never think to consider that the speaker would be so monstrous as to blatantly lie, the norms of ordinary language are repurposed into weapons of deception. Insinuating that something is so, the slanderer hopes to trick others into treating what is a perlocutionary act ("Did you *read* what Jim did?")

as carrying illocutionary force ("Jim has lost his mind"). But such a speech-act is really akin to "Fire!" in that it is possible there is no fire; simply saying it does not make (much less guarantee) it so. If usually where there is smoke there is fire, here is the mere appearance of smoke. The words are calculated to convince they signal something, but nothing is there. Leveling the accusation, the conspirators who resort to slander hope others will not question what they say or what they report others as having said (rumor is a weapon of choice in the arsenal); for simply by the sheer force of having said it they hope suddenly it becomes so. That is what makes slander the pernicious form of lie it is. That language is able to represent what is not as being true or represent what is true as what is not, is what the conspirators exploit to such damaging effect. Language also has the capacity not only to distort what it says by misrepresenting, but to efface the one who does so. In the torrent of words, the slanderers recede into the background, concealed from responsibility behind a veil of rhetoric, which, having brought about the reputed state of affairs it has, directs the attention back to the victim rather than onto themselves. If we thus call these false accusers, ultimately it is because by using words how they have, they put an innocent target on trial.

With a conspiracy designed to assassinate its target with lies, as in the organized smear campaign in the press, or even just the whispers of false friends or disingenuous family, the aim is to impose a meaning on the actions and motivations of the victim that suit the desire of the plotters. They hope to mold the situation so that it conforms to how they want it to appear, so that those in turn who are taken in will think things are just as they appear. The malice involved here is substantial. To twist the fabric of reality for one's own gain, and at the expense of someone else, what kind of heart of darkness is this? And yet not only do the plotters acknowledge the sordidness of their behavior, they expressly take it into account, deploying every precaution available to conceal it.

If we have said something of the motivations and methods governing conspiracy, it is necessary to say a word concerning its consequences. It will be noted that just as the voyeur caught in the hall must withstand the knowing look of the other, so the one attacked by a conspiracy endures the pain of knowing he has been assigned a meaning beyond his control. Only in this case the sentence is worse, for the things themselves do not support the meaning imposed. The power of the plot's spell consists precisely in that—to convince others of something without or despite the evidence. At least initially, others come under its sway even though (or sometimes even because) there is no real evidence for believing any of it. The conspirators are like sorcerers who, waving their wand and uttering "abracadabra," bring into being a state of affairs that only exists in the words. Here, just because it has been said so, something is taken to be so. If, as Sartre says, the meaning of a situation transcends our control, this is an experiential fact the conspirators exploit against their enemy. The voyeur's actions take on a meaning beyond what he was free to give them. Because they invoke others, the situation escapes him. And if others have a say in the meaning of his action, this power to pass judgment is another one of language's powers that the conspirators know only too well. Whether by manipulating events so as to produce a nefarious effect reinforcing the narrative they have crafted, or by discreet whispers that do the same, the conspirators move and live and find their being in silence, hiding behind words that spotlight their victim instead.

Silence is that without which a conspiracy would not only fail to succeed but would cease to *be* what it is. It fuels conspiracy. Though in our culture it has taken on a largely pejorative connotation (we use the term "conspiracy theory" reflexively as an epithet), the concept of conspiracy is acknowledged in the law. In the legal context, a conspiracy is when two or more people get together to do something illegal. There is nothing bizarre about recognizing that conspiracies are accordingly commonplace in everyday life. After all, a criminal without a plan—imagine, say, the bank robber who leaps into an unplanned heist—would not be a very effective one. To further consider our example, it is worth noting the role silence once again plays. The criminal plot by necessity is hatched in secret. Since what it plans to carry out is illegal, and indeed to have formed the mere intention is too, announcing the plot would be to confess one's criminal intent. Hence, the conspiracy, at least in its criminal manifestation, is birthed in silence. Though not necessarily criminal, other forms exhibit a silence no less quotidian: four teenagers arrange to ditch the friend they like the least, or two coworkers at the construction site keep watch so that the boss does not catch them sandbagging. Here again, the success hinges on secrecy's silence. In a way, the same applies even in the case of the surprise birthday party. It too is a form of conspiracy: would it succeed if the attendees had told the birthday boy? Good-natured people who do not want to face up to the scary facts of life will respond by noting that a surprise party, though demanding secrecy is not technically a conspiracy, for it does not intend to do wrong. The conspiracies many people are invested in denying are those requiring careful cooperation on the part of some, even many, to do something bad. That is what offends people's sense of possibility. And yet the incredulity only turns back on itself: if two or more persons are indeed working together to do something illegal or otherwise wrong, *would* they tell everyone about it? Of course not. Far then from seeing the silence of secrecy as an illusion only the paranoid see, it is, as the law acknowledges, not just a feature of everyday life but one of a criminal conspiracy's necessary conditions. If it were not secret, it would not be a plot.

The political scandal is another case. Why else, after all, does the public relations spokesman reply to penetrating but fair questions with a prototypically brusque "no comment"? Whether one looks to Clinton cash scandals or the deaths involving their coterie, the Bush family's funding of the Nazis and the drug trade, or the phantom weapons of mass destruction in Iraq, no one can deny that systematic deception, and the conspiracy necessary to coordinate it so as to manage public perception, is a cornerstone of today's oligarchic political world. Even those who still take corporate news seriously are forced to confront the specter of conspiracy in the headlines: "The Russians Interfered in the Election," "Clinton Obstructed Justice over the Benghazi Investigation." Dostoevsky wrote an entire novel, *Demons*, about political conspiracy, an account that was not crafted solely from imagination but from personal experience with the radical socialist circles that led to his exile in Siberia. His memorable portrayal of the political world of intrigue, subversion, and revolt is so compelling in part precisely because it existed.

If conspiracy perverts truth by dissimulating it, passes itself off as what it knows it is not, seeks to manipulate others to parade as truth an untruth tailored for its own twisted purposes (the motive may be as primal as insecurity), what then are we to say about the mocker? Why does this third figure in our review of silence do openly what the conspirator keeps secret? The conspirator relishes his feelings in private, whereas the mocker makes them public, deriving immense satisfaction in doing so. Describing his nocturnal ritual of observation preceding the murder, Poe's narrator recounts watching the old man in the black room: "Every night about twelve o'clock I slowly opened his door. And when the door was opened wide enough I put my hand in, and then my head. In my hand I held a light covered over with a cloth so that no light showed. And I stood there quietly. Then, carefully, I lifted the cloth, just a little, so that a single, thin, small light fell across that eye."[31] As Poe shows, there is a peculiar glee in the self-indulgence that enjoys knowing what the other does not. But for our narrator this sick enjoyment that constitutes the conspirator's highest pleasure is still not enough. More is needed. But what? When in the next line he goes on to say, "And every morning I went to his room, and with a warm, friendly voice I asked him how he had slept. He could not guess that every night, just at twelve, I looked in at him as he slept,"[32] it is clear that we have crossed a threshold beyond delighting in a secret to enjoying mocking the one who does not know it. Hence, where a band of conspirators uses silence to hide its real intentions, the mocker makes it known that he holds what he does in pure contempt. Even the act of insincere benevolence is intended to hint at the venom beneath it. The mocker derives his satisfaction precisely from subtly taunting the object of his scorn.

A source of a mocker's scorn can be the truth itself. That is why the scoffer hates those who have pursued good. If no one is said to like a do-gooder, that is only really true of those who love evil. Our voyeur was rendered speechless in the face of the just judgment he received in the look of the other. But the mocker sneers at justice. Here there is no shame. There is the anger of being caught, or the frustration of having his will thwarted, or the resentment of seeing someone he dislikes doing well for himself. That is why deprecation becomes a tool of art for the mocker. What better way to make himself feel better than by slighting the accomplishment of the one he envies? And when the success of the other is too much to bear, what better way to compensate for one's overpowering sense of resentment and impotence than by mocking the one who has succeeded? The mocker wishes that the one he mocks would lower himself to his own level. At the heart of mockery then is a lack of self-control. At bottom, it is the weapon of choice for one who cannot control his temper but likes to indulge it. The allure of seeing what acting against his better judgment will bring proves too strong. Knowing that what he will go on to say would be better left unsaid, the mocker relishes the feeling of saying what he knows he should not. Because there is an undercurrent of self-destruction at work (there always is in sadism), a situation that should be treated seriously with respect is demeaned. In having lowered himself to a place where nothing is sacred anymore, the mocker lashes out against anything that reminds him that perhaps some things are noble and worthy of reverence. We are thus reckoning with an astonishing form of perversity: an individual whose pleasure is to belittle what he hates, precisely because he knows that what he hates is good. To mock in this respect is to desecrate something and to enjoy doing so precisely for that reason.

Though mockery is willing to deliver itself over to its own self-destruction, in transgressing silence by saying what should not dared be said, the mocker betrays the underlying insecurity that has incited him to speak. If he meant what he says, he would not have felt called to say it. By making fun of what he does, he is hoping to convince himself as much as anyone that what he scorns is unworthy of admiration. This tactic is a neighbor to the tactic preferred by the conspirator, that by saying something is so, it thereby becomes so. An inherent flaw in the conspirator's intention is that his plot attempts to create *ex nihilo*, which is why eventually it is exposed for the deception it was. Here the mocker's own words aim to achieve what they by necessity cannot. Just because one holds something in derision does not mean it deserves to be, and though the mocker wishes to convince everyone that his attitude is just, he fails. One question suffices to expose the mockery's instability: if one truly thinks as lowly as one does about what one mocks, why say anything at all? If what one mocks does not matter, why does it preoccupy the mocker to the degree it has? It lapses into self-parody, for in saying what he says, the mocker reinforces the opposite impression his words were meant to produce. Consequently, any time encountering the mocker, one response always suffices: "Thou dost protest too much."

At this stage of the analysis, it is necessary to consider a reservation. While it may be that to mock sometimes is to admit that the object of scorn is unworthy of scorn, is that always so? Rather than seeing a performative contradiction in mockery, might it not be seen as consistent, as a form of expressing that one thinks deservedly little of what it does? Is mockery necessarily self-undermining, or can it have its proper time and place, thereby serving a purpose? Addressing these questions will open to a fourth figure of silence, the hypocrite.

If a long tradition culminating with Heidegger has viewed human rationality as a capacity consisting in our ability to account for ourselves by giving reasons to others, holding ourselves responsible to others is to act in a way that is measured by the *logos*. Human action exemplifies the norm at stake in what it involves. In acting as I do, I incur the tacit but always potentially dischargeable duty of accounting for how or whether my behavior lives up to the measure governing it. This accountability calls on our capacity to render reasons. In this way, to be rational is to be able and willing to give reasons for what one does. It is to treat one's actions as evaluable in terms whose measure of success or failure is situated in the light: the space of meaning open to all those who can hold themselves and others answerable to the reasons at issue.

To stand in the *logos* is to hold one's actions accountable in the light. It is to hold oneself open to the assessment of others, to make one's actions inspectable in light of the reasons that justify them. But a question must be asked. If the ability to assume responsibility by holding oneself accountable to others is something we can succeed or fail at, and authentic existence is the existence that takes this task of responsibility squarely on, what are we to say regarding our figures of silence? Can such silence *be* authentic? Immediately, a paradox presents itself. From a certain point of view, being a liar, conspirator, mocker, as with any other human possibilities, is measured by the norm of success or failure. And yet these possibilities constitutively preclude the possibility of ever holding oneself accountable with reasons. To the contrary, they foreclose any possibility of entering into the light of the *logos*, because the measure of success requires avoiding the practice of reason-giving.

Take the liar. As there is no reason for lying, as the leap into evil is without reason, it is impossible to lie authentically. The authentic liar would be the one who is ready to give reasons for what he has done, but there can be no such reasons for what he has done. If to be authentic is to be accountable by giving reasons, the liar, who is always without excuse, has no reasons—*ergo*, he necessarily is inauthentic.

If the authentic liar is a contradiction in terms, so a similar contradiction is at work with the conspirator. Here the issue once again concerns the status of the inherent standards determining success at being a conspirator: keeping one's true intentions secret clashes with the practice of rendering reasons for one's actions. A conspirator who rendered true reasons as to why he has done what he has would be a failure. Far from concealing his plot, which is essential to his aim, he would instead be confessing it, thereby failing at what he is trying to do. Success in trying to be the conspirator demands that he keep it hidden. Rather than requiring he hold himself open to the space of reasons, his trying to be what he is requires that he shirk it. The conspirator is one who like the liar cannot enter the space of reasons authentically, since to do so would be to fail at ensuring his reasons are not brought out of the dark into the light. Thus, acting in light of what it means to be a conspirator entails *not* being answerable for what one is trying to be, since answering to others would mean failing at being a conspirator.

As for the mocker, again there is only the semblance of authentic reason-giving.

Adopting the attitude he does, his rules of engagement treat what he derides as being unworthy of any seriousness, as if providing serious reasons for his judgment is otiose. He has exited the space of reasons, as if justified, when that very question remains open. The mocker therefore excuses himself from the burden of rendering reasons, helping himself to the idea that no reasons are necessary.

The various forms of paradox at work in these figures coalesce with the hypocrite. The hypocrite says one thing but does another. There is disagreement between his words and deeds, which is why he cannot justify the latter by the former. Often a hypocrite falls silent when his inconsistency is pointed out. Yet does not this very same description fit the inauthentic one, the one who is either unable or unwilling to justify himself to others with reasons? Inauthenticity is shot through with hypocrisy. If the authentic life tries to hold itself accountable to others by coming into the light of the *logos*, the hypocrite is the one who constitutively fails to do so. His deeds are not done in the truth, which is why he contradicts himself when he insists that they are. He does one thing but says another. The greatest form of inauthenticity imaginable then would be the one who, having articulated a conceptual understanding of what it means to engage in authentic reason-giving, nevertheless refuses in practice to live up to that understanding all the while claiming that he does. This is the supreme hypocrite, the one who claims to be authentic but is not.

Authentic liar, authentic conspirator, authentic mocker, authentic hypocrite: all undermine themselves. Each in its own way disguises with the lips what is in the heart. One cannot *be* an authentic liar (to hold oneself accountable with false reasons is a pretend responsibility), cannot *be* an authentic conspirator (to succeed as a schemer demands hiding one's reasons, not disclosing them), cannot *be* an authentic mocker (to scoff is to criticize something without offering reasons), and cannot *be* an authentic hypocrite (the practice of giving reasons presupposes the ideal of a harmony between word and deed the hypocrite flouts). Marion in *Being Given* defines Revelation as the saturated phenomenon *par excellence*, as what that work names a "paradox of the second degree."[33] Here we might identify another similarly concentrated paradox in the figure of the one who claims to be authentic but is not, the one who claims to live a life holding himself accountable to others but does not. This is the hypocrite *par excellence*: the most inauthentic character conceivable, the inauthentically authentic one saturated with hypocrisy.

But of course not every silence is pernicious. Far from it. There can be, for one, a silence of hospitality and joy. In a meditation concerning the multiple kinds of silence, Jean-Louis Chrétien in the *Ark of Speech* distinguishes between those that we make and those that befall us. As he notes, there are voluntary and involuntary silences. We may have nothing to say when we are at a loss for words, shocked by what we have encountered. This kind of involuntary silence, however, is very different from when, still in command of our powers of speech, we decline to exercise it. In voluntary silences, we communicate as much by what we chose not to utter as by what we have. We say what we do by not saying what we could have. Keeping silent becomes a way of saying that what has attempted to provoke it does not deserve a response. Whether indecent, improper, or unintelligible, the comment is unworthy of a spoken reply. Silence here is not an evasion of truth, but a form of submission to it. Some scenarios demand a discretionary silence.

This difference between silences that overpower us and those we put to work is peculiar to human speech and silence. Yet as Chrétien observes, there are distinctions within the silence beyond the immediately human sphere of speech. In a section of that same analysis directly inspired by a similar set of meditations from Kierkegaard's 1849 discussion of the lily of the field and the bird of the air, he draws attention to nature's silence. On the beach, there is the cry of the seagulls, the crash of the ocean waves, and the rustle of the breeze. When I stand alone and still myself, there is a profound background silence. It is in this stillness that we hear God, observes Kierkegaard. God speaks through the silence of his creatures. Against this "background of silence from which all sounds emerge," as Chrétien notes, "this silence of nature forms a creaturely silence, it ultimately refers us to the creatures who stand before God, and to the way they listen to or await God's speech."[34] Nature is a "canticle of creatures," a silence that points to the speech of God we will hear if we attend to it.

Returning to the matter of human silence, it is worth noting that to Chrétien's original distinction between the voluntary and involuntary may be added a further schema. It is a tripartite division among forms of inaction. The division is moral in kind. In the first instance, the silence could be one that results from my being overcome by what I have encountered. In the whirlwind of events, I have not yet gathered myself. Sudden news of the death of a loved one leaves us speechless, for instance. These events shock us so badly that they leave us silent. We struggle to find words, but they flee. It is a shocked silence associated with an experience that immobilizes us, an involuntary response referred to in the English expression, "deer in the headlights." There is nothing good or bad about this first form of inaction. Morally, it is neutral. In a second form, the inaction in question is admirable. We deem it good because it exhibits virtues like self-control, tact, or prudence. Sometimes we refrain from speaking, knowing that speaking will only engender pointless strife or further confusion, condone bad behavior, encourage deceit, or so forth. Refusing to speak is a way of choosing not to cooperate with the bad. A variation of such admirable silence is the one friends and lovers share. Silence allows us simply to enjoy each other's presence. It is all that is needed. At ease with each other, we welcome one another in a communion whose mode of exchange has no word to offer, because no word is necessary. The bond, and the mutual understanding underlying it, goes without saying. It is the trusting silence of comfort and familiarity. And relatedly, there is reverence's silence, also admirable. In the hospital room or at the gravesite, for instance, not to speak may be the only fitting form of response. The list of such respectable silences could be extended.

But this second form of choosing to keep quiet, itself estimable and wholesome, is to be distinguished from yet a third kind of silence. Here the silence of inaction is far from praiseworthy. Unlike the first two variants, it is neither neutral nor good, but rather morally pernicious. We have in view a form of keeping silent that assumes the form of evil, precisely because it is indifferent to evil. Refusing to speak out against something tacitly licenses what should be condemned. If the famous adage maintains that evil triumphs when good men do nothing, that includes the inaction of not speaking out against evil. Failure to denounce injustice enflames it. As Bonhoeffer is purported to have said, "Silence in the face of evil is itself evil: God will not hold us guiltless. Not to speak is to speak. Not to act is to act."[35] When we do not speak out against wrongdoing, not only does it continue unabated but the evil strengthens itself. Those who disapprove of what they are witnessing and choose not to voice their opposition are not always exercising the tact or discretion of prudence that sometimes calls for ignoring something. The inaction, rather, is rooted in self-interest and self-preservation. It is thus an evil silence, if only because it leaves evil unchecked out of selfishness.

It is this inactive silence in the face of evil that highlights a moral dimension at stake in the structure of *ratio* characterizing human life. Ontologically, the one who refuses to hold oneself open to the truth by coming into the light of sincere exchange stands in the untruth, either declaring as true what is false (the liar), scheming to bring about something bad that must be concealed (the conspirator), ridiculing the good (the mocker), or claiming to exemplify the good while violating it (the hypocrite). Inaction against evil points to a fifth figure of silence, which we are now ready to mention. This fifth silent one is the coward. The coward is the one who hides in the dark, unwilling to hold himself accountable because he knows that what he has done is wrong. Whether misrepresenting (the liar), thwarting (the conspirator), deprecating (the mocker), or transgressing (the hypocrite) the truth, a more primordial decision to shrink back from the truth has taken place. Arguably, the greatest exemplar of evil is thus the coward, the type who, receding into the dark of silence, attempts to hide from everything—from himself because of what he knows he has become, from others because he knows they know it too, and thus from the truth itself. John lays out with precision this logic of evil and silence. The silent one hides the truth of his deeds because he knows them to be false. Knowing he will be unable to render a convincing account as to why he has done what he has, he does not enter into the light of reasons: "And this is the judgment: the light has come into the world, and people loved the darkness rather than the light because their works were evil" (John 3:19). In turn, his existence becomes one of appearing to be what he is not, as though his deeds are justifiable while he knows they are not: "For everyone who does evil hates the light and does not come to the light, lest his deeds should be exposed" (John 3:20). In contrast, the one who does not do evil lives a life of reason, because he lives a life where he is always ready to give reasons for what he does, for what he has done was done in the light, and so his deeds exemplify the *logos*. There is no need for silence for there is nothing to hide: "But whoever does what is true comes to the light, so that it may be clearly seen that his deeds have been done in God" (John 3:21). As then for the one who does not abide in the Word, this inauthentic one accordingly will have no justifying word to offer when what was done in darkness is exposed.

Sartre's voyeur comes again to mind. Overwhelmed with shame, left speechless when he did not expect to be seen, the voyeur is seen doing what he did not want to be seen doing. If Sartre describes the experience of being apprehended unprepared in the look of the other as horrifying, how much worse a judgment to be apprehended not merely in the look of another man but by God? In the twenty-second chapter of Matthew, Christ relates a parable warning about such a scenario befalling a man who did not learn the seriousness of what it will mean to be brought into judgment until it was too late. Lost in the dark wood Dante depicts, the man had not turned back but pressed deeper into the thicket, stumbling in the dark, and finally reaching the point of no return. For as we continue reading, we learn that having been invited to the wedding feast by the king, the man shows up without a garment. When the king enters the hall and sees him seated at the feast without his garment, the latter is left speechless. There is no time to bargain, no time to rationalize, no time to utter a word—all that can be done is to accept what comes next. He is thrown out, and that is that. The teaching's lesson will make us fear and tremble should we really think about it by putting ourselves into the position of the one condemned. The story warns: unless I change now, what will I have to say for myself knowing I have squandered the gift of life on evil?

A common response to this train of thought warrants attention. What prevents us from denying that there is any eternal judgment? In response to this mode of denial, it is worth noting it does not follow that if I disbelieve something it is not so. I may not believe it will rain tomorrow, but that does not mean it will not. Perhaps it will. Whether it does is not decided by what I believe. The same applies to judgment: that I do not believe there will be a judgment does not mean there will not be one. But the attitude denying there is a judgment succumbs to a deeper problem. No one disputes that the world is a place of injustice and evil. There is suffering, and basically everyone if prompted will say that this is a great concern to them. Who is untroubled over the world's being so far from perfect? Who will admit to being unbothered by such things? To live in our world indifferent to the knowledge that it will not ultimately be put right, that the suffering will be unjustified, that evil will go unpunished, and that the good will not triumph, what is one to say in response to someone who is resigned comfortably to living like this, content to look after himself and his own interests and contentment? When we put the point like that, the reply is that living a good and moral life does not require superstition. Living a deeply humane life does not presuppose any belief in God and the afterlife. Many of this opinion go even further, contending that belief in God, immortality, and an eternal judgment detracts from our moral duties, sugarcoating them with a false hope. It is not too difficult to spot this suspicion's fundamental interpretive dishonesty. If one truly is as good as the objector claims, if living a maximally upright life without faith is possible, if caring for the well-being of others is one's real priority, and if one hates suffering and evil, how does one exist in a world so broken and not die of grief? If anyone can live a comfortable life, relatively apathetic in the face of the supposed knowledge that this is the only world there will be, that there will be no judgment in which good is rewarded and evil punished: can we take this attitude's declarations of sensitivity and clean-heartedness seriously? An existence truly pure but also indifferent to the prospect of judgment is inconceivable. Anyone who embarked on it would be driven to insanity, quietism, or else a broken heart. Experientially, to thirst after righteousness without a judgment is impossible.

In Dante's eighth circle, a place called Malebolge, there is a series of ten ditches, or *bolgoias*. The sinners are forced to march the circumference of their assigned ditch, while being whipped and sometimes torn to pieces by the presiding demons. At this level of perdition, just one above hell's frozen bottom, the sin of fraudulence in all its forms is punished. Each *bolgoia* is dedicated to a particular species of interpersonal, civic, or spiritual treachery—betrayal, treason, lying are among them. In the second ditch, for instance, are those awash in feces, who in this life were guilty of flattery. For Dante, what recently has been made by Harry Frankfurt the topic of light amusement is no laughing matter. In the sixth ditch are the hypocrites, bound in lead. In the tenth *bolgoia* are the liars. There are many unforgettable figures. But the one of our interest is Master Adam, guilty of counterfeiting. He had attempted to pass off false florins, the currency of Florence, each containing only twenty-one rather than the standard twenty-four carats of gold. As punishment, he looks back on the streams and hills of Italy, seeing how what he had then was all he could have wanted, though he had squandered it on the pursuit of false goods: "Alive, I had plenty all I wanted. And now I crave a single drop of water! The streams that, in the Casentino, run down along green hillsides to the Arno, keeping their channels cool and moist, flow before my eyes forever, and not in vain, because their image makes me thirst still more than does the malady that wastes my features. The rigid justice that torments me employs the landscape where I sinned to make my sighs come faster."[36] Twisted into the shape of a lute, face rotting off, and bloated with dropsy, he thirsts for a drink of water. Unable to move, it has become an "impossible dream" simply to be able to move an inch in a year. He is haunted by the knowledge that while alive on earth he had taken what was a field of glory and defiled it with lust, cheapening everything into little more than a field for his own dishonest gain. Master Adam is the chief idolater in the Henryran sense, for he has used his powers of life to pursue his satisfaction in goods apart from God. This is the ultimate counterfeiter, the one who denying who he is attempted to live away from the very God who had given him life.

Dante's underworld is one without hope, we know. But that is not all. We immediately notice that no one there takes any solace in the company of the others there too—everyone is at each other's throats, and the petty jealousies that consumed them on earth are only intensified in hell. The scene calls to mind the position of Sartre, who sees shame and pride as not only fundamental to but exhaustive of the response to the look of the other. Without contesting that these two moods have some role to play in our relations with others, does it not overlook a third possible attitude to being apprehended in the look? We have in mind joy. A relatively obscure text *Opera omnia* belonging to the fourteenth-century Flemish Christian mystic Jan van Ruussbroec depicts heaven as a place where there is a participative union in God without distinction. Those in glory will encounter a "burning and being burned up," yet not one associated with the infernal anguish of hell but with the ecstasy of love: "And for this reason we must lay the foundations of our life in an unfathomable abyss and so we shall be able to sink into love forever and sink away from ourselves in those unfathomable depths, and with the same love we shall raise and transcend ourselves onto those incomprehensible heights and in that love we shall wander without manner and it shall lead us and lose us in the measureless width of God's love. In it we shall flow, and flow beyond ourselves in that unknown luxury that is the wealth and goodness of God and in it we shall melt and be melted down, we shall whirl and be whirled away in the glory of God forever."[37] The contrast with Dante's hell could not be starker. If Ruusbroec's saints are those who will be united as one in the joy of love, it is because they are not turned in on themselves against others, as the sinners in life who knew only to look after themselves. A saint has a heart of love, the lost a heart of stone. And if the latter are unfeeling in the biblical sense of that term, it is because they are calloused to anything besides the pursuit of what their own wills deem valuable. Ruusbroec in the *Little Book of Enlightenment* comments on such figures, observing that a life of self-interest on earth presaged their lonely fate in the hereafter, "For they wish to teach and will learn from none; they wish to revile and be reviled by none; to command and to obey no one; they wish to oppress others and to be oppressed by none; they wish to say what they will and never to be contradicted. They are self-willed and subject to none."[38] It is a self-determination that hands them over to an infernal isolation. In the end, they die alone, jaded and frustrated through a life of lust that never delivered the satisfaction they craved. They do not want to die, for they fear it, but they also do not want to keep living, for they are tormented by a life of lust, worry, and despair.

By now, there will be the stirring of an objection, even if it is not yet one fully articulated. For what are we to make of this seemingly bizarre idea of one alive but dead? Or more to the point, how does the particular way such a one handles his own relation to death affect how we all see our own more generally? As A. W. Moore has pointed out in defense of Bernard Williams and against Thomas Nagel, it does not follow that one does not want to die at every particular instance one is asked so that one thereby desires to live forever. Defending the thesis of Williams's influential essay, "The Makropulos Case: Reflections on the Tedium of Immortality,"[39] Moore argues that death is not always a misfortune. To the contrary, perhaps immortality would be regrettable. In question is an imagined scenario that establishes this subtle yet important distinction. Moore accordingly asks us to consider someone who is given, each week, the option of deciding whether he wants to continue living another week or whether instead he wants to die. Now as Moore notes, it could happen that every single week the man decides he does not want to die, but in choosing each week to keep living, that desire—to postpone death at least one more time—is consistent with a desire not to be immortal. That I do not yet want to die, and may always choose to keep living when asked if I would rather not, does not mean I desire to live forever. The case is fascinating in a certain way, but the issue does not center squarely on determining whether Moore's argument against Nagel is sound. For even supposing that it is logically impeccable as it appears, what the precise spiritual or practical takeaway of the conclusion is remains less clear. On one way of putting the distinction that it establishes to use, we may say Moore has provided the sketch, in the form of a formal possibility, of what we have presently been outlining as an existential actuality. In some quite literal sense, Moore's man is the one who is already the living dead.

It is with this fundamentally conflicted form of life in mind that it becomes easy to see how far from accidental is the central principle of Anton LaVey's Church of Satan, founded in the 1960s in San Francisco, of purportedly rational self-interest. Embodying the teachings of the infamous British occultist Aleister Crowley, its *esprit de corps* is not some fringe movement but one defining the present age. The exaltation of *ego*, a society succumbing to the cult of pride, swept up in the vapid pursuit of nothing but what it thinks will somehow make it feel good, is this not what today is considered normal? It is a society without law, a society whose only law is that there be none but seeking one's own desire. "Do what thou wilt" has become the whole of the law: my comfort, my pleasure, my power, my fame, my honor, my wealth, my reality. We needn't open to a page of Dante to learn the ways of the shade. They are all around us. Family, friends, neighbors, and coworkers who in a few short years have rapidly changed, right before our eyes, now become those who feel for nothing except what they feel will make them feel good, people who have learned perpetually to conform themselves to an increasingly cruel and sick world. We are in a world whose unstated *modus operandi* has become the very Sartrean motif, first immortalized in the play *No Exit*, only someone already under the spell of transcendental egoism's enclosing reserve could possibly endorse: "Hell is other people."

In this society, one of the spectacle, there is no tolerance for sincere empathy, thought, or integrity. Only the appearance of virtue is tolerated. Anything more receives swift condemnation. Righteousness is a dirty word and hypocrisy is king. This is why the political rally, the Twitter campaign, the indignant *New York Times* op-ed piece, and the cable news "debate" are all in fashion. Everyone knows to say that justice for others matters, but everyone resents anyone who acts on it. Barely beneath the din of incessant self-congratulatory rhetoric lies a moral outrage as shallow as the very slogans advertising it. It does not take a spiritual savant to see what really is at work here. Self is god. To those who live this way, in the world with an eye only to what they have to gain or enjoy in it, they are condemned already. If there is a judgment (a fact they are free to deny so long as they want), they have chosen to live unconcerned with the task of readying themselves for it. Seeing God is something they neither desire nor anticipate.

For them, judgment cannot be an event that brings joy. They are unprepared, and so they deny there will be one. It is known that Justin Martyr thought Plato had read Moses and the prophets. Highlighting Plato's treatment of the unjust man's denial of judgment, in chapter 26, "Plato Indebted to the Prophets," of the *Hortatory Address to the Greeks*, he observes that Plato's remarks in the *Republic* regarding the judgment to come are worthy of being heeded. As Justin points out, according to Plato if one is scared of death, that alone means one should be. To be in dread of death is to be unready for the judgment death brings: "When a man begins to think he is soon to die, fear invades him, and concern about things which had never before entered his head. And those stories about what goes on in Hades, which tell us that the man who has here been unjust must there be punished, though formerly ridiculed, now torment his soul with apprehensions and that they may be true. . . . He becomes, therefore, full of apprehension and dread, and begins to call himself to account, and to consider whether he has done any one an injury. And that man who finds in his life many iniquities, and who continually starts from his sleep as children do, lives in terror, and with a forlorn prospect." As for the one who *is* ready, he is so because, as Plato notes, "whoever lives a life of holiness and justice," to him is given "sweet hope."[40] Whoever lives unjustly, focused exclusively on the time leading to the death continually haunting it, meets the idea of judgment in the hereafter with vehement indifference or maybe a flicker of dread quickly explained away as a phantom. The silent one knows only shame or pride, persuading himself that such a future is unreal. It is an attitude of hopelessness that without even seeing it intimates the very judgment it denies.

Finally, before the Final Judgment for which one never prepared, what will there be but silence? Without excuse, the truth will go without saying.

NOTES

1. Dante, *The Inferno*, trans. R. Hollander and J. Hollander (New York: Anchor Books, 2000), 3.
2. Ibid., 47.
3. Edgar Allen Poe, "The Tell-Tale Heart," in *Edgar Allen Poe: Complete Tales and Poems,* ed. Benjam F. Fisher (New York: Barnes & Noble Classics, 2004), 284.
4. Ibid.
5. Ibid., 285.
6. Soren Kierkegaard, *The Concept of Anxiety: A Simple Psychologically Orienting Deliberation on the Dogmatic Issue of Hereditary Sin*, trans. R. Thomte (Princeton: Princeton University Press, 1980), 31.
7. Ibid.
8. Ibid, 32.
9. Ibid., 44.
10. Ibid., 61.
11. Ibid., 63.
12. Michel Henry, *Incarnation: A Philosophy of the Flesh*, trans. K. Hefty. (Evanston, Il: Northwestern University Press, 2015), 174.
13. F. W. J. Schelling, *Philosophical Investigations into the Essence of Human Freedom*, trans. J. Love and J. Schmidt (Albany: SUNY Press, 2006), 23.
14. Fyodor Dostoevsky, *Notes from Underground*, trans. Richard Pevear and Larissa Volokhonsky (New York: Vintage Books, 1994), 13.
15. Schelling, *Philosophical Investigations*, 53.

16. Ibid., 51.
17. Ibid., 52.
18. Henry, *Incarnation*, 191.
19. Ibid., 200–201.
20. Ibid., 203.
21. Ibid., 232.
22. Ibid., 234.
23. Poe, "The Tell-Tale Heart," xx.
24. Jean-Paul Sartre, *Being and Nothingness: An Essay on Phenomenological Ontology*, trans. H. Barnes. (London: Routledge, 2003), 281. Emphasis in the original.
25. Ibid., 289. Emphasis in the original.
26. Ibid., 282.
27. Ibid.
28. Ibid., 284.
29. Ibid., 288.
30. Ibid.
31. Poe, "The Tell-Tale Heart," 199.
32. Ibid.
33. Jean-Luc Marion, *Being Given: Towards a Phenomenology of Givenness*, trans. Jeffrey L. Kosky (Stanford, CA: Stanford University Press, 2002), 242.
34. Jean-Louis Chrétien, *The Ark of Speech*, trans. A. Brown (London and New York: Routledge, 2004), 50–51.
35. Eric Mataxas, *Bonhoeffer: Pastor, Martyr, Prophet, Spy* (Nashville, TN: Thomas Nelson, Inc, 2010).
36. Dante, *Inferno*, 553.
37. Jan van Ruusbroec, *Opera omnia*, ed. J. Alaerts, G. de Baere, P. Mommers, and H. Rolfson (Brill, 1981), xx.
38. Ibid., 118.
39. See Bernard Williams, "The Makropulos Case: Reflections on the Tedium of Immortality," in *Problems of the Self*, ed. B. Williams (Cambridge: Cambridge University Press, 1973).
40. Justin Martyr, "Hortatory Address to the Greeks," in *The Ante-Nicene Fathers: The Writings of the Fathers down to A.D. 325*, vol. 1, ed. A. Roberts and J. Donaldson (Grand Rapids, MI: Wm. B. Eerdmans Publishing Company, 1950), 284.

Chapter Seven

Suffering and Salvation

A Note on Art

As suffering dilates time, riveting us to what feels in the moment to be an inescapable agony whose end is so far distant that it may as well be without one, so language is unable to express what we endure when plunged into the depths of suffering's dark saying. Regardless of what is said of suffering, the reply we muster in response only glances off the surface of what our words struggle to retrieve from the abyss of pathos, having hoped to install a castle of significance upon the tidal shores of intelligibility. The effort is in vain. Our utterance, as the sandcastle, soon disappears. For the waves of suffering never abate, which is why everything, including the words responsible for expressing the suffering that has ejected them, eventually is sucked out to the unbounded sea of silence, to rejoin the whirlpool of experience within whose muteness they had so fleetingly just bubbled forth. And so, as suffering by the very essence of its amplitude perpetually defies our capacity to speak adequately in the wake of what its passage has given us to understand, the following remarks, which will attempt to say something on the matter nevertheless, are brief. And a not unfitting choice! In the end, a note on suffering does as well as the treatise.

Art is not salvation. That is the central thought. As obvious as the lesson may seem, it is one Friedrich Nietzsche never accepted. To exalt art in this way is to bow before the postmodern commonplace, one so prevalent today that we hardly notice it, that sees suffering as a passage to nothing beyond itself. Most think that we suffer without end, or more fundamentally, without purpose. And if art comes to be treated as a form of salvation, as our postmodern condition does, it is because art grapples with the pangs of suffering. And when attention turns to suffering, the issue of salvation cannot be far off.

Nietzsche's own thought that so often returns to art, but also to the affirmation of life in light of suffering, is a thought that strains to articulate a coherent and viable conception of salvation. Here, the task is to understand why in turning to art for justification, Nietzsche failed to affirm life convincingly. Why, we shall ask, does art fail to save from suffering's trial?

To make a start, we note an oddity provisionally. Any thought that attempts to think power, yet ultimately treats suffering as something to be stylized, is thereby powerless. Powerless to make sense of suffering. Powerless to make sense of its own powerlessness to justify suffering. And not just impotent but delusional. Or better, helpless in its choice to hand itself over to a plastic salvation that having affirmed the death of God finds itself thereby unable to affirm life. Life accordingly is reduced to an aesthetic phenomenon, and it is far from clear that this is a good thing. Life becomes wholly a matter of style, of deciding how one as an individual will make suffering one's own.[1] Consequently, suffering becomes a reality delimited strictly within the horizon of our being-toward-death and that alone. Hence, today the venerable (and sacred!) idea that there is a transcendent meaning to suffering is a notion many have learned to laugh at. But should they? It is worth noting that even Nietzsche never did. He took the question seriously. In *On the Genealogy of Morality*, he observes that our modern form of existence suffers from a crisis of meaning because of suffering itself, for it lacks any compelling answer to what might justify that suffering: "The meaningless of suffering, not suffering itself, was the curse thus far stretched over humanity."[2] Ever burdened by boredom, pain, anxiety, and the impending fate of a humiliating death, life stands in need of justification, but fails to find one in willing its own ends.

In what suffering's meaning consists—or whether there is one and assuming there is not, what in turn are we to do about that—is a primary concern for those thinking immediately under the influence of Kant. Persuaded by the basics of Kant's idealism, Schopenhauer for one in *The World as Will and Representation* contends that the world as it is understood ordinarily (the world of empirical reality) is only a representation of true reality and thus an illusion that veils the thing in itself. The key point, however, is precisely that: for Schopenhauer unlike Kant, representation veils, without entirely obstructing our access to the truth of the world, which as he claims is said to consist in will. Existence as we know it is not reality in itself. Existence in the *lifeworld* immersed within a practical field of stably differentiated objects causally and intelligibly related to one another, is not the way those things are in themselves—for independently of our spatio-temporal experience of them they are not even individuated things but rather that which we know-not-what.[3] The realm of *principium individuationis* is appearance, nothing more.

The ordinary consciousness of such existence is far from pleasant, as Schopenhauer notes. It is painful and often even horrific, characterized by a dissatisfaction resulting from an insatiable desire, incessant anxiety, and omnipresent boredom. Thus, the best of all possible worlds according to Schopenhauer would be one where we ourselves do not exist. But as we do, the very next best thing is to die soon. Existence is worthless, and hence the task of it becomes learning how to deny it, to increasingly wean oneself from the lure of a desire whose end is always suffering. His thought's pessimism is deeply metaphysical in that while it affirms with Kant a distinction between reality and appearance, it makes room for a kind of insight into the absolute—the world as will. It is the nature of the will itself that explains why Schopenhauer's thought ends with a denial of existence. We may bracket the many paradoxes arising from the idea that we can access what is said to be the thing in itself, and focus instead simply on what it is said to be, with an eye to the pessimistic interpretation of suffering it entails. The world that in itself is will, says Schopenhauer, is an impersonal, blind-striving without concern for anyone or anything, creating and destroying in a never-ending frenzy of passion. How, one naturally asks, do we know that lying at the heart of existence is a writhing, all-consuming will devouring everything? For one, we encounter glimpses of it within the world of appearance. The things of empirical reality including above all our own lives (our lives as individuals) are ruled by desire. The world as will comes most perspicuously into view in aesthetic experience. This is where, as Schopenhauer claims, we are liberated from egoistic desires and concerns, and thereby freed from the burden of anxiety and pain as we contemplate in serenity the Forms.[4] Interrupting the day's ordinary course of events and the ordinary consciousness as well, aesthetic experience transports us elsewhere than the world of representation. As he says, aesthetic contemplation is "the Sabbath of the penal servitude of willing."[5] This is a world unlike the everyday one, for it is one of primal unity. What is typically experienced is revealed to be illusion, including our existence as individual selves. We may ignore the questions this characterization of aesthetic experience calls to mind. One wonders how, if the world in itself is a frenzy of undifferentiated primal striving, an encounter with it in aesthetic experience can be conducive to the peace of stillness. And if one's own individual existence is an illusion, then who is the one who yearns to escape it? Such questions be what they may, the point of concern is that life, which Schopenhauer here characterizes in terms of futile suffering, is seen to be lamentable, to the point of total worthlessness.

The problem is obvious. For no matter however tranquilizing aesthetic experience may be, its salvation is only intermittent—and hence, as Schopenhauer himself recognizes, it is not really a redemption as it never lasts. And if it never lasts, this impermanence is because the pain it learns to bear by dissociating itself from existence is always imprisoned within a future consigned to more pain and anxiety. Precisely as it lacks hope, it is subject to the torment of a present without abiding peace. For Schopenhauer then, who always thinks within a horizon that has decided to ignore God, existence accordingly comes down to a twofold denial. And without doubt, there is an admirable moral sentiment to Schopenhauer's assessment. To begin with, it is prudentially necessary to deny our ordinary experience, since it is an illusion that only ends in the tyranny of suffering. And furthermore, the will itself lying beyond the representational world must be denied as well. But here the denial is not prudential only—the concern is not to be rid of the suffering originating in our egoistic desires. Rather, this denial of the will is moral, because it is rooted in compassion for others and the suffering that bonds us. Because it is the will that produces the horrific evils taking place within the *principium individuationis*, so in the interest of compassion it must be repudiated.[6] Art, then, makes it possible to endure existence—but that is the most we can expect. Life is not to be embraced, but made to be bearable. Hence, Schopenhauer's final verdict: as life is suffering and therefore not worth living, so it should be denied rather than affirmed. Aesthetic experience points to asceticism.

As for Nietzsche, his is a thinking that remains ambivalent about the value of existence. On the one hand, it is plain from the beginning with *The Birth of Tragedy* that he desires to reject the pessimistic thesis that life cannot be justified. On the other hand, it is exceedingly difficult to see how that existence can be affirmed for what it is, without the intermediary of illusions. In order for life to be affirmed, such affirmation will be possible only as an aesthetic phenomenon. And that, as *The Birth of Tragedy* states, here means an affirmation entailing illusions will be necessary to tolerate life. Thus, when Nietzsche later says in his career (particularly in the *The Gay Science* and elsewhere during the "middle" period) that art struggles against pessimism, this is something of a departure from his initial position, which seemed to assert, with Schopenhauer, that it is not possible to affirm life if it is faced for what it is. To say, then, as Nietzsche for example does in section 821 of the *Will to Power*, "There is no such thing as pessimistic art—Art affirms," simply raises the question of what exactly it *is* affirming. Life—to be sure, but a life seen fully in its truth, or one that is in some way or other aided with illusions?

In *The Birth of Tragedy*, life is not affirmable without recourse to illusion, whether it be Apollonian beauty, Dionysian frenzy, or a combination of both. Art, as Nietzsche makes clear there, does not provide metaphysical *knowledge* justifying life (life in itself is not beautiful), but rather it gives us metaphysical *solace*, placative illusions in the form of myth that makes life bearable. It is illusion then, not the unvarnished truth, that makes life worth living. Life is worth living as an aesthetic phenomenon only then, in this sense, because only art makes what would otherwise be unbearable tolerable.

Far from challenging pessimism, such an understanding of art presupposes it: life is to be endured with the help of illusion, not embraced for what it really is. Without the aesthetic illusion of Apollonian beauty, we would lack the strength to accept the ugly truth of what we could not bear.

The indispensability of illusion for affirming life is underscored repeatedly by the text. In the last analysis, as Nietzsche claims, the Apollonian art responsible for allowing the Greeks to see things with a "profound superficiality"[7] did not affirm things as they were, but rather sanitized them, leaving a shining plastic veneer on all things. It provided a way of seeing them as beautiful, but in doing so the gaze that sees such beauty must always take precautions to be selective and ever partial, cautious to maintain its dreamworld from the intrusion of what would accordingly dash it to pieces, since if one were to look on things otherwise, everything would no longer appear so beautiful and ennobling but rather ugly and horrific. As for the Socratic attitude that places its confidence in knowledge, it too is no less an illusion. First, because it believes that the world as science takes it to be is how the world is. But that equivalence is mere delusion, says Nietzsche. In this regard Nietzsche remains too Kantian to endorse any kind of naive scientific realism. It is illusory, second, because it supposes that the truth is not cause for despair but optimism. It believes the world can be made better if it is come to be known better. That assumption is to overestimate not just humanity's ability to control and improve nature, but to think reality is amenable to any positive fundamental and lasting change. And why think that, asks Nietzsche. Is not there as much reason, if not more of one, to think the world is chaos?

Here one might say: very well then, embrace the chaos! This is the third attitude, the Dionysian. It too is a species of illusion. For even if the orgiastic creative frenzy of Dionysianism revels in what it takes to be the primal unity writhing beyond the Apollonian rationality of individual consciousness, this flight into unbridled and supraindividual pathos is exactly that—a flight, a gesture of escapism from our identity as individuals. Thus, Dionysianism does not so much embrace the suffering of individual existence so much as it transfigures that suffering by dissolving away the very individual who would otherwise have had to face it. In its intoxicating (and thereby narcoticizing) exuberance, it takes metaphysical solace in being what it is not—discontent with being a single individual handed over to suffering, it responds to the suffering of individual existence by embracing a frenzied self-annihilation. The Dionysian is not a genuine affirmation of life but a despair over being oneself.

If existence is unjustifiable without illusion, is that to conclude Nietzsche (like Schopenhauer before him) is a pessimist? The answer depends. Unlike Schopenhauer for whom individuality is said to be worthless because of its suffering, Nietzsche's concerns appear to be slightly different. What matters foremost here is the *meaning* of suffering, or more exactly, what meaning can justifiably be accorded to it. Suffering per se is not problematic. Who can forget his famous criticisms of utilitarianism, which he castigates for the idea that life's value hangs on the pursuit of pleasure and the avoidance of pain? If anything then, his own aesthetic justification of life is an inversion of traditional hedonism. In the later thinking on the eternal recurrence, *amor fati*, and the will-to-power, pain itself becomes the source of pleasure, and hence the source of value. Pain is not that which we affirm life in despite of, but because of. Perhaps illusion is not now so necessary as before, for the very presupposition that suffering is bad (and hence requires a justification) has been largely thrown out the window. As Nietzsche says during this period, if the essence of will-to-power consists in the satisfaction one takes in overcoming the resistance of obstacles standing in the way of one's desired ends, the pain that comes in between us and what we are trying to accomplish becomes something we in turn affirm, since in affirming the end we have, one that is reachable only through the crucible of suffering, we thereby will everything, including the suffering itself, that unfolds in having exercised such power. Now there is a certain satisfaction (prideful to be sure!) intermingled in it, one that, in having willed what it has despite the suffering, therefore sees itself as superior to mere "lower types" who take pleasure merely in pleasure and who, lacking the strength to will their own suffering in the pursuit of the attainment of something great, do not know how to transfigure pain into a true pleasure. A profound nobility is said to characterize such suffering, one making whoever has penetrated to its inner secret accordingly superior to everyone who has not. A pain that delights in pain! A pleasurable pain! A pleasure in the pain! This is what Nietzscheanism reduces to, a kind of masochism that must convince itself that pain is not what it is.

It is one of his thoughts' many inspiring merits that Kierkegaard consistently exposes the false presupposition shared by both Schopenhauer and Nietzsche: he will challenge the claim that suffering has no purpose at all (if any) besides what we creatively give it. His rejection of the aesthetic ideal is highlighted in his no less audacious but sober claim that anxiety, contrary to what Schopenhauer and Nietzsche assume, is not unsurpassable. Against the idea that anxiety is a fundamental *Grundstimmung* of existence, a necessary feature of existence as it must be lived, Kierkegaard will explain how it is not so. Anxiety is not a fate but a decision. In his edifying discourse on the lilies and the birds, he emphasizes that it is possible to overcome the torments of anxiety. But if this is to be done, it initially will be necessary to accept the truth of suffering: that means recognizing in the first place that it does have a meaning, but a meaning that is only evident in the light of eternity. This eternal perspective does not annul the individuality but heightens it. It is not a depersonalizing perspective associated with the Hegelian conception of *sub specie aeternitatis*, one that forgets about oneself by substituting the system of world history for the individual—that sort of fanciful self-forgetting is if anything more in keeping with Schopenhauer's and Nietzsche's respective repudiation of the idea that the suffering of an individual human being can be justified and affirmed truthfully, without recourse to illusions or myth. At the beginning of *Fear and Trembling*, in the section entitled "Eulogy on Abraham," Kierkegaard describes the view of the world as both Schopenhauerian pessimism (a cruel and malevolent primal oneness to be denied) and Nietzschean Dionysianism (as an orgiastic frenzy of chaos to be embraced) see it. It is one, call it the aesthetic view, that if true would rule out any genuine affirmation of individual human suffering as impossible:

> If a human being did not have an eternal consciousness, if underlying everything there were only a wild, fermenting power that writhing in dark passions produced everything, be it significant or insignificant, if a vast, never appeased emptiness hid beneath everything, what would life be then but despair? If such were the situation, if there were no sacred bond that knit humankind together, if one generation emerged after another like forest foliage, if one generation succeeded another like the singing of the birds in the forest, if a generation passed through the world as a ship through the sea, as wind through the desert, as unthinking and unproductive performance, if an eternal oblivion, perpetually hungry, lurked for its prey and there were no power strong enough to wrench that away from it—how empty and devoid of consolation life would be![8]

Given his account of reality that denies human individuality, for Schopenhauer the task of life becomes one of overcoming the very illusion that it is worth living. For Nietzsche things are slightly different insofar as the task instead is said to be one of constructing myths that make affirming it possible. Yet in either case, the single individual's life and suffering is taken to be without any truthful justification. Individual existence must be rejected altogether, or else augmented with aesthetic lies. Taken exhaustively, these two options present a false dichotomy. To assert that they are the only two options would be too quick. Kierkegaard will recommend we walk another way, claiming it is possible to affirm life for what it is (without myth) and hence free from the intrusion of placating lies. There is suffering, but that does not mean life is worthless (Schopenhauer) nor that it can be embraced only via illusion (Nietzsche). The truth is not so frail! To begin with, existing in either of the ways proposed by Schopenhauer and Nietzsche is tantamount to choosing despair. Hence, it should be avoided at all costs. To avoid it successfully, what is required is a form of life that stands opposed to what these two images of an existence handed over to death become. There must be a life that overcomes death, by depriving of it the last word, thereby making true joy possible, not by escape into illusion but through rejoicing in the truth. It is no wonder that neither Schopenhauer nor Nietzsche, for whom both the death of God is axiomatic, were never able to articulate anything besides a tormented pessimism or a manic aestheticism. For them, it is the world and not God that is the absolute. And when we live in the world, entirely consumed with the time beset by the burdens of worry, we bear the weight of existence on our own.[9] But there is nothing courageous in it. It is unnecessary, and so to that extent it also is foolish. To exist wholly dissipated into the time of concern, this is not *life* as Kierkegaard understands it, for without God the resulting existence makes death its lord. Consequently, it is a living death, no life at all.

In a meditation named "The Happiness of Eternity," Kierkegaard characterizes suffering otherwise than do the assistant professors, poets, and voluptuaries alike. For him, suffering should be seen as capable of procuring a point, a view of its purposiveness that Nietzsche himself was of course to reject. And for Kierkegaard, seeing the point to suffering is to see it in perspective, which is to say it must be weighed in light of eternal life. Then its burden is not so heavy as when eternity is neglected. As Kierkegaard says, "For when indeed does the temporal suffering oppress a man most terribly? Is it not when it seems to him that it has no significance, that it neither secures nor gains anything for him? Is it not when the suffering, as the impatient man expresses it, is without meaning or purpose?"[10] To experience suffering as without a point, he says, is to have discarded eternity. The aesthetic stylization of suffering in strictly temporal terms is delusional and not only powerless then, for neglecting the joy that comes with anticipating eternal happiness, it makes suffering heavier than it is or needs to be.

There is an objection waiting in the wings. Is not this way of viewing suffering that Kierkegaard proposes—in short, the way that follows Christ in suffering—itself the illusion? Talk of an eternal happiness? Fantasy! A life-denying phantasmagoria, if Nietzsche is to be believed. As he will continually insist, suffering must be borne without thinking there is anything to redeem our suffering beyond this world. Rejecting the notion that suffering will be redeemed in a world to come, Nietzsche consequently avers that it be embraced here and now, as and for what it is—for him, without any reason or meaning beyond the one we give it ourselves. But here things are not so obvious. For has not Nietzsche contradicted himself? To begin with, his criticism of life in Christ as life-denying overlooks that his own alternatives for how to justify life either resort to illusion or end up being psychologically infeasible—who can truly embrace purposeless pain as meaningful? And if life in Christ is to be derided on the supposed grounds of truth, as if it can be ruled out simply because it obviously is untrue, it is worth noting that what Nietzsche rather thoughtlessly dismisses as myth—we mean here the testimony of Jesus Christ as revealed in his life, death, and resurrection, as recorded in the scriptures and as attested by the Spirit that has quickened anyone who comes to know him personally—is a life that has much more in the way of supporting evidence going for it than anything Nietzsche articulates of his own. And finally, the question as to whether a secular myth—be it Apollonian or Dionysian or tragic—is preferable aesthetically to life in the Spirit, that too is dubious. Was Dostoevsky wrong when he was to note that, even if he were to somehow learn (*per impossibile*) that Christ was outside the truth, he would go with Christ rather than the truth? The beauty of Christ and the life he makes possible is surely more so than what any German philosopher has ever coherently articulated.

Therefore, it is not surprising in the least that someone as Nietzsche, who always wanted to assess human existence in fundamentally amoral terms—beyond good and evil, as it were—could never comprehend the true psychological impulse behind the Christian response to suffering. Not a life-denying escapism but a love of the good that manifests itself just as equally in a corresponding hatred of a world, which, being as evil as it is, therefore is worthy of its righteous disavowal.[11] This is not, as Nietzsche too hastily assumes, a denial of life per se, but simply an affirmation of the fact that reality as we experience it in this present evil world is unworthy of such life—Eternal Life, as it has been revealed and given through Jesus Christ. Thus, if suffering is to be justified, it is not as an aesthetic phenomenon, but a moral one only. Only then does suffering have a meaning, and only then can it be affirmed on the basis of truth, without illusion. To with Kierkegaard invoke eternity in matters of suffering means in part to take responsibility for oneself by hating evil, and hence the world for its evil. But that in no way should be confused with a hatred of life. To the contrary, hatred of the world affirms life, by refusing to seek refuge in the inhumanity of a depersonalized and uncompassionate dreamworld, where others and oneself come to be experienced in the detached and thereby deranged gaze that has forgotten what it is to be human.

To conclude, we simply observe that suffering presents us with a decision. On the one hand, we may choose to endure it alone, experiencing ourselves under the crushing burden of a time leading to death, thereby rendering that time in the interim as one with no point at all. To exist aesthetically in this way, like we and the world are beyond good and evil yet somehow still capable of a redemption, is possible. This is the aesthetic life many choose for themselves. It is possible to exist this way, but there is no peace in it. And as for art which this existence substitutes for God, it may help to save us intermittently from the pain of everyday existence, but it cannot by any means save us from its anxieties. It cannot deliver us from anxiety for the reason that it cannot redeem us from evil; only God can do that. Along the way just described, thus, lies only death. But there is always another way open. We may endure with God in mind and eternal happiness in view. Arguments have been marshaled by philosophers on behalf of both positions. And we have recounted a few of them briefly here. But they are positions, which means they ultimately are reached by having first resolved to take a stand. Pain and intellection, after all, are not of the same order. Suffering therefore always remains a matter of the same form in which it first makes itself known, as an immediate problem for life, and one that thereby renders impossible any resolution through thought alone. Inexorably, suffering accordingly confronts us with a choice. And for that reason, it calls upon the whole heart of our being. The freedom is ours to decide how to meet it. In joy with hope, or not.

NOTES

1. For Nietzsche, an aesthetic response to suffering takes on the weight of a practical imperative, as when in *The Gay Science* (trans. Walter Kaufmann [New York: Vintage Books, 1974], 232) he states that in giving one's character its distinctive style one must "turn oneself into a work of art" (290).

2. Nietzsche, *On the Genealogy of Morality*, trans. Maudemarie Clark and Alan Swensen (Indianapolis: Hackett, 1998), III, 28. Schopenhauer claims life is worthless because of suffering. Or more precisely, it is because the suffering is *absurd*—it lacks any purpose. In his very perceptive *Nietzsche's Philosophy of Art*, Julian Young emphasizes how Nietzsche's both earliest and latest thinking on art seem to end in pessimism as well. Some have criticized the idea that Nietzsche's concern is suffering per se. See Ken Gemes and Chris Skyes, "Nietzsche's Illusion," in *Nietzsche on Art and Life*, ed. Daniel Came (Oxford: University of Oxford Press, 2014), 80–106. Although it may be true that Nietzsche is concerned with the meaning of suffering ultimately, it seems inaccurate to accuse Schopenhauer (and thus Young) as not saying essentially the same. Schopenhauer makes it clear, I think, that his pessimistic judgment of the world is rooted in what he takes to be the evident *absurdity* of life, not just that we suffer. Thus, the matter of whether suffering is justified is part of the matter of whether everything under the sun is vanity—or not.

3. This is a notion that the phenomenological tradition, from Husserl on, has rejected. From the phenomenological perspective, the transcendental one of Husserl especially so, an unknowable thing in itself is nonsense. As he says famously in §41 of *Cartesian Meditations*, "If transcendental subjectivity is the universe of possible sense, then an outside is precisely—nonsense."

4. Often this liberation from desire characterizing aesthetic experience is said to be one of absolute passivity. For an interpretation of what the aesthetic reduction brackets about ordinary experience, where that bracketing is taken not to involve a total passivity but rather simply one of our egoistic and selfish desires, see A. E. Denham, "Attuned, Transcendent, and Transfigured: Nietzsche's Appropriation of Schopenhauer's Aesthetic Psychology," in *Nietzsche on Art and Life*, ed. Daniel Came (Oxford: Oxford University Press, 2014), 163–200.

5. Schopenhauer, *The World as Will and Representation,* vol. 1, ed. Judith Norman, Alistair Welchman, and Christopher Janaway (Cambridge: Cambridge University Press, 2011), 220. For an incredible phenomenological study that analyses the work of art in sabbatical terms (emphasizing Heidegger, not Schopenhauer), see Jean-Yves Lacoste, *Le monde et l'absence d'oeuvre* (Paris: Paris Universitaires de France, 2000).

6. Julian Young notes well that it is Schopenhauer, and not Nietzsche, who offers the more humane response to the world's suffering, since it allows for a human solidarity and compassion that Nietzsche's view of life does not. A purely aesthetic outlook courts monstrosity: "There is, it seems to me, something ugly, inhuman even, one is tempted to add, Wagnerian about a willingness not only to condone but even to inhabit a state of mind willing to deploy human individuals as mere means to the production of artist—god's spectacular, bloody, cosmic epic," *Nietzsche's Philosophy of Art* (Cambridge: Cambridge University Press, 1992), 54–55. For indications of how the Dionysian perspective might lend itself to sadistic cruelty,

see the text itself, Friedrich Nietzsche, *The Birth of Tragedy out of the Spirit of Music*, trans. Walter Kaufmann (New York: Vintage, 1967).

7. An expression he uses in aphorism 4 of *The Gay Science*: "What is required is to stop courageously at the surface, the fold, the skin, to adore appearance, to believe in forms, tones, words, in the whole Olympus of appearance! Those Greeks were superficial—*out of profundity!*"

8. Kierkegaard, *Fear and Trembling*, trans. Edna Hong and Howard Hong (Princeton, NJ: Princeton University Press, 1983), 15. For a notable analysis of the problem of individuality in its specifically German Idealist context, see Michelle Kosch, *Freedom and Reason in Kant, Schelling, and Kierkegaard* (New York: Oxford University Press, 2006).

9. Perhaps the best analysis of the torments plaguing this kind of existence (and which makes constant reference to Kierkegaard) is a relatively recent one. See Jérôme de Gramont, *Le discours de la vie: Trois essais sur Platon, Kierkegaard et Nietzsche* (Paris: L'Harmattan, 2001).

10. Kierkegaard, *The Gospel of Suffering*, trans. David F. Swenson and Lillian Marvin Swenson (Minneapolis, MN: Augsburg Publishing House, 1948), 126–27.

11. This raises the general question of theodicy, including its viability or very possibility. For one attempt, see Richard Swinburne, "Some Major Strands of Theodicy," in *The Evidential Argument from Evil*, ed. Daniel Howard-Snyder (Bloomington, IN: Indiana University Press, 1996) 30–48. But even if one is disinclined to embrace theistic theodicies, at least two things must be kept in mind when it comes specifically to the question of suffering. First, to take the existence of suffering as a *prima facie* problem for theism, as the evidential problem of evil does, presupposes that suffering *is* an evil (a view Nietzsche himself rejects), and second, that as it is an evil, there must be such a thing as the good. But what is the standard of good and evil here? It seems, then, that it is impossible to formulate a traditional argument from evil against theism from a Nietzschean perspective, since the latter either denies that suffering is an evil, or else denies that there even is any genuine moral standard of good and evil by which theism can be criticized. Finally, it should be noted that, to whatever extent one finds theistic theodicies implausible, Schopenhauer and Nietzsche (and others) are in effect attempting to offer secular theodicies: to ask after the question of what makes suffering justifiable is, even in the aesthetic context, to ask what makes it in some sense permissible or in general good or okay.

Chapter Eight

The Light That Lights Every Man

The world is broken, and there is no fixing it. The routine events of our common experience remind us daily that this is not the stuff of an Elysium, where goodness and wisdom are rewarded and evil and foolishness punished. Quite the opposite! Media glorify stupidity and deviancy. Wickedness boasts. Mediocrity prevails. There can be no disputing that in this life happiness is not a destiny. And for that reason, neither is justice.

Hence, the reasons for the impossibility of fixing the world are as layered as they are interconnected. Let us recite some of the most significant. First, if we are frank, it is necessary to acknowledge that it is not even possible for everyone to reach an agreement over what precisely fixing it would entail, or in what that would consist. Politics in practice is never a point of fraternity but of discord. Perhaps the only universal in this domain is disagreement itself: in every time and place, whether it be ancient Rome or Sparta, Napoleonic France or Rwanda and South Africa, there have been calls and efforts to reform society, yet strife regarding how to do so. This leads to the recognition of a second. Forming any particularly vivid conception of this world we wish we could know now is impossible. Of it, there are glimmers only. Conceiving how the world ought to be calls upon our power of imagination as much as it does our capacities for practical or theoretical reason—and for good reason. Here, mostly we are stumbling in the dark. If pressed to specify in any detail what is floating before our mind, our speech and thought are thrown back ineluctably onto this world, and all that we dislike about it. Without doubt a presentiment of a better world exists, but it is received obliquely, arriving reflected from an elsewhere none of us has seen directly.

And so there subsists an indistinct image of a better world haunting our everyday experience of this one, an idealistic world beyond the familiar world, never grasped clearly or distinctly, instead only experienced as a projection in reference to everything we so detest about this present one. Consequently, it is much easier to state all that is wrong with this world than to clarify what the best of all possible worlds would be exactly.

Yet despite the remarkably evident absence of any consensus regarding what the world should be, and despite the corresponding lack of any substantive or comprehensive conception regarding what bringing about such a world would involve precisely, there is a predictable objection and it must be addressed. Against what has just been made plain, this objection will insist on acting as if it does not already see what has just been shown and which everyone sees. Instead, feigning genuine ignorance, it asks: is not to say that the world cannot be fixed thus to condone (or even aid) various forms of injustice (social, political, or economic)? This objection, a favorite of those who like to appear compassionate because they are not, in defiance of what has already been noted about both the brokenness of the world and the limits of our ability to either imagine or produce one better than this one, proceeds undeterred, claiming that acceptance of the world's fundamental imperfectability is quietist, which is just to say a morally objectionable form of defeatism. No matter how many times the objection is used, however, it can always be turned back against itself. Quite evidently, it displays a lack of the same compassion it alleges it sees lacking in those it has criticized. For although it claims to sympathize with the oppressed, at bottom, its righteous indignation in the face of social injustice is embarrassingly shallow. It chastises others for saying the world cannot be radically changed or improved, but it does not ache before the suffering of the world nearly as badly as it pretends. Perhaps it sympathizes the least of all! At a minimum, it certainly does so less than some. For in the last analysis, only someone who has not allowed the horror, sorrow, and injustice of the world to transform him could ever assert, as this objection does so cavalierly, that it is wrong to accept the world cannot be fixed. Only someone who has never truly felt the world's brokenness (or who does not care for it as much as he says) could accuse those of moral lethargy who admit to a powerlessness in the face of the world's overpowering evil and injustice. Hence, contrary to what this objection implied, the real hypocrites are not those who admit to the brokenness of the world and go on living knowing so but those who claim to believe that the world can be radically changed while knowing that it cannot. As for these who are so aghast at whoever accepts the idea of the world's irreparable brokenness, they put on a show. It is emotional artifice. If those who superficially wield this objection confronted the horrors of existence, they would fall silent rather than pontificate about a suffering they dishonor when they cheapen it, having turned human suffering into an opportunity for their shallow and self-indulgent posturing. To be sure, no one can deny that it is self-serving to pretend there is nothing to be done about a situation when looking to excuse oneself from having to address it; and still, it is no less despicable to claim a situation is not without remedy when one knows that it is, all simply with the intent that by saying so, by claiming to see there is hope where there is none, one may appear to others to be more noble than those who are sensitive enough to concede what everyone knows and have admitted to the human impossibility of making the world fundamentally better than it is.

It may seem like it, but to charge this objection with disingenuous optimism is not equivalent to pushing for pessimism. Rather, it is the necessary first step in making room for the real optimism. While a better world may not be attainable by us, the idea for that matter is not a complete mirage. Practical infeasibility is not synonymous with complete incoherence. There is hope yet, but it must be located in the right place, which is why pretending as if political, social, and economic revolutions will produce a perfect world is to claim to be hopeful without really being so. Hope must be honest, for it must persist in the face of what would otherwise drive anyone without it to despair, and here such honesty means finding hope in the face of reality as it is, which as history attests means seeing that there is no hope of there one day being a better world in this one. This is the threshold all true hope must cross. True hope, in short, *is not of this world* because it has the strength to admit that the world as we know it, if left to itself, is hopeless and will remain so.

It is precisely for this reason that Arthur Schopenhauer, looking out upon the immensity of the world's suffering, was driven to hopelessness. For him, pessimism is rationalism for it is to admit what everyone can see plainly. He was not the only thinker to turn to philosophy as a way of coping with our world, so far from ideal. On April 8, 1929, on the occasion of a Festschrift held to celebrate his seventieth birthday, Husserl in reply to his student Heidegger's speech indirectly addresses the sorrow of the world and, echoing Boethius, alludes to philosophy's consolations. As Husserl notes, life in the world as he experiences it was bearable only because of the freedom to think of things as being otherwise than how they really are. "On one point I must demur," he remarked, "and that is the talk about great merits. I have none. Philosophy was the mission of my life. I had to philosophize, otherwise I could not live in *this* world."[1] Husserl's comment is ambiguous between two (or maybe more) senses of the world. On one natural way of understanding the term, the world is the *lifeworld*, the immediate and absolute horizon for all action, thought, and understanding. It is the place of meaning wherein we encounter entities while thereby working out a sense of what it means to be the individuals we are. When understood in this sense, it is the world as the transcendental horizon of possible experience. This sense is the one that has guided philosophical thinking, and the phenomenological tradition above all, to a considerable extent. Yet in the world there is great suffering, evil, and injustice. The world, as we know, and as Husserl's own poignant remark implies, is not simply a place where I perceive an apple tree in blossom or wield a hammer in the workshop. It also is a place of unfairness and suffering. Most fundamentally, it also is a place of death. As for this first sense of world as the transcendental horizon of intelligibility, it thereby implicates the individual to whom everything is disclosed: me (and others too whom I live alongside), a finite subject (or better: a mortal being) handed over to the world's absolute horizon, that of death. Within this transcendental horizon of significance, within this horizon of men wherein we see to our tasks and affairs, things are held hostage to the everyday world's absolute reference frame, the pale horse of our shared being-toward-death.

Death is enough to remind us that this is not paradise. Thus, it raises by straightforward contraposition, however subtly, the subject of utopia, a term originating in Thomas More's work by that name.[2] In many ways the modern heir to Plato's *Republic*, More's classic is a work that we may set to the side along with its ancient forerunner, since so much has already been said about the both of them. For it is the lesser known (but no less intriguing!) works of the genre that here can pique our interest. And it is not novelty that counts. There is a principled reason for selection of the texts to follow. In developing their respective conceptions of the ideal community, these utopian works articulate not just an illuminating account of how society should be, but in doing so they draw attention to what makes the everyday one we all experience so imperfect. To use a rich expression coined by Jean-Luc Marion, they prompt us to *think elsewhere*. And in what follows, so we shall! Not a century after More's 1516 first edition of *Utopia*, the Italian Dominican Tomasso Campanella published *Civitas Solis*, a work many readers have observed may have served as an immediate and direct influence on subsequent Renaissance utopian treatises. For example, only a few years after Campanella had articulated his vision of the ideal community, in 1619 the German theologian Johannes Valentinus Andreae debuted his. It was not long after this work, *A Description of the Republic of Christianopolis*, had appeared that it was already being accused of unoriginality. Borrowing too heavily from the Campanellan vision of the perfect city, Andreae's Christianopolis is said to be in key respects largely indistinguishable from the earlier utopia. The matter of personal or literary influence is not altogether trivial. But even assuming the notion of a considerable influence is true, does conceding that the two are similar mean, as sometimes is thought, that this counts as objection to what they have to say? Far from discrediting the importance of either work, their potential convergence can be seen just as easily as a great merit. After all, utopian literature, which very often is dismissed as being too fantastical, as a mere projection of its author's own predilections, in these two texts at least evinces a similarity in substance indicating something tangible or objective. Are not our utopians perhaps *seeing* something? It would explain the similarity in what they describe. With that philosophical possibility in mind, the resemblance of Andreae's vision to Campanella's can be understood not as a mark of literary unoriginality but as involving something at stake beyond mere literary influence: could there be a transcendent essence illuminating their shared vision? A consensus in view here indicates something more akin to the intuition of an archetype and not, as so often is said against utopian works, the reflection of individual temperament.

As for the work itself, a sea journey is its opening plot device. The choice fits since the work becomes a voyage for the reader who undertakes it. In a tone anticipating Kierkegaard's own critique of Christendom two centuries later, Andreae's work criticizes the social, economic, political, and spiritual condition of the world as he finds it. Hypocrisy, sophistry, and tyranny rule. A pilgrim or wanderer in the world, our hero embarks on a journey looking for escape aboard a ship aptly named *Fantasy*, whereupon he is shipwrecked on the shores of a faraway island. With the sea acting as a metaphor for the world and the shipwreck as one of conversion, the island where the colony of Christianopolis is located represents a kind of heaven. It is a haven from the outside, a refuge from the world, for, running on principles wholly contrary to those of the world's ways, the city (or as commentators have noted, more like a reformed monastery) is one wherein the inhabitants live in universal harmony, governed by the triumvirate of Religion, Justice, and Learning.[3]

Steps must be taken to preserve it, lest it become like the world! To safeguard the community from unwanted intrusion and hence ruin, not just anyone who stumbles upon it is automatically welcome. Accordingly, our castaway hero is submitted to an examination designed to test whether he has the right disposition to contribute to the city successfully. The questioning gently begins with the man who has discovered him ashore. On their walk to the city's gates, the hero's companion stresses that "beggars, hucksters and actors (who make idleness enjoyable), curiosity-seekers (who pry minutely into anything unfamiliar), fanatics (who have no genuine piety), alchemists (who defile Chemistry), imposters (who gives out falsely that they are Rosicrucian brethren), and other similar blemishes on the sciences and arts,"[4] will not be tolerated. Their presence is not permitted. Upon pledging to "hold to the truth and follow goodness,"[5] he is given food and a change of clothes and is entrusted to the care of his first companion's colleagues. The second encounter is draining, for his next examiner, though gentle and friendly and kind like the first, is spiritually intense and perceptive. It is as if he sees the secrets of the heart. Explaining to the hero that life in Christianopolis presents the opportunity to be "freed from now on from the ties of the world,"[6] the hero feels himself being evaluated as to the calmness of his soul and his manner of character. "This he did," the voyager tells us, "with such skill that I felt he could scrutinize my very thought, yet he did it with such kindness that I could hold back nothing,"[7] an encounter so intense and penetrating that when his examiner turns at last to the question of knowledge our hero is flummoxed. How can the matter of knowledge have already not yet been raised, when he is already intellectually exhausted and at the limit of his mind's energies? "'Will you excuse me, my friend,' he said, 'for having chatted with you in such an uneducated sort of way? But do not lose hope, there will be no shortage of people for you in this place of ours who are true scholars.'"[8] If this is just a warmup, casual small talk, what sort of intellectual efforts await inside? The third examiner swiftly resolves the hero's question. The learning is as rigorous as it is expansive. Immediately, he is quizzed about what he has theretofore learned in the world: "He wanted to know from me, if in the most charming way, what I had learned of self-mastery, of service to my brother, of rebelling against the world, of resignation to death, of submission to the Spirit—and what I had learned from contemplating the heavens and the earth, and from a close study of nature. What did I know about scientific instruments, about the structure of languages, and about the harmony of all things? What dealings had I had with the fellowship of the church, the blessings of the scriptures, the kingdom of heaven, the school of the Spirit, the brotherhood of Christ, and the family of God?"[9] Faced with an acute awareness of his own ignorance and humbled by the need to penetrate more deeply into matters of which he possesses only the most cursory acquaintance, the hero is honest, telling his examiner that he knows essentially nothing of such things. And the confession is a success. For as he comes to see, his examiner appreciates his humility and his earnest desire to learn. Delighted with the hero's handling of the situation, he permits the hero entry to the city, as a clean slate prepared to learn the ways of wisdom and goodness. What lies inside Christianopolis?

A description ensues. It is smaller than one might have imagined, with only four hundred denizens. Architecturally, it is square in shape with a series of high outer walls and towers. Inside, there are buildings and gardens arranged within increasingly smaller quadrangles starting from the outer walls until reaching the city's center, at which the college stands. And no wonder a college, as education is paramount. As the hero soon discovers, Christianopolis is not only a place of moral uprightness and spiritual simplicity but of immense learning. While there are spaces for food and exercise (and some entertainment), ultimately the focus is contemplation. Everyone works, for in addition to intellectual learning there is wide craftsmanship. In addition, then, to the gardens and living quarters, there are sites dedicated to various endeavors. On the grounds are a library, archives, printing press, armory (one to be used only and reluctantly for defense), treasury, chemical and astronomical laboratories, pharmacy, museum of natural history (the walls are adorned by illustrations of the Great Chain of Being), arts studio, and lecture theaters. Clearly, the residents do not want for lack of intellectual stimulation. Accordingly, education is a priority, which is why, beginning at six, all children (boys and girls) are introduced into a program that will include grammar, rhetoric, logic, metaphysics, foreign languages, arithmetic, geometry, medicine, jurisprudence, history (natural, civil, and church), ethics, and political science; things can be strange, since there admittedly is a touch of the occult, with theosophy and mystic numbers included in the instruction, though Andreae is careful to emphasize the orthodox intentions of it, along with everything else. And just as education is paramount, so it proceeds in accord with priorities that are reversed from those found outside the colony walls. Inside Christianopolis, emphasis above all is placed on knowing God, and hence in growing in virtue. "The first and highest task they have," as our wayfarer reports, "is to worship God with a pure and devout mind; the second, is to achieve the best and most chaste morality; and the third is to develop their intellectual faculties."[10] Andreae's school is one that does not as ours ban prayer, but rather begins with it, unlike with the world, as he notes—and this is sensible, given the people's stated aspirations, which are summarized in the city's ten-article Constitution that reads as a slightly expanded Decalogue.[11] Knowledge is important but not absolute. Those who advance to the furthest stage of learning, having mastered everything the life of the mind could hope to know, undertake the final step of *unlearning* and hence the putting on of Christian poverty. People of this type are happy by having unlearned everything, abandoned everything, and suffered everything: "There are very few of these people, and it is easy to see that they can only be those who have already gone deeply into everything. Human affairs and human knowledge have already been laid bare to them, and after the uncertainties of the earth the only thing they wish for is the certainty of heaven."[12] In contrast to the academy we have today, which has become a kind of corrupt social welfare system for those who are unwilling (or unfit) to function anywhere else, in Andreae's vision, being a college instructor is not something reserved for moral failures: "Their teachers are not drawn from the dregs of humanity, people who are unfit for any other employment."[13] Teachers of Christianopolis excel in "dignity, integrity, industry and generosity."[14] A far cry from the lazy professor! And if it all sounds a little too stuffy, fanciful, or fanatical, in short, too much like what the contemporary imagination instinctively associates with the media's portrayal of a Waco, Andreae anticipates the objection and does well to turn it back on itself. In the world, he notes, "anyone who seeks the heavens may be judged to be heretical."[15] If then the Christianopolians are a strange people by the world's standards, as Andreae says, it is to their credit.

Andreae's true community prizes virtue and piety without thereby sacrificing the life of the mind. Extolling knowledge as it does, it therefore is bound, and understandably so, to elicit comparisons to Bacon's 1626 *New Atlantis*. But whereas Christianopolis is a community valuing knowledge without ever deifying it, Bacon's island of Bensalem elevates knowledge to the status of salvation. Pure science (and not at all like in Husserl's later philosophical sense!) becomes the highest of human ideals, the engine, we might say, of progress. As the early twentieth-century American sociologist Joyce Hertzler says of it in *The History of Utopian Thought*, "Its new program to attain Utopia was the rebuilding of society in the light of knowledge and discovery. Bacon shared and expressed the confidence of his time that wonderful things were to be revealed; and that nothing was impossible to man just provided he hit upon the right key to nature's secrets."[16] But is that spirit only a relic of Bacon's time? To the contrary, it still is with us. In Bacon's lionization of positive science and the conquest of nature, we see another example of the kind of scientific objectivism Michel Henry has done so well to trace from Galileo on, and which defines our age as well. For Bacon, nature is something to be subdued and exploited. It is a resource, a mine fit to satisfy our intellectual curiosity and practical demands.[17] Hence, the Baconian conception of nature exhibits the blinkered way of seeing nature so famously criticized by Heidegger's analysis of technology and ontotheology. But even more troubling, perhaps, are the political implications. There can be no doubt that this is a technocracy, a place where the scientific experts hold the power, keeping everyone else in the dark so they may sculpt the masses to be fit to do as they are told. Bacon's guardians are the scientists who know best, just as Aldous Huxley and Bertrand Russell would envision later in the twentieth century.[18] And if we find Bacon's fetishism for scientific expertise rather unnerving, it is not so much just because of its slavish prostration at the feet of its limited conception of what counts as knowledge, but because in doing so it detaches itself from any overriding moral considerations of natural justice or human brotherhood. Where the previous conceptions of utopia in Campanella and Andreae had emphasized harmony and even brotherhood, in Bensalem, totalitarianism is noticeably in the air. The Solomon House of Bacon might be an institution of scientific knowledge but not one of justice.

A society premised wholly on the pursuit of science for science's sake is blind. A century after Bacon, Jonathan Swift satirizes a fictionalized Bensalem (or maybe just the actual Royal Society) in part 3 of *Gulliver's Travels*, "A Voyage to Laputa, Balnibarbi, Luggnagg, Glubbdubdrib and Japan." In Barlnibari, the greatest efforts are invested in foolish scientific schemes. There in the Grand Academy of Lagado, Gulliver meets a genius who is trying to turn human excrement back into food, another hard at work trying to transform ice to gunpowder, and a third, who, following in the example "of those two prudent insects the bee and spider," is busy tinkering with the idea of building houses beginning with the roofs down to the foundation. Similar absurdities populate the halls.[19] What sense of progress is being served? An answer to the rhetorical question Swift's text poses is clear. However important scientific progress may be, it cannot provide the absolute ideal for a healthy society, much less any perfect one. But rank scientism is not the only target in Swift's gunsight. Seven years before the publication of his own satirical travel tale, another one, Daniel Defoe's *Robinson Crusoe*, had begun making the rounds. At issue in it is whether the individual or society is primordial. Which is to say, at issue is whether human nature is inherently corrupt or whether instead its surroundings corrupt it. To make headway on the dispute, it is worth asking ourselves a question: would the perfect society need laws, or would it not? There is a conspicuous absence of laws in Christianopolis, where it is presumed that everyone is able, insofar as they wish, to do good. Laws spelling out what should be done are therefore superfluous, for they are already taken to be written on the human heart.[20] The ordinary system of inducements and punishments for managing human moral conduct is thereby removed. Because doing the right thing is a skill as any other, it means that a code of civil law in a community as Christianopolis is unnecessary. Laws are bicycle training wheels; though perhaps necessary at first they are to be discarded ultimately, and if they have not been, then something along the way has gone awry, because things are stunted. But there are still the disagreements among the utopians regarding various matters. Is everything including spouses and children to be held in common? Should there be private property? What is the relation of the individual to the state? What form of political rule, if any, should exist—democracy, monarchy, or something besides? Does everyone work, or not? Are there slaves? Is there a compulsory education system, and if so, in what does the learning consist? What are the community's fundamental aspirations and values? If the community is no longer to be run according to the self-interest of market economies, should money be abolished, or should it be rationed and collectivized, with some play currency useful only within the community to be used?

These specific sorts of affairs are what commanded the attention of the eighteenth- and nineteenth-century utopians, who, almost without exception, took it as axiomatic that individuals are warped by the corrupted societies in which they live. We are not Robinson Crusoes, they held. Individuals are made bad by their surroundings, not the other way around. Thus, if society is to make any progress in eliminating its evils such as crime, poverty, and vice, the economic and social injustices of people's environment must be rooted out and alleviated. As James Harrington's 1656 *Oceania* had already emphasized a century before, key to a just society is a proper balance of property, where property is understood to be land specifically. Monarchy vests land in one; aristocracy in the few; a commonwealth with the people at large. How then is property to be distributed? One solution is to say the question puts the cart before the horse. For perhaps the question of property is not distributing it but of eliminating it. It was Abbé Morelly's *Code la Nature* that, advocating the abolition of private property, was to inspire the thought of Henri de Saint-Simon and others. Contrary, for instance, to the Hebrew Prophets, who had seen social corruption and injustice as due to the sinfulness of individuals, Morelly, in a move foreshadowing Owen, sees everyone as pure products of their conditions. Communism (to use an anachronism) would cure society not only of its economic wrongs; in doing so, it would thereby also cure its moral errors. Such is the social motif developed to even further extremes by the French radical political agitator François-Noël Babeuf, who, influencing the likes of Saint-Simon, aimed to "secure as the aim and end of his system absolute mechanical equality in both quantity and kind of goods, and in their use and distribution."[21] Championing the idea of knowledge and industry, however, Saint-Simon's own vision of organized labor was in some ways more Baconian in spirit, calling for a body of scientific experts organizing the business of society. Society is to be hierarchal, with the experts guiding the less gifted.

In any case, there remains the matter of how to implement these visions. Here it is someone like Charles Fourier who distinguishes himself from his fellow utopians. For although he personally held the science of economics in contempt, and despite his reputation for madness, his systematic works brought about some practical change in industry. (A reputation for madness that is not without at least some justification. Sometimes his prose clearly is egomaniacal, as when he declares in the *Epilogue of Théorie des Quatre Mouvements* that "I ALONE shall have confounded twenty centuries of political imbecility").[22] We may leave aside the bizarre metaphysics underpinning his vision for how a world with more just and humane working conditions would be possible. While he may be faulted for his naive optimism, which thought that there must be some *a priori* social plan conformable to God's will (hence it simply is our job to discover what that plan is), his system of *attraction passionelle*, which was styled as a kind of Newtonian mechanics for the moral world, was not without its practical merits. But at the same time, there is a dangerous side to it, since in arguing that free rein be given to the passions it seems this is a recipe that tends to licentiousness and voluptuousness. When he says, for instance, that civilized morality has twisted us by contorting our desires, teaching "man to be at war with himself, to resist his passions, to repress them,"[23] it is easy to discern anticipations of Freud and the even later critical theory. Whether that is a good thing may be left to each to decide.

Standing in opposition to this general drift of autocratic thinking epitomized by the other socialist utopians is the late nineteenth-century Étienne Cabet, who, contrary to Saint-Simon, elevated the principle of equality to an absolute. Vocation and individualism are thrown entirely out the window. Henceforth, there will be a need for the state to control and dictate everyone's affairs, as no one is to receive special privileges of any kind. Everyone is the same: "Each citizen received from the State all articles he consumed; to all alike homes and furniture were assigned; clothing of the same design and quality made in large quantities was delivered to all; they were fed in social boarding houses. Theirs was a community and equality of goods and work, of duties and rights, of burdens and benefits and enjoyments."²⁴ The preceding list of socialist utopians just considered, though incomplete, raises sufficient associations and influences to be dizzying! And yet no clear picture of consensus emerges. Surveying the course of modern utopian thought, we thus inevitably are still left to wonder: is the ideal society to be democratic or autocratic (Fourier is fine with maintaining private property and natural inequality, while Saint-Simon, Owen, and others can't bear the thought), the state to be abolished or absolute (Cabet practically deifies it, while Fourier never so much as mentions one!), the individual to be left to pursue his vocation or instead made to conform to a community tolerating no difference? It seems we have made no further progress in resolving such questions than had antiquity! The only thing these utopian thinkers ultimately agree on is that our present world is far from being a utopia. Hence, the last line of Joyce Hertzler's *The History of Utopian Thought* is not without its justification, when it says so well: "Utopia is not a social state, it is a state of mind."²⁵

The Psalmist longed to fly away, just as so many of the utopian writers have imagined themselves sailing away. To somehow take leave of what we know for some distant land, to escape the ache, has been a wish of all those who have felt, deep within themselves, that the restlessness they experience, along with the accompanying sense that this is not their home, is because there is indeed such a home awaiting us somewhere, just not here. And it is not merely reflected in Renaissance or late Enlightenment literature. It is transhistorical, which is why the ancients experienced the urge also.²⁶ In one of his characteristically erudite studies, the fairly unknown Cambridge theologian and historian John Ferguson takes up the status of utopian thinking in antiquity. The results are fascinating and they bear repeating. A consensus regarding what the perfect political community involves has always been a point of contention. And there are no obvious answers. For the Greeks, the seeds of utopian thinking are evident in their pondering what form the just *polis* should take. The question is raised in the Homeric tragedies, for instance. A strong utopian impulse can be detected there, as Ferguson says, most notably in how *The Odyssey* portrays the affairs of Olympus, where the councils of the gods unfold on a higher plane than do ours. This, Ferguson suggests, points in favor of monarchy, an impression confirmed directly by Odysseus's encounter with the Phaeacians, whose own court enacts "the ideal of monarchy."²⁷ As he says, it is a monarchy that "is not arbitrary and absolute, however. It is benevolent and paternalistic. It depends on intellectual and spiritual qualities, not on physique."²⁸ Benign and just, it is based on what later theorists, following the terminology of Locke, would call the consent of the governed: "If it be not under the rule of law, it is any rate dictated by custom and convention. It is sustained by the free consent of the governed, who treat Alcinous' words like those of a god."²⁹ Proceeding chronologically, Ferguson notes next that the first explicit debate over the form the *polis* should take is in the writings of Herodotus. "Monarchy," for Herodotus as Ferguson says, "is subject to two defects. First the monarch is not answerable to anyone; second, he is bound to be corrupted by power."[30] What is needed is equality before the law, which apparently means popular power: "allocation of office by lot, officials answerable to the people for their tenure in office, and political decisions taken by the whole people."[31] Such is the view of Herodotus's character Otanes. But things are not so simple. For as Megabyzus chimes in, while it is right to agree with this criticism of autocracy, democracy is even worse, for the people are liable to act with even worse violence and foolishness than a dictatorship.[32] Accordingly, the conversation circles back to monarchy, only this time favorably so, where Darius argues that because there is only one best, and the best is the best possible ruler, there should be only one ruler. Hence, as Ferguson notes, the debate recounted by Herodotus "foreshadows the later analysis of constitutions into six, the good forms monarchy, aristocracy, democracy, the bad forms tyranny, oligarchy, ochlocracy."[33] The difficulty in deciding which among them is the best form of government is not limited to the writings of Herodotus. It is reflected, for example, in the actual political scheme of Sparta, whose mixed form of government resisted any easy categorization. There were two kings and a senate of twenty-six others popularly elected by citizens who were sixty or older.[34] As for the Assembly, it was open to all citizens who were at least twenty, and they met in the open air, but its power was very restricted. And finally, in addition to these common institutions, there was the ephorate, a committee of five whose origin, says Ferguson, "is wrapped in obscurity."[35] The main source we have for this is Plutarch, but even there nothing about the evidence given is decisive. Whatever its origins, it wielded considerable power. For Plato in Athens, there of course is a similar autocratic strand running continuously in his thinking from the *Republic* to the *Laws*. However, whereas the former was invested in the notion that a rule of infallible rulers was possible, by the time of the latter, Plato has abandoned this hope. Human nature is too frail to seriously permit such illusions. To preserve justice, there must be laws, since absolute power corrupts, just as Lord Acton said. As Ferguson remarks, "It is powerful individuals, not laws, who constitute the main danger to freedom, and Plato intends his laws to maximize real freedom."[36] All political idealizations come to grief with human nature. For it remains that however we wish to explain it, comparatively few people choose to live the kind of virtuous lives necessary for instituting a just community.

In the *Politics*, for example, Aristotle will claim that just as virtue is necessary for individual happiness, so the same can be said of a community's happiness. The problem is obvious. If so few individuals are truly virtuous, what hope is there of ever realizing a happy community? There are various methods one might suggest to bring it about. Education is always one proposal. But no amount of education can force individuals to be virtuous, which is, in the end, Aristotle's idea of a happy community that remains precisely that, an idea. Ferguson's subsequent analysis of the many other utopian thinkers from the classical world (Diogenes and the early Stoics included) culminates with the thesis that no matter what their stated particulars, all end up confronting the inherent problems plaguing what Augustine in *The City of God* names the "city of the world." The latter city, says Augustine, is the name for the city ruled according to the self-interest of men. It is not simply (or even primarily) a physically locatable *polis*, but rather a description of the state of an individual's heart, as well as the totality of all those who are similarly disposed. As Ferguson explains it, this distinction between the two cities is a difference owing to their respective loves: "The first is sacred, socially constructive, pursuing the common good for the sake of the fellowship of heaven, obedient to God, quiet and peaceable, preferring truth to false praise, friendly desiring for others what it desires for itself, seeking the good of the neighbour. This is the love of the good angels. The second love is ugly, selfish, ambitious and authoritarian, usurping the place of God, restless, troublesome, hungry for praise, envious, forcing the neighbor for its own ends. This is the love of the evil angels."[37] And hence, "These two loves mark off from one another the two cities, the one of the righteous, the other of the wicked."[38] Thus the takeaway is as simple as it is historically attested, though many people still do not like to hear it. Human political arrangements will not save us, only God can.

The work of the already mentioned early twentieth-century sociologist Joyce Hertzler is in this context worth returning to. In her book on utopia, she recognizes how the utopian element in ancient philosophers detailed by Ferguson went back further. Tracing such an impulse to before the Greeks, she begins with the Prophets of the Old Testament. "Among another people and in another literature which antedated that of Greece by several centuries we find numerous utopian expressions by men, who, as social critics and social architects, were the equals if not the peers of Plato. We refer to the Hebrew prophets."[39] In turn, she examines some of the most remarkable of them, beginning with Amos, Hosea, and Isaiah, then Jeremiah and Ezekiel. Amos, on Hertzler's telling, was a social reformer who was disgusted by the injustice and corruption of his society and imagined a better one founded on the principles of fair play and integrity. At the time, these were both departures from the norm. Worship of God "had degenerated to a Saturnalian orgy. Revelry and tumultuous carousings marked the festivals: drunkenness and indecency together with the most licentious debaucheries were common at the local shrines."[40] Consequently, though society was materially prosperous, it was rotten to the core morally, for, as she notes, Amos saw the superficiality of its luxury: "It was luxury of the few at the expense of the toil of the many; consequently social injustice was rife."[41] Amos was a prophet denouncing social sins, those that wronged the neighbor, and hence, as Hertzler summarizes, his was an ideal extolling a new social ethic of justice, one based on an awakened spirituality that saw the universe as under God's control for a moral purpose.[42] But how is this rejuvenation to take place?

Where Amos rebuked his society for relishing a prosperity that rested on a moral decay, it is Hosea who proposes that the only way out is through renewed spiritual loyalty to God. This will require a society open and committed to divine love. "The central idea of Hosea's teaching," as Hertzler says, "expressed throughout his pages is that fatherly love is the foremost attribute of Jehovah and that it alone is the great reconstructing force of which society can avail itself in order to work out its redemption."[43] But even if we are right to locate the source of possible social rejuvenation in divine love, how are we to get others to see it for themselves and to act accordingly? Here, Hosea's message of redemption is taken up by Isaiah, who further deepens it by emphasizing the focus already placed on love by Amos and Hosea, noting that only faith in God will mobilize such love. "Isaiah," as she comments, "more emphatically than any other, insists that mankind endures, progresses, attains perfection, not so much by means of material forces or the prevalent doctrine of economic necessity, as by the purely ethical and spiritual forces."[44] When a city or nation is in spiritual destitution, everything else about it suffers rot too: "When these essential forces are not in the ascendency, the life of nations as well as of individuals is doomed to wastage and destruction; when they are, there will be advance, enlightenment, happiness without end."[45] Isaiah's Messianic hope highlights that, without the moral commitment and participation of individuals, the Kingdom of God cannot be established. It is on this basis that Jeremiah deepens the call for individual spiritual renewal. Salvation is not merely a collective one for a nation, but of the individual souls who will one day meet God's judgment in eternity. "It was Jeremiah," as Hertzler accordingly notes, "who first made the soul of the individual the true seat of pure religion and the individual conscience the basis of social ethics; who first explicitly formulated the new idea of moral freedom and responsibility."[46] It is this new birth in character that Ezekiel for his own part accentuates, as with Jeremiah before him. If social change is to occur, the individual must consciously desire this change, a desire whose sincerity is thus measured by whether the one who claims to desire it has taken responsibility for his own character, through resolving to shape his will in conformity with God's righteousness. As Hertzler summarizes, "the community and nation as a moral and religious unit disappear and its people become self-willing moral agents, each of which pursues independently his own way, wholly unaffected by the rest, responsible only for his own acts, working out his own salvation or his own doom, his outward lot harmonizing with his inner character."[47] Revolution begins in us.

The difficulty of instituting a just *polis* not only vexed the Prophets, the Greeks, and modern utopians, for it is still with us to this day, as Hannah Arendt shows when tackling the problem admirably in *The Human Condition*. The task she sets for that work is refreshingly honest—"to think what we are doing."[48] As she notes, our current predicament is twofold. Whereas the Greeks had a *polis* (however flawed), we do not. For them, the household and public were separated; the former pertained to the bodily necessities of life, whereas the latter was the place of freedom, the place of word and action. What today we call society, so she argues, was to them unknown. There used to be a genuine distinction between private and public, but that distinction, as so much else, has for us been obliterated. The point might sound abstract. But it is attestable. For instance, does not what commands so much of what we today call politics concern affairs which the earlier Greek perspective would have relegated to the private sphere? As she says, "Society is the form in which the fact of mutual dependence for the sake of life and nothing else assumes public significance and where the activities connected with sheer survival are permitted to appear in public."[49] Hence, as the Greeks understood, "Without mastering the necessities of life in the household, neither life nor the 'good life' is possible, but politics is never for the sake of life. As far as the members of the *polis* are concerned, household life exists for the sake of the 'good life' in the *polis*."[50] At the same time, what should be a matter of the public sphere has been made impossible, for we lack any true venue for deed and word. What we have instead is mass society, an amorphous blob of jobholders toiling in meaningless work to secure a paycheck for the necessities of life. Observing what she sees in the 1950s, Arendt's astute description highlights what has only become more glaring since she wrote it: "The point is not that for the first time in history laborers were admitted and given equal rights in the public realm, but that we have almost succeeded in leveling all human activities to the common denominator of securing the necessities of life and providing for their abundance. Whatever we do, we are supposed to do for the sake of 'making a living'; such is the verdict of society, and the number of people, especially in the professions who might challenge it, has decreased rapidly."[51] This soulless labor—this labor is not work, not in the sense Arendt attributes to the ancient's *vita activa*[52]—is supplemented by the vain and often degrading amusements of mass entertainment, to numb the pain and to foster the false sense that by indulging in them one thereby is not alone. The most pernicious form of isolation is the one that believes itself connected to others when it is not. This is the illusion created by mass entertainment and epitomized by contemporary social media.

World of work and dwelling, world of meaning: such is the world that also becomes, as Arendt notes, a world whereby self-understanding is possible. And for the Greeks, that meant the possibility of achieving great deeds immortalizing themselves. And yet, even for them, self-transparency remained impossible. While the world provides the horizon in which meaningful activity takes place, a comprehensive definition of man eludes us. As she says in the midst of an analysis on the conception of worldhood heavily indebted to Heidegger, "The moment we want to say *who* somebody is, our very vocabulary leads us astray into saying *what* he is; we get entangled in a description of qualities he necessarily shares with others like him."[53] As perceptive as Arendt's analyses of worldhood in the *The Human Condition* are, they fail to explicate another conception of the world, the one as it is presented in the Bible, which is to say, as a place of evil, where selfish desires incite all manner of suffering and depravity. This other sense of the world is missing from the analysis, one that *The Banality of Evil* brings into comparative relief. The world in such a sense, as dominated by great but extraordinarily quotidian evil, is one of lust. It is of this phenomenon that the Apostle John speaks when he says, "Love not the world nor the things in the world. If anyone loves the world, the love of the Father is not in him. For all that *is* in the world—the lust of the flesh, the lust of the eyes, and the pride of life—is not of the Father but is of the world. And the world is passing away, and the lust of thereof, but he who does the will of God abides forever" (1 John 2:15–17). When Arendt talks about the human world (or the world as human), she means what takes nature and builds and constructs something durable. This is work. But as she admits, even such relatively durable things in the end are fragile and fleeting. Destined to pass away, the greatest of all pagan exploits, those of an Alexander or a Caesar or an Odysseus, fade. The only thing that does not, as John accordingly observes, is not any deed done in and for this world, but the one who, doing what is right eternally, thereby prepares himself for the world to come.

It is that eternal perspective, with the transformation its love of God effectuates in whomever so chooses to live in the light of it, that is capable of establishing an earthly community no longer bound by death. Not circumscribed by death, for it looks to a life promised beyond it through the Resurrection of Jesus Christ. Because it is no longer bound by death but rather knit in love, the bond between those who have been unified together through it cannot be severed by anything, including the power of death itself. This community, which is dispersed invisibly on earth and stretched across the ages of those past and those yet to come, is the body of Christ. It is this body, the body of believers, that Jean-Louis Chrétien so beautifully explores in his work *Symbolique du corps* on the Song of Songs. The members of the church, which is to say the body of Christ, are many: teeth, nose, lips, neck, hair, breasts, belly, hands, legs, and feet. Everything has its appointed function and everything accordingly works together. They form a unity of purpose across their variegated difference.

In a wonderful chapter regarding the portrayal of the neck in the Old Testament text, "Du Cou," Chrétien returns to a favorite subject of his, humility. "In the Bible," he observes, "the neck is not described in terms of its physiological functions, but is evoked for its powerful significance."[54] The symbolic significance lies precisely in its physical power itself, but not primarily in its power to sustain the weight of the head. More importantly, it is because of that power that it is able to submit itself, to bow to a power above it in an act of symbolic but no less real obedience. Here, Chrétien has in mind the obedience to God. While the prideful are stiff-necked, refusing to bend their necks to God, the humble are those who do. As Chrétien notes, when through the obedience of faith the heart bends its neck (there is a spiritual tradition he describes that has seen in the heart its own members) in submission to God, a new life begins. There is nothing mundane about this choice to submit, since to relinquish one's power, as he says, "implies in effect a personal relationship with Christ,"[55] which in turn implies, as he makes explicit at the end of the same paragraph, that this "obedience is nothing but humility."[56] Quoting approvingly the twelfth-century Cistercian monk John of Ford, Chrétien notes how this life in Christ, as a member of his body, makes possible true life, because it initiates one into the only community on earth where each is accepted for what one truly is and has become, a child of God. "Thus humility," John of Ford says, "which is the mother of virtues, presents itself first of all as an ornament of honor by a spirit of sweetness and its modest reserve (necklaces). Secondly, it fortifies patience, then, through the contempt for earthly realities and the hope of heavenly ones, it elevates (David's tower). Finally, by the very chaste contemplation of its Bride, 'triple praise of the neck of the Bridegroom,' it marries the bride with the Word of God (tower of ivory)."[57] As Chrétien says elsewhere in another book, *Pour reprendre et perdre halein*, our most common of words (in the sense that we hold and share them in common) are those we use to name the most universal of experiences they express—breath, way, temptation, attention, peace, softness, abandon, wound; and if they unite us, ultimately it is because, as those who have entered upon the Way of Life come to see, everything was already waiting to be united by the Word that has brought us together. This is why, as those who have become brothers in Christ know, even a friendship survives death—not only is there always remembering so long as the one of them is still alive (a point Kierkegaard made poignantly in *Works of Love*), but the future holds the promise of a reunion in flesh and blood! Consequently, summarizing John of Ford's point about the importance of humility for community, and stressing in turn how the human neck's powers of motion symbolize how without humility true community is impossible, Chrétien says, "Such is the 'triple praise of the neck of the Bride,' which corresponds to humility towards oneself, towards others, and towards God."[58] Here Chrétien's intention, as so often, is to signal to us a joy that will be ours if only we would choose to seek it for ourselves. As his analysis of humility implies, nobody who has not yet submitted in obedience to God will know the joy of meeting a fellow traveler, who, already laboring for some time on his own way, has found the way by also having done the same. For a moment, however briefly, they are brought together, encountering and recognizing one another as fellow pilgrims passing on the same road. It brings a smile to the face, leads one to run like a child again, sometimes even to leap with joy! As for the memory of these moments so pregnant with eternal promise, it remains. Upward and onward into the Everlasting Arms.

It will be said that not every road has a destination—some simply end, even in nowhere. That is true. But some journeys do have a destination. And this is one of them. The destination is not of this world, for it is the city of God. New Jerusalem, where there is no night, where there is no lie, where there is no evil, where there are no tears or sorrow, only love and joy. Peace!

> And he showed me a pure river of water of life, clear as crystal, proceeding out of the throne of God and of the Lamb. In the midst of the street of it, and on either side of the river, there was the tree of life, which bare twelve manner of fruits, and yielded her fruit every month: and the leaves of the tree were for the healing of the nations. And there shall be no more curse: but the throne of God and of the Lamb shall be in it; and his servants shall serve him: And they shall see his face; and his name shall be in their foreheads. And there shall be no night there; and they need no candle, neither light of the sun; for the Lord God giveth them light: and they shall reign for ever and ever (Rev 21:1–5).

The Kingdom, already reigning within those who have been born of the Spirit, buoys us on. In an *elsewhere* concealed from the foundations of a world that cannot know it, propelled on by the Spirit's undulations, I receive myself as the one I have become, as a son of God, sustained by the One who has made all things new, to the very depths of the heart. Here no longer handed over to the world's cult of death, I live: "crucified with Christ: nevertheless I live; yet not I, but Christ lives in me" (Gal 2:20). As for all those who choose to embrace these rivers of eternal life, they speak of the same transfiguring flood, a revolution within the depths of a life now found. A life, they know, that is now no longer one of despair but of victory.

What John saw approaches. Trembling in expectation, the creation groans. As do we! All you who are upright in heart: rejoice.

NOTES

1. See *Becoming Heidegger: On the Trail of His Early Occasional Writings, 1910–1927*, ed. Theodor Kiesel and Thomas Sheehan (Evanston, IL: Northwestern University Press. 2007).

2. Dubbed by some the "English Socrates," it is well known that More lived an intriguing and eventful life, culminating in the dramatic circumstances of his death by martyrdom. But he was not always so perfect, it must be admitted. Despite creating a space for religious tolerance in his fictional Utopia, he did not extend an equal spirit of tolerance when acting as chancellor in London. Often he was involved in the torture, imprisonment, and execution of those deemed unorthodox. This is by no means to suggest that his hypocrisy negates the importance of his work on utopia, but it does serve to underscore that if utopia is so hard to achieve on earth, it is because even the men who write about it fail to live up to their own standards of the idealized community.

3. Andreae, *Christianopolis* (trans. Edward H. Thompson [Dordrecht: Kluwer, 1999]), 187. To return for a moment to the subject of Campanella's influence, it will be noted that Andreae's triumvirate is indebted to the Power, Love, and Wisdom of *Civitas solis*.

4. Ibid., 158–59.
5. Ibid., 159.
6. Ibid., 160.
7. Ibid.
8. Ibid.
9. Ibid., 160–61.
10. Ibid., 220.
11. Ibid., 190–91.
12. Ibid., 249.
13. Ibid., 218.
14. Ibid., 219.
15. Ibid., 188.

16. Joyce Hertzler, *The History of Utopian Thought* (New York: The Macmillan Company, 1923), 148.

17. Though his criticisms of scientific objectivism are presented in many of his works, probably the two most powerful statements are in *Barbarism* (London: Continuum, 2012) and *I Am the Truth: Toward a Philosophy of Christianity* (Stanford, CA: Stanford University Press, 2002). Lacoste, for one, does not hesitate to emphasize the extent to which this modern conception of nature is inquisitorial to the point of resorting to torture. To know its secrets, nature must be compelled to cry out: "Calculation or measurement are already to participate in a logic of the stranglehold. We know more however since Bacon, to whom we owe the equation of experimentation and what we must call torture. According to Bacon, experimentation is intended to force the object to 'speak.'" Jean-Yves Lacoste, *Être en Danger* (Paris: Les Éditions du Cerf, 2011).

18. For perhaps Russell's clearest statement of the technocratic pretensions for society, see *The Impact of Science on Society* (New York: Routledge, 2016).

19. Swift, *Gulliver's Travels*, 198. If it is a habit of contemporary academicians to drone on for pages in the acknowledgment section of their books, self-congratulatorily flattering their impressive friends, so this was the habit in the Grand Academy of Lagado. At the very end of his tour, Gulliver explains the method of anagrams to one of the professors who is working on a method to discover political conspiracies. Gulliver relates the professor's amusing reaction, "The Professor made me great Acknowledgments for communicating these Observations, and promised to make honourable mention of me in his Treatise," 211.

20. An interesting connection between utopian thought, on the one hand, and theories of natural law, on the other, is readily evident. For if, as some have accordingly imagined, utopia would not require any civil law, is it not because already promulgated in the consciences and minds of men there is no need for the law to be exteriorized when it has been thus understood? The laws of government become at best redundant, at worst misleading or inaccurate. The idea that the ideal society would therefore be lawless, in that codifying justice and morality would be otiose, is not a notion limited only to utopian literature, of course. The question arose as well

in the context of eighteenth- and nineteenth-century discussions in English political economy regarding the relationship between natural law and property rights. For an excellent work that takes up the matter of distributive justice (along with other matters) within the intellectual legacy bequeathed by John Locke, see Daniel Layman, *Locke Among the Radicals* (Oxford: Oxford University Press, 2020).

21. Hertzler, 190.

22. As the passage continues, it becomes only more self-aggrandizing, even if it is meant to be slightly facetious: "and it is to me alone that present and future generations will owe the initiative of their boundless happiness. Before me, mankind lost several thousand years by fighting madly against Nature; I am the first who has bowed before her, by studying attraction, the organ of her decrees; she has designed to smile upon the only mortal who has offered incense at her shrine; she has delivered up all her treasures to me. Possessor of the book of Fate, I come to dissipate political and moral darkness, and, upon the ruins of the uncertain sciences, I erect the theory of universal harmony: Exegi monumentum aere perennius," *Selections from the Works of Fourier*, trans. Julia Franklin (London: Swan Sonnenschein & Co, 1901), 14.

23. Ibid., 55.

24. Hertzler, 206.

25. Hertzler, 314.

26. It almost goes without saying that such a thesis is contestable. Bernard Williams, for one, in his work *Shame and Necessity* (Berkeley and Los Angeles, CA: University of California Press, 1993) contests it, adopting a view with historicist tendencies, by accentuating what he takes to be the different forms of self-understanding characterizing people of the ancient world from ours. It would be unwise to overlook such differences, where they do exist. But these differences being whatever they may, it seems that their presumed fundamentality can be exaggerated, or at the very least given undue precedence. Is not a human being a human being?

27. John Ferguson, *Utopias of the Classical World* (Ithaca, NY: Cornell University Press, 1975), 14.

28. Ibid.

29. Ibid.

30. Ibid., 26.

31. Ibid.

32. Ibid.

33. Ibid.

34. Ibid., 32.

35. Ibid., 33.

36. Ibid., 79.

37. Ibid., 184.

38. Ibid.

39. Hertzler, 7.

40. Ibid., 10.

41. Ibid., 11.

42. Ibid., 13.

43. Ibid., 18.

44. Ibid., 24.

45. Ibid.

46. Ibid., 32.

47. Ibid., 39.

48. Hannah Arendt, *The Human Condition* (Chicago: University of Chicago Press, 1958), 5.

49. Ibid., 46.

50. Ibid., 37.

51. Ibid., 126–27.

52. The kind of dreary labor Arendt sees characterizing our time is marked by the kind of repulsiveness Fourier had thought it was so crucial to overcome. For him, labor must be reorganized to satisfy our instincts: the *papillone* (the need for change and variety), the *cabaliste* (love of intrigue), and the *composite* (pleasure at once in both mind and body).

53. Ibid., 181. What Arendt in this passage identifies as man's essential indefinability can be attributed to our being made in the *imago Dei*, as God himself defies any such complete conceptualization. Just as God transcends any definition, so too do we. For a substantial analysis along just these lines, see Jean-Luc Marion, *In the Self's Place: The Approach of St Augustine*, trans. Jeffrey L. Kosky (Stanford, CA: Stanford University Press, 2012), 230–89.

54. Jean-Louis Chrétien, *Symbolique du corps: La tradition chrétienne du Cantique des Cantiques* (Paris: Presses Universitaires de France, 2005), 125.

55. Ibid., 127.
56. Ibid.
57. Ibid., 129.
58. Ibid.

Index

Andreae, Johannes Valentinus, 166–168
Anscombe, Elizabeth, 102
Anselm, 7, 26
Aquinas, Thomas, 26
Arendt, Hannah, 69n20, 177–178, 182n52, 183n53
Aristotle, 7, 81, 99, 111, 174
Augustine, 18, 21, 22, 24, 26, 124, 174
Austin, J. L., 134

Babeuf, François-Noël, 171
Bacon, Francis, 169
Bechtol, Harris, 115n13
Benton, Matthew, 38n6
Blondel, Maurice, 114n9
Bonhoeffer, Dietrich, 120
Brague, Rémi, 114n7

Cabet, Etienne, 172
Calvin, John, 21, 26, 127
Campanella, Tomasso, 166
Camus, Albert, 2, 10n8, 21
Carnap, Rudolf, 129
Chrétien, Jean-Louis, 13, 93n17, 97, 107, 123, 141, 178–180
Churchill, Winston, 105–106
Clement of Alexandria, 22
Clement of Rome, 22
Coyne, Ryan, 10n10
Crowley, Aleister, 147

Dante, 118, 143–145
Davidson, Donald, 97
Defoe, Daniel, 170
Descartes, René, 7, 68n1
Dika, Tarek, 10n10
Dodd, James, 34
Dostoevsky, Fyodor, 2, 86–87, 91, 112, 119, 126, 136, 158
Drummond, John, 39n23

Ellul, Jacques, 52, 53–55, 113
Eusebius, 24
existentialism, 1; question of God in, 2–3, 9

Falque, Emmanuel, 10n7

Hadot, Pierre, 31, 33
Harrington, James, 171
Hegel, G. W. F., 101, 110
Heidegger, Martin, 2, 3–9, 15, 27, 34, 35, 37, 43, 100, 120, 137, 139, 169
Henry, Michel, 45, 53, 69n10, 108, 123, 125, 127, 169, 181n17
Herder, Johann, 126
Herodotus, 173
Hertzler, Joyce, 169, 172, 175–176
Hobbes, Thomas, 49–51
d'Holbach, Baron, 126
Homer, 173
Hopp, Walter, 10n8

Hume, David, 30, 71n97
Husserl, Edmund, 2, 27, 34, 37, 44, 98–99, 100, 120, 124, 160n3
Huxley, Aldous, 169

Ignatius of Antioch, 24
Irenaeus of Lyons, 22, 60

Jacobi, C. G. J., 126
James the Apostle, 107
Janicaud, Dominique, 10n1
Jankélévitch, Vladimir, 80–84
Jerome, 26
John of Ford, 179
John the Apostle, 178
Justin Martyr, 13, 23, 25, 31–32, 147

Kant, Immanuel, 22, 24, 35, 152
Kearney, Richard, 94n22
Kierkegaard, Søren, 2, 10n4, 10n8, 13, 14, 35, 52, 65, 74, 79, 112, 123–124, 127–128, 156, 158, 179

Lacoste, Jean-Yves, 7, 8, 14, 16, 18, 115n18, 181n17
Lactantius, 25
Layman, Daniel, 181n20
Leibniz, Gottfried, 126, 129
Levinas, Emmanuel, 46, 100
Lipps, Theodor, 44
Locke, John, 173, 181n20
Luther, Martin, 26

Malebranche, Nicolas, 13
Malpas, Jeff, 99
Marcel, Gabriel, 2
Marion, Jean-Luc, 39n25, 93n17, 98, 100, 114n10, 122, 140, 166, 183n53
Marx, Karl, 108
Merleau-Ponty, Maurice, 16, 34, 48, 117, 120
methodological atheism, 2; dogmatism of, 10, 27, 34, 35; existentialism's relation to, 3, 9; Heidegger's understanding of, 3–9
Moore, A. W., 146
Morelly, Abbé, 171
Murdoch, Iris, 10n8, 50–51

Nagel, Thomas, 146
Newton, Isaac, 172
Nietzsche, Friedrich, 2, 151–152, 154–155, 158

Origen, 25
Owen, Robert, 171

Pascal, Blaise, 13, 18, 123
Patočka, Jan, 34
Paul the Apostle, 15, 32, 61, 67, 85, 112
Pelagius, 26
Plantinga, Alvin, 21
Plato, 50, 107, 147, 173
Plutarch, 56–63, 173
Poe, Edgard Allen, 119, 129, 137
propaganda, 52; mechanism for coping with loneliness, 55; rooted in denial of individuality, 52; triviality of, 53–54
Proust, Marcel, 47

Romano, Claude, 47, 49, 69n23, 122
Rousseau, Jean-Jacques, 49–50, 56, 63–64, 66, 71n97
Ricœur, Paul, 21, 85
Russell, Bertrand, 20, 130, 169, 181n18
Ruussbroec, Jan van, 145

Saint-Simon, Henri de, 171
salvation, 22; as aesthetic ideal, 151–152, 153; as eternal reward for love of God, 22, 176; as goal of philosophy, 33, 36; from hatred of others, 63
Sartre, Jean-Paul, 2, 7, 15, 21, 110, 117, 131–133, 143, 147
Scheler, Max, 18, 44, 120
Schellenberg, John, 13, 19
Schelling, F. W. J., 126–127
Schopenhauer, Arthur, 126, 152–153, 156, 165
Shestov, Lev, 2
solipsism, 41; Cartesian legacy of, 43, 47; ethical failure of, 46
Spinoza, Baruch, 126, 131
Stein, Edith, 44–45
Swift, Jonathan, 170
Swinburne, Richard, 161n11

Tertullian, 68

theodicy, 161n11
Tolstoy, Leo, 88–91
transcendental egoism, 46; cause of violence, 101, 103, 109; in relation to forgiveness, 74; myopia of, 50, 147

utopia, 112; history of, 166; in ancient Greece, 174; in Old Testament, 175

Voltaire, 21, 71n97

Williams, Bernard, 63, 146, 182n26
Wittgenstein, Ludwig, 33, 98

Young, Julian, 160n6

Zeretsky, Robert, 71n97
Zermelo, Ernst, 130

www.ingramcontent.com/pod-product-compliance
Lightning Source LLC
Chambersburg PA
CBHW032128010526
44111CB00033B/276